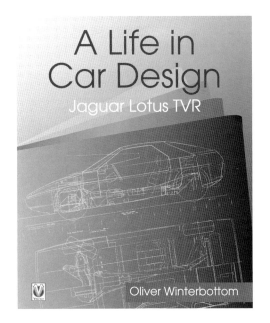

A Life in
Car Design

Jaguar Lotus TVR

Oliver Winterbottom

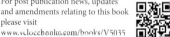

www.velocebooks.com

First published in March 2017 by Veloce Publishing Limited, Veloce House, Parkway Farm Business Park, Middle Farm Way, Poundbury, Dorchester DT1 3AR, England. Fax 01305 250479 / e-mail info@veloce.co.uk / web www.veloce.co.uk or www.velocebooks.com.
ISBN: 978-1-787110-35-9; UPC: 6-36847-01035-5.

A Life in
Car Design

Jaguar Lotus TVR

Oliver Winterbottom

Contents

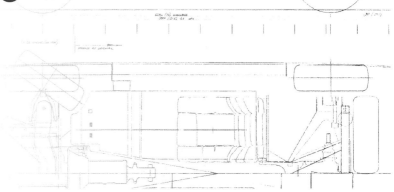

Dedication
To Wendy, Anne and Jane.

Introduction

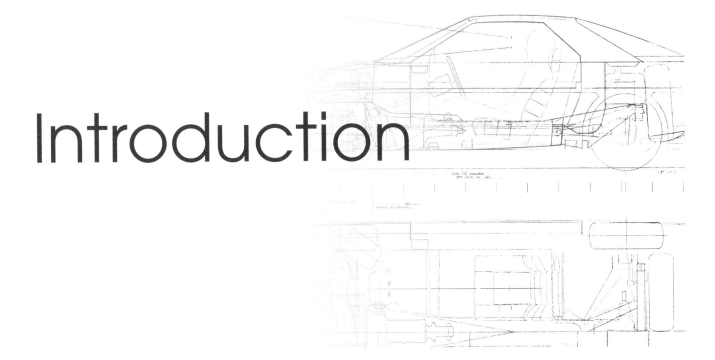

Throughout my working life I have often been asked what I do. "I am a car designer," has been my reply. "Oh, that must be exciting," they usually say. Well, it has been exciting – and frustrating, wearying, worrying, depressing and, above all, exhilarating. Throughout my career, new technology completely transformed working methods. In the 1960s, when I started in the business, the industry was using tools and processes little changed from Victorian times. By the beginning of the 21st century, a total revolution had been wrought by the microchip and the computer. Before, we used Imperial measurements – now, we use metric. These changes have made a huge impact on the accuracy, control and reliability of the motorcar, and I have been lucky to work through that evolution; this book shares the story with you.

The tale traces my life from my upbringing, joining Jaguar Cars in 1961 as an engineering apprentice, through my creative years there and at Lotus and TVR. As a change, I had a short time designing luxury seagoing boats. Later on, I worked for General Motors in Detroit, USA, and completed my career in China, retiring in 2009. Many of the projects described were stillborn. While this poses the question of what might have been, it is still not unusual today for ideas to bud and then wither. Some could have changed the course of history in a beneficial way, while others would probably have marked the demise of the perpetrators. As life progressed, I attained more senior positions in the industry. Sadly, for me, that marked a gradual departure from the drawing board and experimental workshop.

A few years ago, I had the opportunity to become involved in the vehicle safety sector. This was a new and exciting area in which to operate, with the bonus of hopefully being able to reduce the personal suffering caused by road accidents.

To keep the story interesting, I have introduced some projects and aspects of motoring history hitherto known only to a few, but this is not intended to be a marque history or technical guide. I hope it gives an insight into the events behind the creation of various products. I have included many illustrations, some of which are the only remaining record of projects. Copies of engineering drawings are in some cases damaged or lacking in clarity, but are here as a necessary part of the story.

In the course of the story, I have ventured my personal opinions on various events and stress that these are just that: personal. They do not necessarily reflect those of others.

It would be nice to think that this tale gives more people the desire, or hopefully passion, to join the world of creative engineering. I found the (often hard) work, very enjoyable, and, today, take great satisfaction seeing my past efforts on the road. It makes it all worth while.

Finally, I would like to give my thanks to all those who have helped in the production of this book. To the copyright holders of the illustrations, and the friends who jogged my memory, without whom, this could not have happened. To Ron and Brenda Middleton at Focalpoint, Norwich, who gave up so much time to digitise the many historic drawings, and last, but not least, to my late wife, Wendy, who had the patience to allow this work to encroach throughout the whole of our home.

Oliver Winterbottom

The author with his 1966 award-winning model.

Photo acknowledgements

General Motors Cadillac Historic Services 137, 140
Jaguar Daimler Heritage Trust 11, 12, 19-22, 24, 26
Malcolm Griffiths/*Classic & Sports Car* 6
Millbrook Proving Ground Ltd 147
Toyota (GB) PLC 142
TVR Engineering Limited 83, 84, 87-91, 93, 94

All other photos: author's collection, or by permission.

Chapter 1
The beginning

I was born on 24 February 1944, in Ashford, Kent, and was immediately forced to take up residence under the hospital bed as protection from an air raid. Once this alert was over, life became more conventional, with Rowna, my mother, taking me home to New Romney by the sea. My father, Walter (always known as Frosty), who, in normal times, was a family doctor, was not present at my birth, as he was serving in the Royal Army Medical Corps.

My grandfather, Archie Winterbottom, provided the link with engineering – which had a long family history. An ancestor had driven locomotives for the Caledonian Railway in the 1850s, and his grandson, Archibald, had covered nearly every sector of engineering. A Lancashire man, he was an apprenticed engineer to a textile machinery maker, later joining the Caledonian Railway, and then the Argyll Motor Company. He then transferred to yet another branch of engineering: shipbuilding. Moving to Shanghai, he qualified as a Chief Engineer Marine, before joining the Rising Sun Petroleum Company, running oil refineries in the Far East until the Second World War. Following service in the Navy in the Faroe Isles, he retired to England, and kept me amused with his enthusiasm for railways.

My father was born in Oldham, Lancashire, and attended school in Shanghai before coming back to England and public school. He took up medicine, qualifying at St Mary's Hospital, Paddington, where he found the two loves of his life. One was Brooklands motor racing track, the other was my mother.

My mother came from Lincolnshire and provided me with another link to motor cars. A cousin was Raymond Mays, founder and driving force in the creation of ERA and, later, BRM racing cars.

1944 saw the arrival of the V1 flying bomb directed at London. The House in New Romney, with its large orchard, became the site for a barrage of American heavy anti-aircraft guns. When, one day, my mother found a large piece of shrapnel in my pram, she decided to move away to a safer spot. In a letter to Archie, she relates, "while life is not too comfortable, at least Oliver finds any form of bang amusing." Eventually, my father came back from Europe, in late 1945, and plans were made for the future. My parents squeezed me into their MG TB sports car and headed for Olney, in North Buckinghamshire.

My father was a major influence, with his love of motorsport and cars. 14 May 1949 was the first motor racing event that I can remember: the British Grand Prix at Silverstone. I was only five years old, and, not surprisingly, found the cars very noisy, the worst offenders being the 500cc cars. This visit to Silverstone was to be the first of many.

Frosty was keen to participate in sporting events – his biggest achievement occurred on January 22 1950. Glasgow was the start of the Monte Carlo Rally. After a difficult drive through blizzards, my father and the car's entrant, Norman Hiskins, got the privately-entered Hillman Minx to the finish in 70th place. This was to be the peak of my father's motorsport activity, and was all the more commendable, as the only deviation from standard specification was a pair of fog lamps. Lucas 'sponsored' these – they had to be returned after the event!

My mother, who successfully navigated my father on many club rallies, was also a significant influence. She had qualified to attend the Slade School of Art in London. Unfortunately, her father died and, with him, the necessary funds for her to take it up. She was a skilled watercolour artist, and encouraged me to draw and paint throughout my childhood.

In 1952, at the tender age of seven, I was sent away to boarding school in Staffordshire. The school brochure, written during the war, stated, "Boys are allowed to have an occasional cake, also fruit and eggs, if obtainable. Parents are specially asked not to send tuck to their boys, except on birthdays." So we got cake once a year.

My parents, and the school, encouraged reading. I found books with motoring subjects the most appealing, and still have a number of them today. At school, we would write to car manufacturers for their brochures, and one made a lasting impression on me. Writing to Jaguar in 1955, I inquired as to why I had seen photographs of a racing D-Type both with and without a tail fin. The reply was thorough, explaining that the car changed as it was developed. Also with the letter came brochures, photographs, and – top for school credibility – a silver lapel badge. My father and his friends thought the response very positive, so Jaguar had done the right thing.

However, sometimes these requests for brochures would backfire, as the address Smallwood Manor (if the word school was omitted) was taken a bit too seriously by the motor industry. The Headmaster had to put a stop to the practice, when an Armstrong Siddeley arrived at the door, at 11 o'clock one morning, for a boy to test drive. The demonstration driver was not pleased to learn he had driven all the way from Coventry to sell to a ten-year-old.

When I was eleven, a friend of my parents, Ian Boswell, came to dinner. Ian was the owner of the Tickford Coachworks, from 1943 until he sold it in 1955 to Aston Martin. I had made a drawing of a car, and Ian, shown the drawing, commented encouragingly. From that moment, I was committed to becoming a car designer. I called the car Hector, and many future Latin lessons were devoted to designs for the Hector Motor Company.

My father's enthusiasm for motor cars brought various people to our house. I remember David Murray and the Ecurie Ecosse team coming to dinner, the arrival of a works Sunbeam Rapier with David Humphrey, and various local personalities with Alfa Romeos, Lancias, and, later, a Lister Jaguar.

I then entered my father's old school, Denstone College, located on top of a windy hill in North Staffordshire. It was a building of massive local stone, with lofty ceilings and ecclesiastical arches, housing the accommodation and obligatory chapel – all at the mercy of the sort of weather one would expect at the southern end of Britain's Pennine mountain range.

Notable changes were that science became part of the curriculum, and Latin was starting to get a bit hard. Sport and games were tougher; in the winter, rugby reigned supreme. For some strange reason, I was made a second row forward, a role I for which I was not really built, being underweight for my fairly considerable height. Having my head trodden on half the time did not endear me to the game, although some people seemed to relish it. The alternative, if you were not picked for head squashing, was the compulsory cross country run, disliked by most participants, as they traversed the sticky clay hills around the College. Not noted for my rugby skills, I became a successful member of the school Cross Country running team. Another sport I took up was rifle shooting. At Christmas, the school organised a competition with a Christmas cake as the prize. The scarcity of food was often at the forefront of my mind, so I anticipated the prize with relish – and won it. As a result, I was invited to join the school team. I finally managed to shoot the highest score of the year – twice; so I could shoot straight – and then run away – better than most.

Twice a week, the school had Combined Cadet Force parade. This junior army (and air force) was run on fully professional lines; uniforms and boots had to be immaculate. Much marching up and down, and drill, was performed, along with classroom lessons on how to run a platoon, or war, or whatever. At that time, compulsory National Service was still in force, and I counted myself lucky to be one of the first to miss it. Starting off in the Army section, I worked to get my exams, so that I could then escape to the Royal Air Force Cadets, which did rather less of this marching about, and had a big attraction: a motor transport section.

With my father and his new Vauxhall, which I don't think he liked very much.

Mac, a mechanic at the local village garage, was contracted by the school to teach motor mechanics to the RAF cadets. On Tuesday evenings, he taught the small group the basic principles of the Otto Cycle, and how to strip and rebuild an engine. Under his supervision, an RAF surplus Standard Vanguard Pickup was stripped of its body, and, besides being used for maintenance purposes, was also employed to give rudimentary driving lessons. I could handle the Vanguard with aplomb, but later experiments riding and falling off a motorcycle put me off two wheels forever.

In 1958, I bought *Automobile Year,* and it became a major influence. From it, I became interested in the work of the Italian coachbuilders – so far in advance of British motor industry. In a letter to my parents, I made some scathing observations on the new MG Magnette. I saw it as a lost opportunity to rival the Alfa Romeos and other small GT cars from Italy. Besides books, I was a subscriber to *Sports Car and Lotus Owner* magazine, taking great interest in something with which I would later become deeply associated.

One day, I cycled with a friend over to Derby and visited the David Buxton showrooms, which represented Lotus in the area. Buxton was running the works Team Elite in GT racing and on the showroom floor was a Lotus Elite. I was allowed to sit in it and was totally 'sold' on the car. Of course, I couldn't do more than aspire to it then; it would be a very long time before I got to drive one.

I had enjoyed art classes at my prep school – including winning the annual art prize – but Denstone did not have such a luxury. Nor, in those days, were there 'Technology' courses, so, when I suggested that I wished to be a car designer, the school was somewhat surprised. The headmaster brought a gentleman from Rolls-Royce, Derby, to talk to me about engineering careers, but I felt they were perhaps a bit too engineering and not enough motor car!

My father had discussed this with Lofty England of Jaguar, whom he knew well, while at a Silverstone meeting. England suggested he bring me to Coventry.

So, in February 1961, my father took me to Jaguar Cars in Coventry for discussions on apprenticeships. Part of the visit was a tour of the factory, and, during the course of it, we came across what I first thought were D-Type racing

My version of a racing car in 1952.

cars on a production line. Sworn to secrecy, I was told it was the new E-Type road car. Scarcely able to believe such a machine was going into production, I had to wait three weeks before its announcement in Geneva.

Fortunately, Jaguar accepted me as an apprenticed Automobile Engineer. Denstone may not have educated me in art or technology, but it gave me a firm grounding in self-confidence, and the ability to live with diverse other folk. Thus equipped, I began a career in the motor industry.

The 1956 works Mille Miglia Sunbeam Rapier outside our home.

Chapter 2

Jaguar engineering apprentice

Mid-September 1961, I caught the train to Coventry, and then a Corporation bus, which duly arrived at the Main Gate of Jaguar Cars Ltd, Browns Lane, in the far north of the city. Reporting to the Personnel Building, a drab concrete block alongside the Executive Offices, I found my new colleagues, the Jaguar apprentices for 1961. They were a pretty exclusive bunch: Jaguar only took about 24 per year.

Apprenticeships had a long history as a way of learning engineering. When my grandfather was an apprentice, his parents had to lodge a sum of money as a 'premium,' from which he would have been paid. Fortunately, this practice had ceased by the time I reached Jaguar, although the pay was pretty 19th century. I had five years ahead of me, to work in various departments of the business, with time to attend technical college for academic qualifications. I have no doubt that it was a superb way to enter the world of engineering, and adulthood.

My first day in the Apprentice School introduced me to the world of the machine tool. My background had not exposed me to the lathe, or the milling machine, so the instructor, Bob Andrews, had his work cut out. Next to the Machine Shop was the Lecture Room, and, in one corner, was the Apprentice Supervisor's office for one Joe Barker, and, more importantly his secretary, Felicity. If Joe was out when Bob gave a lecture, the apprentice's concentration was diverted to Felicity, who, being some years older and wiser, took no notice.

Christmas 1961 saw me finish my time in the Apprentice School, with the successful completion of the Bob Andrews Standard Test Piece: an adjustable tap wrench. My New Year assignment was the Machine Shop at the old Daimler works, in Radford. I was put in the Jaguar Gear Cutting Shop to work alongside a tool setter on the hobbing machines. This was a very boring period for me, and the time spent there was an introduction to the tedium which motor vehicle – or any other – mass production entailed.

The next move was to the Fighting Vehicle Department, also at Radford, where the Daimler Ferret scout car was built. Placed in the Experimental Department, I found life much more interesting. The Daimler Ferret was a two-man scout car, composed of a fully welded steel monocoque hull, sitting on double-wishbone suspension to all four wheels. A Rolls-Royce four-litre petrol engine, mounted longitudinally at the rear, drove a pre-selector gearbox. This was very similar to the transmission on ERA racing cars, which allowed one to steer with both hands when actually changing gear. The driver sat at the front, with the steering wheel tilted the opposite way to a car, due to the angle of the armoured hull. The danger of this was that one could turn it the wrong way when reversing, from some strange quirk of human ergonomics.

The transmission had the forward and reverse gears between the gearbox and the axles, so the vehicle could use all five gears in each direction. This gave a governed 60mph (100kph) in both forward and reverse very good for a scout car caught by surprise and needing to retreat, but not so good if you steered the wrong way at maximum speed in reverse. I took (and passed) my Jaguar company driving test on a Ferret, which also entitled me to drive all other company products, including the 150mph (forwards) E-Type – and the 60mph (backwards) Ferret.

I participated in the activities of the experimental group that was developing an amphibious version of the Ferret. The armoured hull was encased in a glass fibre box, containing foam to provide buoyancy, while the propulsion was by two Dowty ducted propellers, under the central gearbox. These were rather badly sited, hanging under the centre of the hull: they were very vulnerable, when entering or exiting water, if there was a steep bank. As a result, they usually got squashed upon entry, and the four-wheel drive to the knobbly tyres was all that was left to propel the machine.

Much testing was done in some ponds at MIRA. After a short journey from the Works, testing usually lasted a few minutes, until the jets detached. With full power, the wheels could manage 4mph (6kph) in still water. The vehicle floated very deep, with only the top of the turret showing, so it was extremely hard for it to climb out onto the bank, if there was no beach. A second, standard, vehicle was taken along to perform towing duties.

One day, the pair of Daimlers set off from MIRA to return to the factory, and a certain competitive spirit led to a race breaking out. Approaching a large floral-decorated roundabout in Nuneaton, the two Ferrets were neck-and-neck, with only space for one. With barely a bump, the one that I was navigating took a route straight across the middle, scattering ornamental tulip bulbs in all directions. Upon the return to Radford, my job was to lie down, under the thing, and remove a metal plate, which held back all the smelly, oily, muddy water that had leaked in during the day.

A big event followed: I was asked to accompany a full-production Ferret to Scotland for its annual sign-off trials. The 1962 trial was to be the last one required regularly for the Ferret. If it came through without defect, it would be accepted in perpetuity, as it had performed so consistently in the past.

Starting bright and early from the factory, the tank was filled with petrol, and the gun removed, to travel separately in an accompanying Vauxhall Victor. Apparently, it was illegal for civilians to drive around England with a working gun. Contemporary photographs suggest this rule was not too rigidly enforced, as it is clearly in place on one of our coffee stops. We headed north, stopping overnight en route, with the vehicle securely locked in Chorley munitions factory. The next morning, crossing Shap Fell, the driver was greatly assisted by my instructing him on the oncoming traffic status. I was high in the turret, which gave advantageous

The Daimler Ferret scout car in the Radford Works prior to the Scottish trip.

The Daimler Ferret, with its gun mounted, en route to Scotland.

views ahead, over the stone walls. While progress may seem slow by modern standards, it was the traffic, not the old roads, which held us up, as the Ferret could maintain its maximum speed most of the time.

The inspecting Major and Army driver were staying at the Selkirk Arms Hotel, in Kircudbright, while I, the official Daimler representative, had bed and breakfast in a cottage down the road. The trials went well, with the cross-country driving especially spectacular.

The Ferret fired its gun, discharged its smoke canisters, went through a full road test, and fuel consumption trial, and finished with an evacuation through the emergency hatch in the side of the hull. It all took three days and was passed successfully.

Not long after the trip to Scotland, I moved to the Jaguar factory at Browns Lane again, having thoroughly enjoyed playing with fighting vehicles, and I attended various departments, from Exhaust System Welding to the Service Spares Stores.

In an interview with Joe Barker, I explained that I wanted to be a body stylist, and that my training was going nowhere near that part of the business. Barker listened intently, and then suggested that, perhaps, a course on vehicle body building in Birmingham might be appropriate. I had to undertake to get myself there at my own expense, and thus I started to attend one day and

one evening per week. Meanwhile, Barker also arranged for me to enter the Experimental Body Shop, under Harry Rogers.

1964 arrived, and work progressed in the Body Experimental. All the wooden models used to check the development steel panels were made there, along with the wind tunnel models. Malcolm Sayer, the aerodynamicist, would draw these, including detail of the engine bay, and, if an open car, the interior. They were then sent for test in the quarter-scale wind tunnel at MIRA.

While I was in Harry Roger's shop, models were being made of road-going versions of the XJ 13 racing car. The project was shrouded in secrecy, even within the department, and the model maker had to cover them up during tea breaks. At the same time, the lightweight E-Type was being built in the Competition Shop next door – exciting times.

I was put to work at a bench between two people who were complete opposites. One fellow was a straightforward young pattern maker, who was friendly and helpful to me, while the other was an elderly, self-confessed communist. Spotting the 'privileged' background that he believed I had probably had, he pontificated his extreme dogma to any that would listen (not many). Given the close proximity of the workbenches, it was just as well that I managed to ignore most of Albert's jibes, and eventually got to quite like the old man. He was close to retirement, and spent most of the afternoons asleep in the toilets, which gave me and everyone else a break.

Jaguar was tooling up for the 'S' version of the Mark II, and I had to make the pattern for the fuel door hinge. It took me a long time, but I got it right in the end. Some of the Technical College work at Garretts Green was helpful, but, in the main, I had to pick it up as I went along. Each workman had his own tool collection, valued at hundreds of pounds, and most had homemade tools, such as spoke shaves, which could reach the places other tools could not. My meagre collection of tools was kindly augmented by my colleagues, a very trustworthy act on their part.

I also made some wooden scale models of car body design ideas, and, by the time I left the Body Experimental in the early summer, I was quite a good wood shaper.

The summer of 1964 saw me pass my Vehicle Body Building examinations, and I joined the Body Drawing Office, working alongside Cyril Crouch, the Assistant Chief Body Engineer. Cyril was fond of being taken out to lunch and had a jolly disposition, and I got on with him well. Work was going on for the revised Jaguar Mark X – the 420G; and others were laying out the body lines for the new Daimler limousine, built on a stretched Mark X floor. Most of my fairly lowly work was to draw up the smaller modifications to the 420G.

The drawings were done on a material not dissimilar to greaseproof paper, with a very hard traditional wooden pencil. If the drawing was for a component to be used in production, the original was passed to a team of tracers. These girls (they were always female) traced the drawing onto linen cloth using pens with Indian ink. Dimensions were always Imperial inches and 64ths.

While I was working there, a young body engineer, Phil Shepherd, left Jaguar to work on a body engineering contract in Germany; a pioneer to the immense contract industry that has grown up since then. It was considered very daring, as everyone waited for his first home leave to find out if the idea had worked. Of course it had, but the concept of leaving a lifetime employer was new, and, despite the greatly increased money available, few others dared to follow him at the time.

I wanted to be a body stylist, as they were known then, but my progress at Jaguar was thwarted, as it had no styling department. Instead, Sir William Lyons worked with Fred Gardner, in the Experimental Workshops, and Chief Body Engineer, Bill Thornton, to build up full-size models of future ideas. He insisted on them being made in metal, to ensure they flowed and were true surfaces, and, once he was happy with them, they were drawn out on aluminium sheet with a steel scriber. After the

dimensions were taken, through various points on the surface, the curves were generated from French or ships curves, or by using flexible splines. Until the advent of computer-generated surfaces, this was the only way to create the curves, with, obviously, tiny variations each time they were translated.

Now, as Sir William acknowledged that he would one day retire, there was to be a new Styling Department. Ahead of time, I heard that it was coming, and managed to find out that the new man being brought in to run it occasionally called at the Sportsmans Arms pub, in Allesley. I went there 'on spec' and, following the description of the person, introduced myself to Doug Thorpe, asking for a position in the new department. I didn't succeed at first, and another apprentice left the drawing office to join the fledgling department at the Radford works. However, I kept trying, and submitted some drawings of my design ideas, and, after a couple of months, I joined as the department apprentice.

The embryo Jaguar Styling Department was located on the first floor of the office buildings at Radford, alongside the Daimler Company showroom. The space was painted out in white, and the long thin room was lit from two windows at one end, and a skylight contraption, similar to an undernourished greenhouse. Doug Thorpe had a small private office in one corner, while we – for some time, just I – had a drawing board and table in the main space. An angled wallboard ran down one side, for the creation of full-size body line drawings, and a turntable was located at the end of the room, for the presentation of clay models up to ⅜-scale. Two clay modelling tables were freestanding nearby, with a small clay softening oven. A number of pinboards adorned the walls, for the display of Doug's highly professional, and my totally amateur, drawings.

When I first arrived, work in the Styling Department was all based on ideas for the forthcoming XJ6 saloon, which, in 1965, had styling based on a large version of an E-Type Jaguar with four headlamps. A similar frontal design reappeared later on the XJS. The idea was very advanced and exciting, but accommodating the E-Type curves on such a large vehicle tended to add too much weight to the design. Gradually the ideas moved towards a shrunken Mark X style, but with a rise over the rear wheels, and a rear deck not unlike the contemporary Lancia Fulvia.

Our most popular medium for presentation drawings was French Papier Canson – rag paper – in a variety of colours, with the drawing made using Cumberland Derwent crayon pencils. Highlights, and deep shadow were emphasised with gouache paint. Later, I produced a number of drawings using charcoal, but the need for the constant use of fixative, to prevent smudging, slowed up the work. After I had begun to attend art school, I moved to airbrush work, but that was also very slow, due to the need to cut masks, to prevent overspray around the areas being worked.

For models, we used a clay/wax material imported from the USA. It has remained the mainstay of the automobile design world and was heated to a mild temperature to soften it. We then applied it to a wooden basic armature, and shaped it with various home made tools. Most of these were adapted from sharpened pieces of hacksaw blade. I soon became fairly proficient in this, probably as a result of my work under Bill Rogers, but I never came to love the waxy smell, or the way that clay found its way under nails and into clothing. We modelled both exteriors and interiors, but it was the exterior work I preferred.

Joe Barker supported this work by sending me to Coventry College of Art, where I joined a Technical Illustration Course. In those days, there were no specific automobile design courses available. Here, I worked on various projects involving drawing, illustration, and even printing and photography. Among the projects that I carried out was an entry in the IBCAM design competition that required a detailed design and coloured drawing of a small family car. The resulting airbrushed entry managed a commended award. There were a number of professional design competitions in those days against which I could pit myself, and they were a good way of measuring my skill against recognised industry designers. I had a number of commendations in these, which helped my confidence – and my standing – in the department.

One of the most memorable of these was the Concorso Grifo d'Oro Bertone, a car design competition announced in the press, in March 1966. I immediately contacted the organisers in Italy, and received the instructions and chassis drawings around which a car body was to be designed. The instructions asked for the design to be submitted to Bertone, the organising coachbuilding concern, by a date a few weeks later.

The competition required a design to be delineated over a chassis drawing supplied by Bertone. I immediately encountered a problem: the views of the front and rear of the chassis would have overlapped the drawings of the finished body. Taking the same size of paper, and carefully redrawing the competition symbol of the Griffon, I redrew the body drawing to lie within the paper size comfortably. I produced a three-quarter front view of the design using crayon on 16 x 20in (400 x 500mm) coloured paper. A design thesis had to be written explaining the philosophy behind the design. Finally, I made a tenth-scale model. Finished in bright Italian red, the model had solid windows, painted black – all identified by the monogram 'CI,' to preserve anonymity during judging.

I rushed the design to completion – working at home, in the office, and at art college – and dispatched it to Italy. The entry had taken much hard work, all under extreme time pressure.

Shortly afterwards, I received a letter which not only confirmed the safe arrival of the package, but also explained that the spring deadline was not for the complete finished job, but was the closing date for applications to enter. It went on to apologise for the incorrect translation of the competition rules, and added: would I like the entry returned to me, as the closing date was in August! I decided that I had done all I could, and that the entry should stay at Bertone. Now all I had to do was wait.

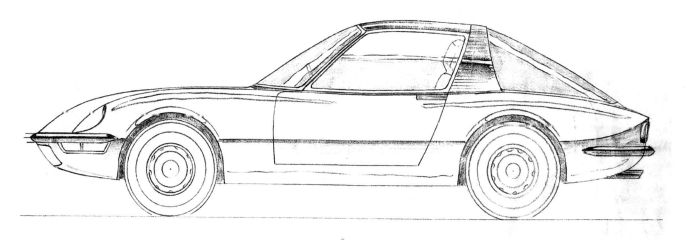

A pencil drawing of my design for the Bertone Concorso Grifo d'Oro in 1966.

My apprenticeship was approaching its end. There was no guarantee of a position at Jaguar once an apprentice had completed his three- or five-year training, and this had caused some difficulties for me back in January 1966. Following my commendation in an IBCAM design competition, the Ford Motor Company had contacted me, and asked me to attend an interview. The result was that it offered me a position, with a salary of £1200 per year. This was an enormous sum, as I would only expect to get £750 to £800 at the end of my apprenticeship, nine months later – assuming I was offered anything at all. There was also the attraction of discounted Ford products – as Jaguars were expensive, its products were not attainable on my likely Jaguar salary.

I responded that I was interested in the job, but only if Ford would wait until September, so that I could finish my apprenticeship. Ford said it couldn't wait, so, with some reluctance, I dropped the whole thing. It was probably the right thing to do, as an indentured Automobile Engineer at Jaguar is held in high regard.

In the meantime, changes were afoot. Sitting down to tea on 12 July 1966, the assembled Jaguar apprentices were shocked to learn that the company had just lost its independence. The evening news announced the merger of Jaguar with the British Motor Corporation. This brought luxury and sporting cars, plus buses from Daimler, and heavy trucks from Guy, into the group that already had Austin, Austin Healey, Morris, MG, Riley and Wolseley. This new group was to be called British Motor (Holdings) Ltd, and commanded a 44% share of the British market. The creation of BMH was to have an effect on me through my work in the Styling Department, as Sir William became involved in the future model policy of the whole group. But that followed the end of my apprenticeship – now fast approaching.

As September 1966 drew near, I waited to hear whether I had secured a permanent staff position in the Jaguar Styling Department. The company confirmed a place for me that summer, and I drifted towards having a proper job, aged 22½.

www.velocebooks.com / www.veloce.co.uk
Details of all current books • New book news • Special offers • Gift vouchers • Forum

15

Chapter 3
Jaguar staff stylist

Mid-shaving, one Saturday morning, at the end of August 1966, prior to going to Silverstone, I answered the telephone: an Italian voice told me I had won a silver medal – Grifo Argento – in the Bertone design competition. My parents and I were euphoric. Later that day, the effect of shaving only the right side of my face became both obvious and irritating.

The Concorso had attracted 5374 applications. Alexander Neumeister, from Stuttgart, in Germany, won the gold, with a beautifully built model which featured transparent windows, and an interior. It is perhaps interesting to ponder what might have happened had the application deadline been correctly translated into English.

Jaguar was delighted with the news of this success, and assisted in getting maximum publicity for itself and me, circulating it to all the national daily papers, and international motoring and business magazines. My prize was an air ticket to Turin, with accommodation provided, and Jaguar's biggest contribution was to extend the visit, so that I would have plenty of time to enjoy the motor show, and absorb the city of coachbuilding.

The first day, I toured Bertone's premises, with its lines of pretty Fiat 850 spyders and the equally pleasant Simca 1000 coupés. These models were built in quantity, and formed the mainstay of the Bertone Carrozzeria. However, like all Italian coachbuilders at the time, it was the low-volume and one-off designs that touched the heart and hit the headlines.

Giorgetto Guigiaro had been Chief Designer at Bertone since leaving Fiat, and, some 21 cars later, he had just departed for a short spell with Ghia. He left many fine designs at Bertone, but it was a one-off prototype which stole the show for me. The Alfa Romeo Canguro, with a fibreglass skin over a tubular chassis from the racing Tubolare, was so fluid, so well-proportioned and balanced, that I have never forgotten the impression it made on me when I was allowed to sit in it. The Bertone factory tour culminated in a visit to the workshop, where a forthcoming Turin Show star exhibit was frantically being prepared and repaired.

In those days, each major country held its Motor Show every year: Paris in October, followed a few days later by London, and then, four days after that, Turin. Bertone and Lamborghini had cooperated to produce the legendary Miura, and the prototype was continuing development in Modena, while Bertone finished a second car for exhibition use. This had been rushed back from the stunned crowds at Earls Court, over the weekend, in time for refurbishment, prior to Turin opening three days later.

There must have been six people working on it, tapping out dents, re-spraying scratches and fettling the interior trim, all in a small workshop. At one point, a panel beater, who had tapped out a near-invisible dent in one door, threw his hammer over the roof of this priceless car to his colleague, working on the other one. Such was their confidence in each other's skill that the thought of dropping the hammer never crossed their minds. The painter ran round with a small gun, blowing in any imperfections, using his free hand as a fast and mobile mask to prevent overspray. The Lamborghini Miura was smugly in place at the Valentino Park Exhibition Hall before the show opened.

The first afternoon in Turin, we visited the exhibition

of the winning designs in the Concorso, which had been laid out under the colonnades in the Via Roma, Turin's main street. Here, the models, incorporating both the designer's impression and the bodylines drawing, were displayed on specially made tables.

The following morning, the prizegiving took place in a fine building, and I was privileged to shake the hand of the great man himself, Nuccio Bertone. His father had founded the business in 1912, but it was Nuccio who had brought the firm into the limelight, and had built, in the early 1960s, his state-of-the-art factory for specialist car construction, at Grugliasco. Like Sir William Lyons, Bertone did not style the products himself, but was the selector of designs and designers.

Following the presentation of the silver Grifo, we went to the opening of the Motor Show. Here, the showstopper was to be Ghia, or, more accurately, Guigiaro. He had been brought in to revive its fortunes, in late 1965. Twelve months later, he stunned the automobile design world with a presentation that may well be a record for the simultaneous release of diverse product by one designer. These were the De Tomaso Pampero, a mid-engined spider on the Vallelunga chassis, the De Tomaso Mangusta with a V8 Ford engine mounted midships, the Vanessa (built on the Fiat 850), and, finally, the Ghibli, residing on the Maserati stand.

Jaguar was, of course, exhibiting at the Turin Show. John Morgan, its Export Sales Director, was in attendance, and acted as my host, once the Bertone proceedings were over, and while I stayed on another couple of days at Jaguar's expense.

A couple of notable events failed to come to fruition. The first was an attempt to get me a ride in the prototype Lamborghini Miura down at Santa Agata, shelved due to travel and time constraints. It has recently emerged that this was probably the car being refurbished at Bertone, to allow the press access to only the second car of its generation.

The second was my television debut. BBC2 had been running for a short time, and was transmitted only in the London area. Special television sets were needed to pick up the 625-line pictures. John Mills produced a motoring program called *Wheelbase,* as part of the new channel's speciality role. I was interviewed at the exhibition, on the Bertone stand. Beforehand, Mr Mills discussed the questions he would be asking – though, in the event, he deviated from the planned script completely after two questions, but I got through it fairly happily. I expressed the view that British motor industry had nothing to compare to the designs behind us on the Bertone stand. I thought Britain should take notice, or we would lose competitive appeal.

The model and drawings on display in Turin for the Bertone competition in 1966.

The Grifo d'Oro Bertone 1966.

He stayed with Jaguar for many years, being most interested in interiors. A little later, two more apprentices joined, Chris Greville-Smith and George Thompson. Chris later raced sports cars, taking over the Phantom Clubman's car in which I had a hand. George came to Coventry from Glasgow. He had an unmistakable 'line' that I have continued to see emerge through his various employers' products over the years. Very quiet and unassuming, George was a natural, and he did a lot of very good work, much of which was never used.

The department's work was still mainly for the forthcoming Jaguar XJ6, code-named XJ4 – the market name being a last-minute creation. Stuck for something better, the powers that were decided to commandeer the project name, but alter the numeral to the number of engine cylinders. This actually led to some later confusion with other XJ experimental programmes.

Besides working on scale-model interiors, we did some work for Sir William Lyons on a variety of vehicles within the newly joined BMH Group. Sir William probably felt uneasy about being asked to assist with vehicles unlike typical Jaguars. I produced a number of stylish designs for coupé Minis, based on the longer van wheelbase. These were never adopted, but the redesigned front for the standard saloon was eventually released as the Mini Clubman in 1969. Jaguar was never publicly connected with that project, which is often seen as spoiling the 'classic' Mini front end. However, at the time, the Mini wasn't a classic, and Austin/Morris saw a freshening of the design as essential.

1967 saw the publication of the first American safety regulations, and all our work had to start taking them into account. At the time (and often since), I felt that, while the auto industry could certainly do things to make cars safer, it seemed that it was on the receiving end of the bulk of the measures, when, in fact, other areas, such as road engineering, with issues such as the placing of telegraph poles on the outside of bends, should also have received attention.

It was a big change of direction for many in the industry, brought up on the dictum: 'we don't build cars for people to crash them!' This new focus on safety resulted in my attending a crash test of the E-Type at

My parents' home was 55 miles from London, and BBC2 could not be received by standard television equipment there. Living locally was a family friend who was a television enthusiast and, with the aid of a very tall aerial in his garden, he could access the new channel. Very kindly, he invited me, my parents and friends to watch the programme. Being a good host, he laid on food and drink for all the guests. Well, the report of the show was there, but no mention of me, which I found embarrassing, to say the least. I slunk off, never to trust television producers again!

The end of my apprenticeship merged seamlessly into my appointment as a staff designer in the Jaguar Styling Department. The department was growing slowly, with, first, the addition of another apprentice, Colin Holtum.

MIRA, in 1978, the first of what were to become, for me, many. The facilities were all in the open, and the test car was propelled into the barrier by being towed by another car. On at least one occasion, the tow car (not the Jaguar) failed to have enough power to achieve the correct impact speed! The E-Type, with its generous front overhang performed, extremely well.

A quarter-scale drawing signed 'Designed and drawn OCW,' dated 5 August 1968, marks my first proper, serious car design that could have proceeded, had circumstances permitted. Titled Project XJ21 2+2 (wide track), it depicts a plan to re-body the E-Type Jaguar. The substructure was preserved from the two-plus-two platform with the 105in (2667mm) wheelbase; only the interface with the skin panels needed modification to suit the revised contours. The drawing carries a data box, which describes the following:

- Engine: V12, with either petrol injection, or carburettors
- Cooling: Two air intakes. Total area 680sq in. [The cooling of the V12 was obviously causing some concern, hence the attention to this aspect]
- Suspension: Front track 58in (1473mm); Rear track 58⅝in (1489mm) – as XJ4 saloon. [Interesting that the intention was to commonise at least the rear suspension with the then-unannounced saloon to become the XJ6]
- Tyres: Dunlop A70 VR 15 SP Sport
- Lamps: 4 x 5¾in headlamps with Clear Hooters [a local company] retracting units; all other lamps to world regulations

The overall dimensions were given in inches, and feet and inches.

Jaguar E-Type crash test MIRA. I am in the centre, in the light coloured coat.

I modelled the design in clay, and finished it with aluminium window frames and wooden foil-covered bumpers. It was spray-painted in Jaguar Carmen Red (despite our being aware of Dynok peelable plastic skinning, we never used it). As a result, the clay was discarded when the model was dismantled. Following the successful presentation of the model to Sir William Lyons, I drew out the full-size bodylines. However, Jaguar's engineers were very busy completing the XJ6, so the project came to nothing. Later the E-Type was fitted with the V12 engine and wider track suspension, but the body had only minor modifications.

Sir William was elected to the Royal Institute of British Architects, and this brought some interesting little jobs back to the office. One of these was to develop an idea of using moving pavements in London to reduce pedestrians' need of road transport. Compared to modern airport 'moving pavements,' it ran three times as fast, with three belts running alongside the fast belt at 'stations.' People would have stepped from one to another, to give the necessary acceleration and deceleration. Whether people would have enjoyed travelling at twelve miles per hour, erect, and what would have happened if the motor stopped suddenly, we will never know, as this was also a stillborn project. Later, this idea re-emerged as the Travolator, often used at airports.

Another job that Sir William brought in was closer to the motor industry sector: a bus designed to plug into the forthcoming Boeing 747 Jumbo jet airliner. Twice the size of any other civil airliner then in existence, London Airport was working out ways of loading and unloading passengers from the 747 without losing the onboard conditioned air, which would take a long time to replenish.

Aircraft were still boarded by external steps at the time, and the size of the 747 would have left a long walk from the terminal. The vehicles were to be built on four Daimler 33ft (10.05m) bus chassis, arranged two-by-two. This would make a vehicle with a 66ft (20.1m) wheelbase (there were no axles in the centre) and a width of around 16ft (4.87m). A flexible trunk joined the upper deck of this two-floor vehicle to either the aircraft, or the terminal building. The airport authorities could not comprehend a plane with a wingspan twice anything then known, taxiing up to a terminal.

Designated a 'mobile lounge,' there were to be two versions: one, for economy class passengers, had as many bus seats as would fit – probably around 200. The other had 60 first class chairs, and some facilities for ground stewardesses serving cocktails, etc. Powered by one rear-mounted engine, it would be driven out to the aircraft, and plugged in, to allow boarding. One problem was the considerable height of the Boeing floor, so the ramp stuck up like a unicorn's horn. Presentation drawings were made – one in particular is worth a mention: we wanted some human figures to give it scale, and, as no one in the department wished to draw the figures, suitably-scaled pictures were sought in magazines. We will never know if Sir William ever spotted the Duke of Edinburgh as the bus driver!

Eventually, they made the loading trunk at airports long enough to

Quarter-scale clay model of the rebodied Jaguar E-Type 2+2 V12.

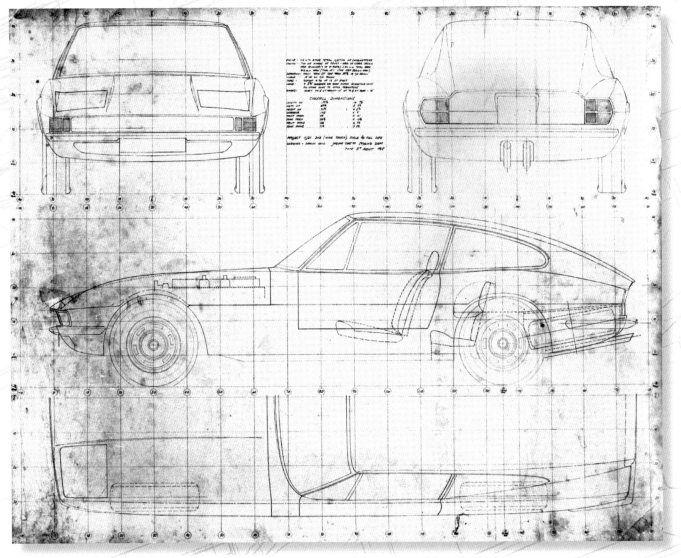

My general arrangement drawing for the Jaguar E-Type 2+2 V12.

dispense with the mobile lounge altogether, and none were ever built. These trunks became the now-familiar Jetway.

The autumn of 1968 brought the launch of the XJ6, to worldwide acclaim. The car was a huge success, and I had managed to get two items through to the production car, without the design being changed. One was the centre bright metal road wheel trim – the knave plate, and the other was the face-level vent on the outboard ends of the dashboard.

Various offshoots came from the XJ6, and, one day, Sir William came into the office and said he wanted a stretched version, with 4in (100mm) extra in the rear passenger length. I was assigned to work out how to cut and splice in the extra length, as the car did not have its maximum

height, width, wing line, in the same place. I calculated what to do, produced the full-size drawing on a Thursday, and was staggered to see a finished car on the Monday following. A car had been cut and steel sections let in, butt-welded, sanded and painted over a weekend. While not drivable, it gave the 'Old Man' a chance to assess the package quickly. Unfortunately, when he closed it, the back door fell in half, the welding not having the necessary integrity for the blow. The long-wheelbase XJ6 went into production, as an option, some time later.

I also drew the lines for the two-door coupé XJ6. The engineering challenges of that job comprised: dropping rear quarter glass into the body; and how to ensure a droop free passenger door. This design also went into

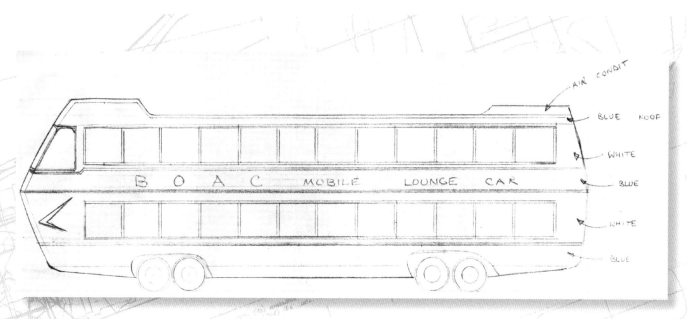

A sketch of the airport mobile lounge.

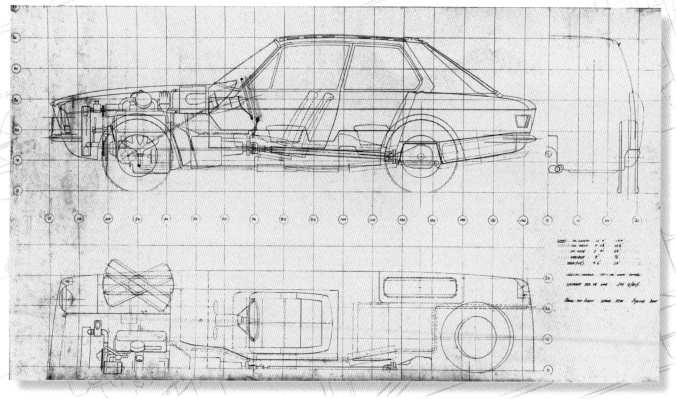

My general arrangement drawing of the proposed Jaguar 'small car.'

production, unlike the convertible we planned, on the same platform. Jaguar often planned designs for many variants of its cars, such as estate cars and limousines, but rarely proceeded with them.

In 1967, Leyland Motors, the truck-building concern, bought the Rover Company. Rover had itself bought the famous Alvis Company, in 1965, so Leyland, who already owned Standard-Triumph, now represented a large segment of Britain's motor industry. 17 January 1968 was the day that Leyland Motors merged with British Motor Holdings – which included Jaguar Cars Ltd – to form a huge conglomerate of motor interests. It proved hopelessly cumbersome to manage, and was in difficulty before it even began, as so many members were old rivals. Jaguar and Rover were potentially at war, with Jaguar getting the proposed mid-engined Rover BS coupé scrapped. It also got the proposed P8 Rover large car dropped from corporate plans, as it could have been a threat to Jaguar's new saloon. Sir William fought his corner in the Leyland boardroom from a position of strength, and continued to call upon the Styling Department for assistance. I remember producing a design for a Leyland gas turbine coach, as one of these offerings.

1969 was an eventful year. My personal transport became a Sunbeam Imp Sport, which was a nice car to drive; but I got the chance to drive an even nicer one, when Geoff Dove, a long-time family friend, lent me his Alfa Romeo 1750 GTV. The loan was part of the concept study for a new small saloon for Jaguar, which, while Sir William supported it, was championed by Lofty England. It was quickly decided that the Alfa did not have enough rear seat room, and that 4in (100mm) extra was needed in that area.

Mike Kimberley was assigned to help me with the mechanical layout of my first new vehicle. He was to become an important part of Lotus (and my story), later. Mike had worked with the small team developing the XJ13 Le Mans car. He was to be found in a secure upstairs office in the Engineering Centre, alongside Malcolm Sayer. The room had a pleasant, relaxed atmosphere, as they worked on future concepts specifically for the company directors.

The small Jaguar was being considered, because the new XJ6 was larger than the Mark Two models. The Daimler V8 250 was going out of production in 1969, while the Jaguar 240/340 models had gone a year earlier. Some customers wanted the luxury and performance without the bulk, and Lofty England, the ex-Competitions Manager, could probably see little racing potential in the big car.

The overall length of 164in (4166mm) sat on a 96in (2438mm) wheelbase. The roof was 4ft 2⅞in (1292mm) high and the overall width 64in (1626mm). The frontal styling had single 7in diameter headlamps. To keep the front low, the tops of the lamps projected above the peak of the bonnet. The Daimler 2.5-litre V8 engine was located over the front wheels, mated to a Jaguar gearbox. A dotted line on the plan view indicated a proposed Jaguar XJ V8 engine at 920mm wide.

Alfa Romeo had 118hp in its GTV, so Daimler's 140hp should have given fine performance, assuming the weight had been similar. Quarter-scale models were made for the body design, and Mike Kimberley worked up a sensible mechanical package, with assistance from Malcolm Sayer. No doubt due to the Leyland clash of interests, the project was axed as being too close to Rover – or so we were led to believe at the time.

3 December 1968 is the date on the drawing of my proposal for the car that became the XJS. Code-named the XJ27, Malcolm Sayer had already drawn designs for a 2+2 coupé on a shortened XJ6 saloon car platform. The wheelbase was reduced behind the driver's seat by 6.8in (173mm). The car was to replace the E-Type, which was proving difficult to sell in the late '60s. Sayer's proposal looked much like the final production car, but with twin circular headlamps in place of the special units used outside the USA.

We had to take care to preserve parts of the XJ6, as was demanded for cost purposes, but the rear seat pans were new. They were scalloped back 64mm from the original saloon car position, while keeping the structural members unchanged, to make enough space with the shortened wheelbase. The front bucket seats were based on those in the E-Type. The passenger door was 45.2in (1148mm) long, and contained a 'USA side impact bar' 40mm wide by 300mm deep. The windshield was direct glazed for a flush transition into the roof, which was helped by having a double curvature crown on the top of the glass. The rain gutter was indicated as being down the inside of the screen pillar. This design was used, in similar form, on the Lotus M50 Elite of 1971.

A 27-gallon (123-litre) fuel tank was located over the rear axle, filled from a fuel cap in the vinyl-covered 'feature' quarter pillar above the rear wheel. The spare tyre lay on the boot floor, which required modification from the parent saloon, and I recall that the rear structural longitudinal member was shortened some 4in (100mm) from the original. Dunlop tyres of E 70 VR 195 x 15 were the specified rubber. The drawing shows considerable detail of the base structure, sealing, glass drop, and important mechanical features, and therefore can be seen as a coming-of-age point for me – as a car designer, rather than just a stylist. A quarter-scale model was built, and interested Sir William enough for him to approve the next step.

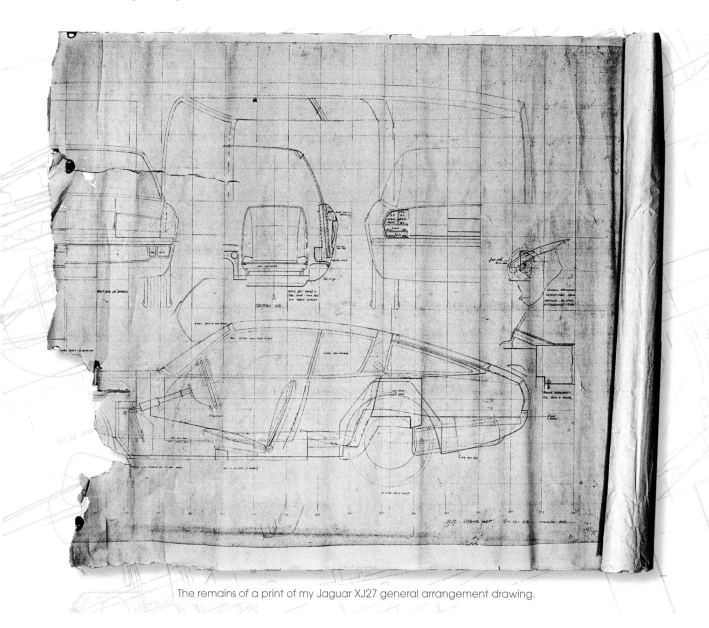

The remains of a print of my Jaguar XJ27 general arrangement drawing.

At Jaguar, this comprised a full-size steel skin model; Sir William would not view clay or plaster models as the final stage of design. First, I had to draw the body lines full-size – not only the transverse sections, but also the waterlines and light lines. The waterlines were sections parallel to the ground, which checked out the smoothness of the panel, and gave detail to the ends and places of rapid change. The highlights were tangents off the wing forms, to estimate the effect of angular light reflections. This information was delivered to the Competition Shop at Browns Lane, where Bob Blake the ex-Briggs Cunningham panel beater, was to make the wooden egg crate checking fixture, upon which the panels would be fitted.

The process involved cutting all the sections in plywood, making detail corners in carved mahogany, and building up a full-size model. As Bob progressed, wooden splines (long straight grained pieces of wood, about a quarter-of-an-inch square) were laid along the body, to check that the curves presented by the sections were fair without humps or hollows. Happily, the work needed no modification and, in due course, it was finished; I was very pleased with the result. I was thrilled and excited to see my design transformed to full-size for the first time, and the egg crate was moved to Fred Gardner's Body Experimental Shop for the skin to be made.

This was the first time I had seen one of my ideas

turned into a full-size model. In those early days, I used to try hard to imagine what the finished car would look like. Later, I became used to the transformation, and could imagine the design as a finished car while it was still on paper. This attribute was severely tested when it came to boats, where the scale was of a larger magnitude. Part of this visualisation skill also allowed me to 'see' components and details from the three-view drawings, whether it be for cars, houses, or civil engineering.

Bob Blake was not involved with the panelling of the steel skin, as it was entrusted to Fred's shop – where one was not welcome to visit. Fred ran his empire as a tyrant, removing even legitimate visitors with colourful language.

Some days later, Fred called me up to the workshop to explain why the rear wheels were so far inside the body. We checked the position of the wheels, and found it to be correct, so Fred suggested, in his expressive way, that the designer was both incompetent and inexperienced. Mystified, I put my hand under the edge of the wheel opening and found that the panels were nowhere near touching the wooden sections. I suggested that, as the splines had lain over the surface correctly before cladding, the problem was in the panels, not the design. Gardner would not accept this, and I left the workshop very disappointed. I heard nothing more, until, a few weeks later, I discovered that the model had been sent to the Jaguar scrap yard, and broken up. While not perhaps the greatest design, its lack of a fair showing always mystified me, although I suspect that some of the old hands at Jaguar probably arranged for its early demise, as they had traditionally worked up new designs with Sir William.

Bill Heynes, the Technical Director, masterminded another stillborn design. It occurred in the summer of 1969 when the Jaguar E-Type was not selling at all well, and the Reliant Scimitar GTE had just been announced as a sports estate car. Heynes had a large dog, and had difficulty getting it into his E-Type, so he asked me to design an estate version. Heynes tended to keep away from the body activities and leave it to Sir William, but, in this case, he got involved. The design featured a large 'picture window' on a steeper, more angular, rear end. The E-Type estate did not progress beyond the drawing stage!

The spring of 1970 brought an opportunity for me to make a bit more progress. As mentioned earlier, Sir William was participating in the policy and management of the new huge group formed as British Leyland. The group recognised that there were overlaps, and a proliferation of parts and designs, and wanted to rationalise them. Jaguar was asked to send a full-size model of the interior of the forthcoming XJS to Longbridge, for a corporate design review, and we had only six weeks to get it ready.

I had been working on ideas for the interior, but no hardware existed. Asked if I could meet this deadline, I promised to get a satisfactory wooden model done in time. This involved getting Percy Leason's Trim Shop, at Browns Lane, to do the seats and all the trimmed surfaces, while the Radford Pattern Shop built the models. First, a buck (which was a replica of the floor), bulkheads and tunnel had to be made, before wooden models of the dashboard, centre console and instrument pack could be upholstered and fitted.

The floor was carpeted, and representative pedals, steering column and switchgear were made and fitted. The centre console contained a Philips radio/cassette player, a first at Jaguar and, indeed, one of the earliest in the motor industry.

I wrote an ambitious plan to ensure that all would be ready on the day and, on this one occasion, was allowed to do overtime. The job was ready on time, despite many expectations otherwise – which didn't do me any harm – but it did not go to Longbridge, as the meeting was postponed at the last minute!

All this work was going on at the old Daimler factory in Radford. At about this time, the department moved to Browns Lane, where much more space was available and the full-size models could be made next door, under Bob Blake's control, Fred Gardner having retired. We held great hopes that the new studio would reflect the latest up-market architectural fashions, such as we had all seen in articles on Ford, and other big design studios. The reality was that, beyond painting part of the old Experimental Body Shop white, and constructing basic metal-framed storerooms and Doug Thorpe's office, nothing else was done, except the flooring. The team was very disappointed as indications had, originally, been very different.

The work at Jaguar was proceeding slowly, so it was a relief to get some interesting unpaid work from some friends. Richard Cresswell was an ex-Jaguar apprentice, and worked in the Experimental Road Test Department with his colleague, Peter Taylor. Richard's brother raced a car in the Clubman's Formula, and we decided we could do better, and would build our own. I took responsibility for the packaging and appearance of this machine.

It had to be front-engined, rear-wheel drive; the power unit of 1600cc, and aerodynamic wings and slick tyres were permitted. The body was as low as possible, with the top of the engine housed in a blister. The driver lay in a reclining driving position, on the right side of the car, while there was theoretical space for a passenger on the left. Mudguards had to be fitted, so that the car was 'road legal,' although it had no lights. Our apartment became not only the drawing office for the project, but the

My Jaguar XJ27 quarter-scale clay model.

The Jaguar XJ27 interior model.

About this time, Jaguar got hold of the new BMW 2800. I, and many of my contemporaries, saw this as a direction for future Jaguars, but senior management thought it 'not appropriate.' Another design which met with the same indifference was the Pininfarina-bodied BMC 1800, with its sleek aerodynamic and airy lines. It was beginning to seem that little progress could be made at Jaguar. That the XJS was going toward production with a body style I disliked, did not help.

The previous year, in October 1969, I had married Wendy, who encouraged and supported me until her untimely death in 2014. As my Jaguar efforts were being thwarted, especially over the XJS design, she agreed that, perhaps, it was time for a change. We contemplated taking an hotel in the far north of Scotland, but that plan failed to materialise; so, when the prospect of moving to another car company arose, it was welcomed by us both.

This came via one of my former colleagues at Jaguar: after teaming up on the small

furniture was rearranged to create the seating buck, so the cockpit could be a snug fit for Richard. The Cresswell Clubman's car, after coming a fine second in the Shell Championship, was eventually taken over by Chris Greville-Smith as the Phantom.

Work in the Jaguar Styling Department consisted mainly of continuing the interior design and mock-up work for the XJS interior. Work on minor changes for the V12 E-Type was still ongoing, with it now moving into pre-production. One of these changes involved the use of a rear lamp, modelled on the unit used on the Alfa Romeo that I had borrowed from Geoff Dove. This also turned up on the Lotus Elan +2, so Geoff, as an Alfa dealer, had done a good job selling lamps!

car project, Mike Kimberley had moved to Lotus, at the beginning of 1970, to work under its new Chief Engineer, Tony Rudd. Lotus was in the process of developing a four-seat sports car, to take the company 'up-market,' and Colin Chapman was looking for some fresh design. Mike thought of me, and arranged for me to meet Colin in the October of 1970.

The interview with Colin Chapman went well, with a discussion on which recent Italian designers we preferred – something which we found that we agreed. I had brought a portfolio of my work, that included designs for a replacement Lotus Seven, which took some cues from the Cresswell car. The result was that Lotus made me an offer of a salary plus company car. I drove

The very successful Cresswell Clubman's car.

home in high spirits, having promised to discuss the offer and reply promptly.

Jaguar responded by offering to match the salary, but without a car (which would have required a change of status to management). The result of further negotiations was that Lotus agreed to increase the salary, with a Ford Escort as company car, for the position of Manager, Body Styling and Design. Jaguar could not compete, and, as I assumed I would get no further there until Doug Thorpe left or retired, I gave my notice to leave at the end of December 1970.

Sir William called me to his office for a chat about my departure. He showed me some proposals for the future in British Leyland, including the Range Rover and a new Austin Healey 3000 successor. The Range Rover arrived shortly afterwards, but the Healey never made it

to production. During our discussion, I explained that I would like to return to Jaguar one day, but felt that I would increase my experience by working elsewhere in the meantime. Sir William agreed, and wished me well in my new venture. That the Chairman took the time to discuss my future was most flattering, and I treasure the event to this day.

A leaving party at a small country pub, where the beer was dispensed in jugs, marked the severing of my connection with Jaguar after ten years and three months. It had been a privilege to work there, and my association with the company has always been treated with great respect by the rest of the world's motor industry.

On New Year's Eve, 1970, my wife and I set off towards Norfolk, where I would take up my new position with Lotus Cars.

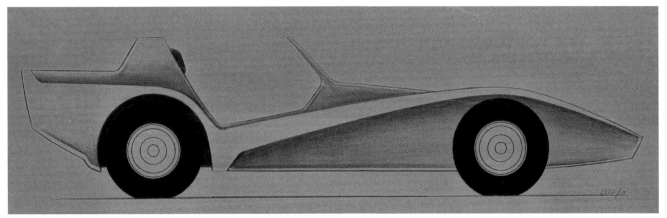

My 'Lotus interview' sketch for a Lotus 7.

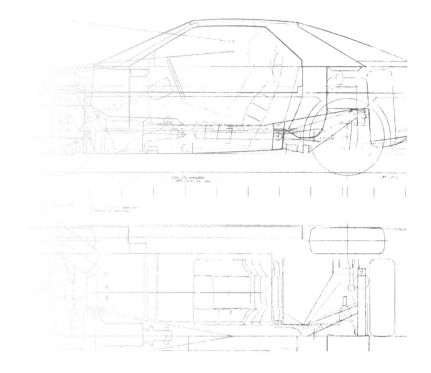

Chapter 4
Lotus

On New Year's Eve 1970, I drove with my wife, Wendy, into Hingham, Norfolk. It was snowing as we arrived to spend a few hours with the Kimberley family, reuniting the partnership of our Jaguar days. During the evening, the conversation turned to Lotus and, in particular, to the impressive new facility in which the company was now located, and where I was about to be based.

Colin Chapman had started building lightweight 'specials' at his Hornsey home, in North London, in the late 1940s. He quickly gained a name as a designer who thought through every detail in order to save weight and optimise function. He earned a reputation as a pioneer, and it was the development of the Type 14 Elite, built around a glass fibre monocoque, which prompted the move to more spacious premises, at Cheshunt, Hertfordshire.

In due course, the Elite gave way to the commercially-much-more-successful Elan. It was the planned expansion of this range, plus the spectacular growth of racing car production, and the operation of the factory's own Team Lotus – by now a dominant feature of the racing scene right up to Grand Prix level and the Indianapolis 500 – which led Chapman to seek yet another location, one which would accommodate whatever further expansion the rapidly growing company might require in the years ahead.

Hethel, three miles from the market town of Wymondham in Norfolk, was a former Second World War airfield. The runways and perimeter road of the airfield provided the company with its own on-site test track, and landing facilities for Chapman's aircraft. The offices, workshops and vehicle assembly buildings were all brand new, and surrounded by landscaped gardens. The main office was a trendsetter, being open plan – it featured on a number of media programmes – while the directors had a fine suite of offices, alongside the panelled boardroom.

Lotus Cars Limited was a busy place, building the two-seater Elan in open and closed forms, its larger sister, the Elan Plus 2, and the mid-engined Europa. Lotus twin-cam cylinder heads were machined alongside the assembly area, and the company had a high quality Paint Shop. Nearby, in Potash Lane, Lotus Components was making the Seven, and a range of racing cars. The trim and upholstery were also produced close by, in the stables of Ketteringham Hall, which Colin had recently bought.

Life at Lotus began, for me, on January 4 1971. My working space was at the back of the open-plan main office, with Team Lotus, under Maurice Philippe, on one side of me, and the production control staff, under John Pettifer, on the other. The reception area, with a car and engine on display, was presided over by a lady at a semi-circular desk. The visitors' seats had been converted from ones used in the Europa, had perilously short legs, and were inclined to trap any occupant who was unwise enough to sit in them!

Tony Rudd, Colin Chapman's Technical Director, sat immediately beyond the reception area, facing his Engineering Department. Rudd had structured the department with Mike Kimberley in charge of vehicle engineering, and Stefan Williams running powertrain. Everything was operated on a small-team basis, so Stefan had just three folk (later to be joined by a couple of others) to help with the new Lotus 907 engine, which was then under development.

The vehicle group comprised Ian Jones, who had come from Vanwall as Colin Chapman's first draughtsman, in 1956, and was responsible for all the outline layout work and presentation drawings of future ideas; Chris Dunster, who worked on body and chassis; Derek Sleath, who had a major input on the body engineering side, assisted by Kevin Youngs; two others working on chassis and suspension; and Ken Baldwin struggling stoically with the electrical work.

It didn't take me long to realise that morale was pretty low; there had been a lot of redundancies before Christmas, as the Elan had been selling slowly, and the Renault-engined Europa was struggling with lack of power, and various practicality problems. My own biggest problem looked likely to be working with Ian Jones, because he had been around for so long. However, Ian was not without a sense of humour, and stories were legion of his past exploits; amongst them, the tale of the origin of the 'British Standard Foot.'

Lotus designs were always a bit cramped across the footwell and pedals, so Colin Chapman had asked Ian to research the ideal size, or 'golden minimum dimension,' for pedal spacing. Ian had made some attempts to find the typical allowance for a shoe – but without much success – when he got a call to report to Chapman's office. Standing on a sheet of drawing film, he traced a pencil line round his shoe, and titled the resulting drawing 'Standard Foot BS 47690.' Chapman used this for some time, as his infallible template!

Another tale comes from a time when Ian needed to fill the newly constructed fishpond in his garden. Deciding that a couple of fish from the pond outside the Lotus front door would do, he brought a net and a large container to work. At lunchtime, he was concentrating on snaring these fish, when he became aware that a shadow had fallen across him. Looking up, he was challenged by Hazel Chapman, who was rightly possessive of all

things Lotus. Ian had no immediate answers, so, to create a diversion, he slid gently into the water. Hazel was so shocked, and, unable to continue the conversation, she promptly left! Ian and I soon became good friends, and work could progress.

The first project was the badging for the Elan Sprint and the Elan +2 S130, which were powered by a big valve version of the twin-cam engine. Concurrent with that, work was progressing on the Twin-Cam Europa.

The original Renault-powered car had been intended for export to France, and the headlamps were set too low for North America. In order to make the car legal for the USA, it had been jacked up on its suspension, so that there was virtually no rebound movement left, resulting in it being very skittish. Press articles were scanned for criticism, and the car's shortcomings listed, to enable the product profile to address as many as possible. (I did just that, in 1990, when the Esprit S4 was being considered.)

Among other items that were addressed, such as more engine power, was the need to improve rear-quarter visibility. The first attempts had been either to put windows in the high rear fins (see photo below), or to make them of acrylic perspex, but these contrived solutions would have been very hard to engineer, and had potentially poor durability – as well as looking bizarre. Marking out a line on some tape affixed to the body, I cut off the whole fin with a diamond cutter. Charlie Prior, of the Pattern Shop, stuck some plywood into the cavity with body filler, leaving room for a thin skin to be modelled as a replacement. With the application of some matching Lotus Yellow paint, the idea was ready for viewing. At first, the response was shock, but, after we'd made an adjustment to the lines between roof and rear deck, the change was accepted.

Colin Chapman, however, had the last say: he casually mentioned, "Of course, the car must have an aerodynamic performance equal to, or better than, the original car"!

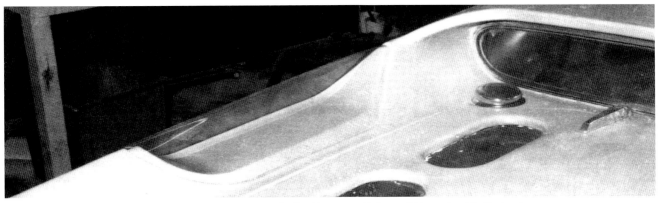

The plastic 'wndow' proposed for the Europa, which would have had limited value.

New engine ventilation holes were also designed, which kept the rain from wetting the ignition system on the engine; the Renault-engined car was almost impossible to start on damp mornings.

Initially, we had concerns that the rear of the body – by now made of much body filler – would fall apart if driven, but time showed that it was either very robust, or under-stressed, as it was run for some 12 months without even cracking. To maintain secrecy, false fins were taped on the back, but after a time these were often dispensed with. So off we went to the wind tunnel at MIRA, where measurements showed that the car had a much higher drag than before, and lots of front lift.

After some investigation, we uncovered the reason for the apparent high drag: when the first tests were made on the Europa, in 1965, Chapman had ordered his engineers to go to the wind tunnel and not come back until a reading of 0.3 had been achieved. Since this figure was actually out of reach, they 'adjusted' the frontal area on paper, which conveniently secured the target figure of 0.30. The bigger the frontal area the lower the drag coefficient would be!

The Twin-Cam had a significantly bigger frontal area, anyway, due to raising the whole car to get the headlamps to US-legal height, while revisions to the under-tray brought the floor back down to give a bigger cockpit. The first test session finished with a true drag figure in the region of 0.34, but the lift still needed curing.

Chapman suggested some air dams on top of the bonnet to spoil the airflow, but, when tested, this did not work, although a chin lip under the air intake produced a perfect balance, and reduced the drag to 0.33. Chapman however, said that he never wanted to see an 'add-on' spoiler again, and decreed that future shapes would have to work without them. The prominent lip that went into production was a 'market first.' Other work on the car included new paint colours, with metallics being added to the range, and the option of beige interior trim, as well as the usual black.

Lotus was a busy place, and another project needing my attention was the new 2-litre, four-seat model, code-named M50. This was the first of a whole range of planned models, which also included an M51, with a 4-litre V8 version of the new engine in the same car, and the M52 and M53, these being 2+2 variants with 2-litre and 4-litre engines, respectively. These cars were to end the kit car business, which was losing its attraction with the coming of VAT, the value-added sales tax, in place of the previous purchase tax. Under the old system, cars assembled by the owner had been exempted. This range of vehicles was planned to grow Lotus into a serious production car

manufacturer, offering alternates to such companies as Aston Martin and Jensen. The gestation of the M50 had been long and hard, and for much of what follows, I am indebted to a surviving notebook of this project, which was passed to me by Gerry Doe.

Ian Jones had written the initial specification for a four-seater on 14 November 1967. Brian Luff received outline approval from Chapman to develop the project, to get a detailed proposal on 6 December, and a model was presented by the stylist, John Frayling, on 19 January 1968. The project was then announced to vehicle engineering employees on 12 March, with a full specification following nine days later.

It specified: four seats, 2-litre engine on a 102in (2591mm) wheelbase, and a top speed of 126mph. The acceleration to 60mph was targeted at ten seconds, helped by a kerb weight of an ambitious 1848lb (838kg). The notes state that it would have a monocoque structure body with "simple (clamshell) mould."

To put these targets into perspective, a 1965 Jaguar 3.8-litre S Type could reach 60mph in 10.4 seconds, and the Alfa Romeo Guilia GTV in 11.1 seconds. The Jaguar weighed in at over 3647lb (1656kg)!

Paul Haussauer issued a new, and more ambitious, performance specification on May 27, which listed an (ambitious) frontal area of 14sq ft and a Cd of 0.35. Tyres were specified as C70 Goodyears, and a projected 0-60mph time of seven seconds.

On June 12 1968, John Frayling presented his model, styling renderings and outline drawings to 'ACBC' (Chapman) and Dennis Austin, Managing Director. The following day, Progress Meeting No 1 was held between Brian Luff, (engineer), Martin Long (purchasing), Paul Haussauer (engineer), John Cox, who became the engineering buyer, and Gerry Doe, who ran the Drawing Office and became the legislation expert. Luff stated that M50 had priority over the engineering work on the current production models, and the results of the styling meeting held on 18 June 1968 were:

1) Front track to measure 56⅛in – an increase of 28.6mm to 1426mm

2) Engine to be designed so that the camshaft gear is ⅝in (16mm) clear of the underside of lid (bonnet), as laid down by John Frayling [a statement giving apparent total power to the body designer!]

3) Pop-up headlamps to be considered

4) Clearance to be allowed for 7in wheel rims. [For the time, this was huge – the Europa of the day had 4.5in rims]

5) Overall height to be no greater than the Elan +2

On 4 July 1968, the full-size draft was officially opened by Chapman and the ten lines laid down – these were lines dividing the design into 10in (250mm) cubes. A few days earlier, the provisional parts list was issued, something Chapman always insisted on at the start of a program, to use as a cost indicator as well as a work list.

John Frayling presented a modified model, on 10 July, with alternative body shapes, and ACBC chose the shape retaining the maximum number of Lotus features: sharp nose; small intake hole; notch back; fixed recessed rectangular headlights for the home market, 7in diameter pop-ups for the USA, in the same recess. Three days later, Gerry Doe noted that his most optimistic estimate of the drawing office work involved was 261 man-weeks, with 436 the most likely figure, and 667 man-weeks as his most pessimistic prediction. Perhaps due to its date: the 13th, someone else has written "Gerry – Balls."

Frayling was back again two weeks later with a revised model, and Chapman requested further changes to increase the family likeness. By 13 August, Frayling had models in glass fibre, with two rear-quarter variants ready for wind tunnel testing.

The notes now have a gap, indicating that the program was proceeding to plan, while the latter part of 1968 was concerned with the engine. On November 27, the policy committee decided to proceed with the Vauxhall engine; then, by December 17, it was to be a Ford; but, in January 1969, the specification of 'Lotus Engine' was issued. The new engine was to be the forerunner of a major move 'upmarket,' designed as a straight four-cylinder, with the block canted at 45 degrees, but also a 4-litre V8.

In mid-June 1969, Colin Fish passed the first quantity of prototype parts through his quality checks; and it appeared that all was well, until September 11, when Colin Chapman requested that a backbone chassis design be prepared. By late November, the notes had become somewhat desperate, as they indicate "structure totally undecided – backbone, perimeter frame or foam-filled (glass fibre) monocoque. Rear suspension doubtful. Transmission modified – gearbox at the front." There were many ideas (and hopes) that the M50 could use a transaxle at the rear, throughout the life of the project. However, there was: "Very low morale and lack of management interest"!

At the beginning of July 1970, eight months later, prototype mould-making of a fastback shape, as approved by Chapman, began, and it had been completed by the time I had arrived at Hethel, on 4 January 1971.

John Frayling was still retained to work on the car, and I visited him, with Derek Sleath, at his home in Pangbourne shortly after my arrival. This could have been a bit difficult, as I thought (correctly) that I had been brought in to take over as the Lotus designer. John was fairly subdued; he had probably lost interest in a job over which he had enthused some two-and-a-half years earlier, and that had then nearly died some 14 months later. However, he was both friendly and courteous.

On February 9, we got the results of model wind tunnel tests on the Frayling shape, and they exhibited extreme lift at both axles. The car would have lost considerable road adhesion at speed; this caused Chapman and Rudd to abandon that shape. The prototype mould was scrapped,

John Frayling's Lotus M50 as shown in the company annual report.

My quarter-scale model of the M50 (Elite).

and Gerry notes that there was still no finalised body/chassis structural design.

On my birthday, February 24 1971, a steel backbone chassis was adopted, and I started design studies on body shapes other than potentially high aero lift fastbacks.

During the first Saturday morning in March 1971, Chapman, Rudd and Kimberley joined me at my drawing-board in the main office. It was very informal, and I sketched ideas as the others debated them. The challenge was to maintain good headroom for the rear seats, without the car becoming excessively long, which conventional fastback designs tended to be. After an hour-and-a-half, Colin agreed a rough sketch of a wedge shape with a cut-off high tail, like an estate car. This sat on a wheelbase of 98in (2489mm) and 59in tracks, front and rear (1498.6mm)

Two weeks later, I presented a quarter-scale model, which was officially adopted by the board (meaning Chapman), pending aerodynamic testing; and full-scale design work commenced. It is interesting to note that in the previous autumn, a 2-litre Elan +2 was built as project M60, but the package was poor, due to the space needed for the 45 degree-angled engine. However, I was aware it was still a distant rival for the future four-seat sports car.

Colin Chapman himself designed the basic M50 chassis and suspension, employing a radius arm at the rear, which determined the location of the heel board at the front of the rear seats. The long rear seat pan was a direct consequence of this.

The M50 project was chasing some radical ideas to try to improve both profitability and product integrity, and a key to this was the desire to make the body in one piece

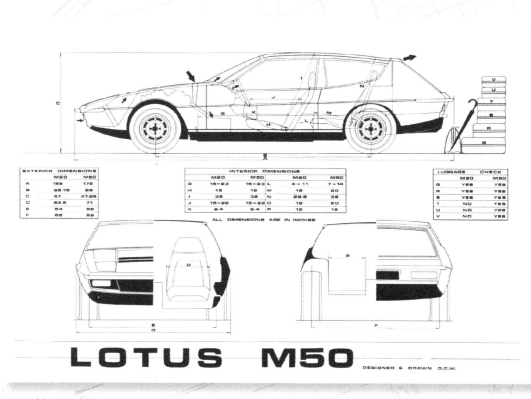

EXTERIOR DIMENSIONS		
	M20	M50
A	168	172
B	85·75	88
C	47	47·25
D	53·5	71
E	54	58
F	56	59

INTERIOR DIMENSIONS						
	M20	M50			M20	M50
G	18-23	18-23	L	4 - 11	7 - 14
H	19	19	M	18	20
I	39	38	N	29·5	38
J	15-22	15-22	O	19	20
K	5·4	5·4	P	12	18

ALL DIMENSIONS ARE IN INCHES

LUGGAGE CHECK		
	M20	M50
Q	YES	YES
R	YES	YES
S	YES	YES
T	NO	YES
U	NO	YES
V	NO	YES

LOTUS M50

DESIGNED & DRAWN D.C.W.

My drawing presented with the model to show comparative dimensions with the Elan Plus 2.

without the need for paint. Typically, the Elan needed something like 14 parts of the mould brought together. As the moulds wore in use, this left excess resin showing along the joint lines. These had to be expensively removed, and the surface faired in by hand. The floor space needed to allow simultaneous lamination into a full set of body moulds was considerable, so, although the M50 moulds were very large, they took up much less space. To achieve this, and remove the extensive hand work, the car was to be constructed from a top and a bottom moulding, joined around the maximum width of the vehicle. This meant that the mouldings could not have undercut (re-entrant) shapes, or the part would get locked in the mould. At this stage, the glass fibre was to have been laid-up in the tools by hand, on top of the 'paint' finish. This 'in mould' finish would remove the need for a long, expensive paint process.

To help research the 'in mould' colour finish, various experiments took place on factory cars, Tony Rudd having an Elan +2 in yellow gel resin, while the Jim Russell Racing School were loaned a Lotus Seven finished in orange resin. However, when this car came back to the factory for assessment, removing an advertising decal from the bonnet revealed that

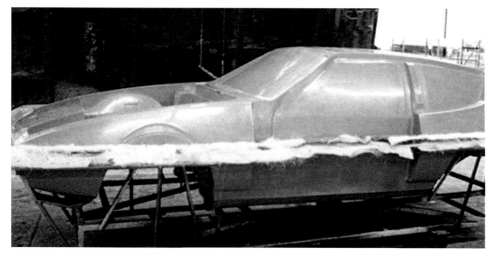

The two halves of the M50 body with no 'undercuts,' which created a design challenge.

Some of the Europa Team. Left to right, Keith Loader, Mike Kimberley, myself, Chris Dunster, John Freeman, Dennis Jewell, Roger Constable and Roger Becker.

a major change of colour had taken place over the summer. I tried this car one afternoon, and it took me quite a time to get out of it afterwards – not due to excessive enthusiasm, more to do with personal excess size.

An additional issue with the two 'simple' piece mould approach was the need to make the undercut areas as add-on items. The sills below the doors were made from glass fibre, and bonded in place. The roof gutters, however were decreed by Chapman to be made from aluminium extrusions. Colin had started his career as a structural engineer with The British Aluminium Company, and he was keen to use it for all the 'bright trim.' The section I designed would have been bent to shape, polished and bright anodised. However, it had to be quite thick to meet the manufacturing process so, later, many were changed to rolled sections. I found that if the section was cut back locally, then bent to shape, I could make a tapered design. The original bumpers and rear quarter window finisher used this trick. The windscreen post posed a bigger problem, and I designed it as a formed metal fabrication – of which, more later. Although the theory was fine, in practice these parts took up a lot of development time, and, worse, they were expensive, cancelling out some of the savings from the body-making process. With the body shape restricted to no undercut shapes, I faced a challenge with the styling.

In March, I visited the Geneva motor show. I joined Chapman and Fred Bushell, Lotus Finance Director, on Hethel airfield sometime before dawn, from where, having cleared Customs through the special arrangement Lotus enjoyed, we took off in the company's Piper Twin Comanche.

Emerging from a taxi at what turned out to be the rear of the exhibition building, Colin attempted, without a ticket, to get past a large security man. "Don't you

know who I am?" he demanded, when challenged, "Colin Chapman of Lotus." "Never heard of you, and anyway you need a ticket," was the response. Rebuffed, Colin stumped round to the ticket office at the front of the building, muttering something about "there wouldn't be a show without people like me."

Luckily, there wasn't a queue, as he would never stand for them, and would have gone straight to the front, to everyone's annoyance. Once inside the show, he spent a very long day, discussing exhibits, car by car, giving me a privileged insight to my employer's thoughts. One comment I remember in particular – he said he thought that Eric Broadley of Lola was the designer he most admired.

Leaving for the airport that evening, I tentatively asked if there was any chance of some food, as we had not eaten all day. Colin, acting as if he had forgotten the stuff existed, enthusiastically made for the airport cafeteria, where he purchased vast quantities of rich chocolate cake. His sweet tooth was well developed, but after such a long day without food, it was not exactly what I was looking forward to. As the plane circled to gain enough altitude for the mountain crossing to France, I enjoyed simultaneous pangs of hunger and the effects of over-indulgence of sickly cake, so I asked for permission to smoke. Although Colin didn't himself, he surprisingly gave the okay.

While I puffed away in the darkness of the aircraft cabin, I heard the pilot and Chapman discussing how to eke out the fuel to make sure we could get home without stopping. Suddenly, there was silence and the Piper took on the flying characteristics more strongly associated with a house brick that an aircraft. While an elegantly planned French town came up to meet us, Chapman was to be seen frantically reaching for the fuel tank changeover lever, and, just in time, the engines spluttered back into life, accompanied by a Chapmanesque comment regarding the efficiency of our fuel tank utilisation.

It was also in April 1971 that, one Saturday morning, the first prototype Europa Twin-Cam emerged from the workshops to run three shakedown laps of the Hethel test track.

With the M50 approved for build as a full-size model, work commenced on the full body layout and surface lines drawings. All the known 'hard points,' such as the engine and chassis, were laid out on a massive roll of drawing film, and the accurate shape put round them. Colin was on 'our side' in ensuring the engine was as low as possible, forcing the engine designers to utilise a shallower oil sump, with its capacity maintained by spreading its shape as wide as possible. He then specified that the inside of the bonnet was no more than ¾in (19mm) clear of the highest point on the powertrain. In practice, the height of the front was dictated as much by the size of the brake servo on the bulkhead. As the drawing progressed through the early summer of 1971, the detail shapes were released to the Body Pattern Shop, presided over by Charlie Prior.

A system that caused us much anguish was the gearbox. Originally, we planned to use a semi-automatic that Automotive Products was developing for Alfa Romeo.

When Alfa decided against it, Automotive Products told us that it would no longer be viable to make it just for Lotus. A few weeks went by, with a large white space on the layout drawing in place of the transmission. The next candidate was a Holbay Sunbeam Rapier five-speed – the specification demanded five speeds, rare at the time – but that eventually fell by the wayside. Tony Rudd then came up with the suggestion that Lotus could package the difficult bits from a Maxi gearbox into a rear drive configuration. It first saw the light of day in the Elan +2, but, despite vigorous testing, was subject to criticism in the M50. The problem appeared to be the consistency of the Austin components – which weren't.

Aerodynamic testing of the quarter-scale model had shown that the shape was fine by the standards of the day, but, nevertheless, we made use of the new model wind tunnel at Specialised Mouldings, in Huntingdon. This company, run by Peter Jackson and his brother, had made a name for itself in the competition car body field. To expand the business, Peter had brought in the ex-BRM designer Peter Wright, who installed a quarter-scale model wind tunnel, a new feature being its ability to draw off ground surface air, to better represent real life.

I remember many trips to Huntingdon with Ian Jones in 1971: Ian, to oversee some early modifications to the

The model in Specialised Mouldings' quarter-scale wind tunnel.

Quarter-scale wind tunnel testing was also carried out at MIRA.

A retouched photo of the model, showing the proposed USA bumpers.

The full-size M50 model at East Carlton Manor for directors' approval in July 1971.

The rear view shows the understated tailgate finish: unfortunately, later made bigger and brighter.

Moonraker motor yacht (a company which Chapman had just bought), and me, to talk to Peter Wright about the M50 wind tunnel work. Peter always got worse figures for the M50 than MIRA, due to the boundary layer improvements in his tunnel, but, as events turned out, the car could surpass both wind tunnel standards.

I set off for the 1971 British Grand Prix at Silverstone, on the morning of Friday practice, with my wife, Wendy, alongside, as she was working in race telephones. The full-size M50 was being finished ready for presentation the following week, so the workshops were painting it, and applying chrome tape to the brightwork. Chapman was also at the Grand Prix, having arrived by plane.

Walking in the paddock, I heard Wendy calling for me through the public address. I assumed there was no hurry, but as the calls became more frantic, I thought I had better report. Once there, I was told that Chapman needed me at the factory immediately to review the model.

Mystified, because I assumed Chapman to be fully engrossed at the race, I had forgotten the brief journey time the company aircraft needed, so, leaving Wendy with £5 to provide overnight lodging, I left for Hethel by road. These were the days before bypasses, and this was a Friday in holiday season, so I put my foot down in my mighty company Ford Escort, and managed to be at Lotus in two hours 20 minutes.

Chapman had stopped work on the model, and was arranging to bring John Frayling in, to seek his advice. I noticed that he did something like this on a number of occasions, when he needed moral support for a big decision. John came up with some suggestions, which included altering the rear wheelarches, tail lamps, bonnet, and the rear roof blip. All but the increased roof blip were subsequently scrapped, and the original design readopted, but, until then, it was a difficult time for me. What I found hard to accept was the total change in enthusiasm shown by Chapman over a mere two days.

Two weeks later, the full-size model was moved to the grounds of Chapman's house, at East Carleton. It was put on display for a time, during which the directors, with Colin and his wife, reviewed the shape, approving it for full-size prototype mould-making. The model was 'dressed,' complete with windscreen wipers and number-plates, and even had real tyres, with a portion sawn from the tread to simulate correct standing height. Glass fibre wheel models were vacuum-sprayed with aluminium to realistic effect. Various comparative vehicles stood alongside, including the Chapman family Mercedes, as well as the current Lotus models. I must say, I thought it made the others look pretty dull.

Chapman became very keen on Glitterflake – particles of aluminium sprayed with clear resin as a body finish – and Europa sills, and Elan +2 roofs treated in this way were sold for evaluation. The clear resin would gradually go brown, and there was no successful repair system, as the finish had been applied from 'inside' the moulding. It was possibly fortunate that the experiments failed, as the Glitterflake finishes (which came from the USA customising industry) were probably too garish for European tastes. Another by-product of the Glitterflake finish was the mottled appearance of body panels when photographed. The flakes, orientated to give a perfect mirror, would dominate the flash lighting.

Colin wanted these ideas to work, so the designer – that was me – was employed to carry out his requirements. Nowadays, it seems that the freedom from restraint some designers enjoy means that they dictate to everyone else. In the face of any restriction, they threaten that the product will be a disaster, unless they can do exactly what they want – they would not have lasted long with the 'Old Man'!

In the spring of 1971, following examination of hand-laid production panels, we found that the resin was not impregnating the glass fibres as well as it should.

Controlling the hand process was very difficult, and we thought that an injection-moulding process might work better. We looked at one called Resinject, but it quickly became apparent that tools powerful enough to squeeze the resin out through the small gap between the inner and outer tools would have to be extremely strong and heavy. Conventional tools for plastic injection mouldings in industry are made of steel, and are subjected to very high pressures, but Chapman wanted to get the

An injected M50 upper body being removed from the outer mould. The inner mould is behind.

result with lightweight, low-cost glass fibre tools which could be made at Hethel.

He came up with the idea of using atmospheric pressure to push the tools together, this being done by applying a vacuum prior to pumping in liquid resin to a matched pair of tools, pre-filled with the reinforcing glass fibres. This ingeniously harnessed nature to provide the necessary clamping pressure. The first part to be made in this way was the removable luggage boot box in the back of the Europa Twin-Cam. This was an ideal shape as it was symmetrical, and the early parts were so good that Chapman would demonstrate their assets by jumping up and down on an upturned example. However, whole cars and, later, boats, would prove more difficult.

Through the summer and into the autumn of 1971, suppliers of components for the M50 were being selected by John Cox, the buyer, supervised by Richard Morley, who was soon to become Managing Director. The car was highly specified, including air-conditioning – a rarity at that time – and a comprehensive radio and tape player.

Among the most fought-over items were the alloy road wheels, and much personal entertainment was dolled out to try and secure the contract. Lotus Purchasing and senior engineering staff believed that the Ford Motor Company could well follow the business, wherever Lotus should place it, which was very significant to potential suppliers.

While work went on with the M50, we were excited about the London Motor Show at Earls Court, as it saw the launch of the Europa Twin-Cam to a very favourable press and public.

In the meantime, one Friday in the summer of 1971, a mile from the factory, I went to pass a Reliant Robin three-wheeler. As I drew alongside, the Reliant suddenly turned right, putting a long gash down the side of the company Ford. Despite the police supporting me over the incident, Colin Chapman took the view that I deserved a Lotus company vehicle driving ban for six months, and said that I was lucky to keep my company car. In the end, the ban was lifted earlier than Chapman specified. A trip was planned to the Turin Show in Italy – Mike Kimberley and I were to drive a Europa Twin-Cam prototype there, and visit Glaverbel glass in Belgium on the return. Mike managed to get the ban lifted, to enable us to share the driving.

Leaving Hethel early in the morning one day in November, we had got as far as Colchester when the throttle linkage broke; we managed to fix it, using a pencil and tank (duct) tape. We finally arrived in Aosta, via the Great St Bernard Pass, after midnight. Starting early the next morning, running at 120mph-plus down towards Turin, I discovered that, where the sun had not penetrated, the road was still coated with ice, so I eased up a bit! We duly arrived, and parked the car outside the exhibition hall in the Valentino Park, where it created much interest. We started back the next day, driving as far as Martigny. The following day was a Sunday, and we made good time to the lunch halt near Dijon, where a quick snack lunch turned out to have many courses. Reaching Paris in time for the Sunday night traffic jam, we faced long delays before running fast towards Brussels. In Charleroi, we found our hotel in darkness, as it was after midnight again. We were up early for a meeting at the glassworks, where Glaverbel was making the large double-curved windshield for the M50 in chemically-toughened and laminated glass – thinner and lighter than normal glass. While there, we got a garage to weld up the exhaust, which was failing. That evening, we caught the Ostend-to-Dover ferry, and arrived back at Ketteringham in the middle of the night. A typical Lotus trip, then!

Christmas; and Lotus gave each of its employees a turkey, which, in 1971, was worth quite a lot of money. Chapman also held a cocktail party for senior staff. Christmas Eve was a working day, but things became more social after lunch, and, at three o'clock, my colleagues and I filed into the board dining room, for sherry and mince pies with the directors.

For 1972, the Imperial Tobacco Group decided to change the sponsorship branding for Team Lotus from Gold Leaf to John Player Special, so the cars' livery was changed to black with gold coach-lining featuring the JPS monogram, which was an interesting development for me, because it gave me the opportunity to use this theme on road cars. Later, when the team mechanics found that the gold stained easily with oil, they changed to yellow, but, for the road cars, we stayed with gold.

The Europa Twin-Cam had been launched successfully, so now there was time to develop a more powerful one. The Twin-Cam Special utilised the big valve Lotus engine, producing 126bhp, with a Renault-based five-speed transmission. The body was distinguished by having gold coach-lines. The interior offered a light beige trim, and a hand-trimmed dashboard crash roll. Perhaps fortunately for the world at large, the idea of writing 'Lotus Europa Twin-cam Special' in Watneys brewery script down the

length of each rear quarter on the approval car did not survive the presentation to Colin!

The cars would pull 124mph on the level, and a hill could bring 134mph-plus. 0-60mph took 6.5 seconds at a test weight of 899kg, which was not bad for a 1600cc car. The price was around £2500, dependent on options. This enormously successful car was developed while work continued on the M50; it was most rewarding when its sales proved to be so good, and it won accolades from the press, including being named 'Best Car of the Year 1972, Sports Cars.'

The new year proved to be a very exciting time in the M50 project. 4 December had seen a running chassis, fitted with rudimentary mudguards and cockpit, complete laps of the test track. A number of problems manifested themselves, which required revisions to the rear suspension geometry, consisting of the relocation of the radius arms, a revised front anti-roll bar design to increase steering lock, and changes to the steering geometry. While the chassis was undergoing these alterations, I was involved in laying out the interior. Chapman examined my work on 14 December, and did not approve it, so my work went on, with many concept sketches to indicate exactly how it would be made, before Chapman would permit further work 'in the flesh.'

He would never approve an idea to go beyond the sketch stage until I had demonstrated 'how' the design would go together. He absolutely refused to allow any attachment screws to be visible, so I had a merry game working out how the 'last' bit would cover everything up – and stay put. Colin had given me a good example of just how simple he wanted a design to be, earlier in the

A retouched photo, while I pondered gold lining for the Europa.

The final result: the Lotus Europa Twin-cam Special.

year. A salesman arrived at Hethel to demonstrate flock finishes. Chapman became involved, and, for a few hours (luckily), the interior was going to be smothered entirely in furry flock, rather than trimmed!

On January 13 1972, the first prototype bodyshell was completed in the hand lay-up moulds. The sills and the scuttle were reinforced by moulding closed box sections, encapsulating rigid foam, which acted as a former – a feature subsequently used in the Lotus Esprit. Through February, the prototype was being assembled and I was asked to install an interior mock-up. I was given only four days to do this, so everyone in the Vehicle and Pattern Workshops was involved, various parts being made either in wood or metal, depending on the skills that were available. After working virtually round the clock, an interior was duly presented, although much still needed to be done to make it all fit together properly. Chapman was unimpressed with the quality of the result, and said so, which I thought a bit unreasonable given the extremely short time involved, and the total lack of professional trimmers available.

My M50 interior, with the thin front seats – later becoming much thicker, reducing interior space.

The first M50 MIRA full-size vehicle wind tunnel test. At this stage, the car still retained a 'European' bumper.

quarter views shown in the press were done while the actual car was being completed – Guigiaro, being an accomplished artist, liked to work on these presentation drawings in the quiet of the weekends.

Around this time, Colin invited me to join him and Hazel, Guigiaro, Tony Rudd and Mike Kimberley at his home at East Carleton for dinner, where I was served the weakest gin and tonic I had ever tasted. It could have been to ensure I said nothing embarrassing, as later, when working on the marine projects, he served me the strongest I have ever had!

On March 14 1972, the first complete prototype lapped the test track, driven by Dennis Jewell, the Development Workshop supervisor. With a rudimentary version of my interior design and the hand lay-up bodyshell giving weights not seen in the later production cars, the two prototypes were rapid cars indeed, and I once saw an indicated 142mph early one morning; the acceleration was equally exciting. On March 29, the M50 passed its 30mph frontal barrier testing at MIRA.

The partially completed M50 went to MIRA for the weekend of March 4/5 1972, where wind tunnel tests were run, followed by a door strength test on one side, and a roof crush test on the other, both of which were well above the compliance requirements for the USA. Meanwhile, I had encouraged Colin to meet the Italian designer Giorgetto Guigiaro, at the 1972 Geneva motor show, and they discussed ideas for him to show a Lotus-based car at the Turin show the following November. This was to become the Esprit.

Chapman, always the opportunist, formulated the idea of a stretched Lotus Europa chassis as the base for Italdesign's Turin car, so that it could eventually be turned into the Europa replacement. Obviously, this would use the forthcoming four-cylinder and V8 engines, so the car would be bigger than the Europa. On March 22, Ian Jones and I prepared quick paper concepts for Ital's guidance, which were taken to Turin two days later – the first of many visits to that city. I got on very well with Guigiaro, and suggested that the Maserati Boomerang show car could act as the theme for the Lotus; as it happened, that idea stuck.

During April and May 1972, Chapman, Rudd, Kimberley and I visited Italdesign a number of times to view and approve the styling direction. Guigiaro presented basic outline scale drawings in tenth-scale – there were never coloured perspective views. The coloured three-

Chapman's enthusiasm for all things Guigiaro brought the decree that Italdesign was to produce a design for the M50 interior. I had faced a difficult time with the interior, as the Lotus Trim Shop was located in the stables at Ketteringham. Production was running at a high level and the trimmers were hard put to keep up. There was no provision for experimental work and it took a non-existent second place. The resource to make the models and moulds for the interior was no better. Charlie Prior was busy with inner panels and bulkheads for the M50, so I found progress very slow. At least moving the work to Italy meant something would be happening. A meeting was held in Turin, where the interior job was agreed, and I returned home to Norfolk in the Chapman Piper Navajo, arriving around midnight on a Thursday night. By lunchtime the next day, Malcolm Bell (an ex-Rolls-Royce engineer recently recruited to the team) and I were picking up a 3½-ton rental truck. After loading a prototype M50 body at the factory, we went home for a few hours' rest and packing, before returning to start out for the ferry at Dover at 1:30am the next morning.

The Ford Thames Trader was not a rapid performer, with a maximum speed of 60mph, but we had consumed most of the diesel fuel by the time we had cleared the Dartford Tunnel some 100 miles from Hethel. Stopping at the next service station, we headed for the pumps, as one does if you are a motorist. Of course, in those days there were few diesel cars and we found there were no diesel pumps under the overhead canopy. Also, we had heard strange noises above, but our attention was drawn to the garage attendant, who came out of his pay box, literally hopping mad. He was hopping not only because he had only one leg, but also because we had removed every strip light in our path as we drove under the canopy. "Oh, that's why the diesel pumps are over there," we said, as I gave the irate gentleman my Lotus Design Manager's business card from my lofty position in the passenger seat. We deemed it best to fill up elsewhere, and we never heard again from the garage.

Arriving at Dover, after littering the A2 with broken glass from the truck roof, we went to a shipping agency, as we had no reservation for a boat, and, while in the second-floor office, we watched with fascination the stormy English Channel break high over the breakwater in the outer harbour. Eventually loaded, we repaired to the bar, where we noticed that all the windows were covered with storm shutters, so we took up station against a vertical pillar would afford us a good clinging post. In due course, the ship began to move, so Malcolm and I held on, knowing better than most of the other passengers what was likely to be ahead of us – and then the ship rose about 30 feet vertically, and dropped immediately afterwards. People were thrown over tables laden with glasses, several cutting themselves and falling to the floor, with furniture going everywhere.

We were fine, until people started being sick, whereupon we left the floors awash with glass, blood, beer and vomit, and went above to the deck, where we shivered as we watched a full-blown Channel storm in progress. We decided to take a chance on lunch, so we presented ourselves at the cafeteria, where there was literally a ton of food and no customers. We were made most welcome by the staff, and given enormous portions. Seated at a table, we each had to hold a plate and a beer bottle in one hand, while forking the grub with the other; anything left unclutched was immediately hurled around the ship. Once we had eaten, we remained their sole customers, until we began the grim walk back to the vehicle decks, upon our arrival in France.

Leaving Calais by road, it was slow-going, as the storms impeded the truck, and, as far as Paris, we could not exceed 45mph. The night was very dark, although the wind abated, and eventually we reached the Swiss boarder at Vallorbe, where the carnet papers had to be stamped to ensure the legality of the precious cargo.

With dawn coming, we descended to Lausanne, where we planned a rest down by the lake. However, Lausanne had trams with overhead cables, and we had not been able to ascertain the height of the truck, despite our best attempts since the English garage incident. Seeing the road down to the lake passed under a very low bridge, and that the tram wires were also lowered, I refused to drive under it. Malcolm was adamant that he would not be involved in a three (or many more) point turn on a steep and busy main road, so I walked under the offending construction while Malcolm drove. The clearance was certainly minimal, and Malcolm admitted afterwards that it might have been a bit close!

So there we were, sitting in a truck on the promenade of a fashionable Swiss resort, unshaven, having travelled for 31 hours. Following a bracing walk, we left town for the Grand St Bernard tunnel, where we were meeting Giancarlo Perini, Guigiaro's personal assistant. After snatching another couple of hours' snooze, we duly met Perini, who had arranged permission with the authorities for the truck to drive on that Sunday and return on the Monday, which was a public holiday – the Italians ban goods vehicles on those days.

We still had 85 miles to go to Turin, and Perini was in a hurry – discovering the outer limits of Ford truck roadholding while descending the Alps proved frightening. We unloaded the M50 body at the Via Tepice works on the Sunday evening, and then were whisked off to dinner, which proved to be at Guigiaro's home, with his wife and children. It was a thoroughly pleasant evening, during which Giorgetto spoke much more English than usual (he usually claimed not to speak it), and I spoke more French (his second language) than usual. We finally got back to our hotel at midnight, and enjoyed a brief sleep, before being back on the road, by eight o'clock the next morning.

The non-stop drive back to Norfolk became quicker once the engine governor failed – the truck's performance improved considerably. We crossed a calm English Channel early on the Tuesday morning, only to be held up at Dover Customs, because the truck was empty. The authorities thought this odd, so they shut themselves into the cargo space to ensure there was no contraband.

Later, the rental company was to accuse us of deliberately disconnecting the speed governor, which we hadn't – we would have done it much sooner if we really had planned it; 2000 miles by underpowered truck in three-and-a-half days, with little motorway and with two crossings of the Alps had been hard work. Malcolm and I worked out that we had done 56 hours 'work' by the time we had returned.

Travel was commonplace at Lotus, and the company aircraft were in use most of the time. Colin Chapman used his Piper Navajo for his own trips, which left the Twin Comanche for company use. Various pilots were retained, although many succumbed to the difficulties of pleasing Chapman. The flying trips were usually done in a day, and Lotus had an arrangement with Customs and Excise to clear the passengers at Hethel. However, the rules did not permit any import or export of goods through the works airfield; these had to be cleared through an international airport.

On one occasion, I was bringing some aluminium bright trim sections back from the chosen supplier Iralco, in Southern Ireland, and they were needed in a hurry. The cost and time of landing at, say, Birmingham, and declaring the goods would probably have delayed us for a couple of days, so this, plus the wear and tear on the aircraft and the landing fees, encouraged us to plot avoidance. On this occasion, the pilot of the day suggested that a feigned engine failure might work. Radioing ahead to Hethel, he explained that he would land on only one engine. Once we had landed, in the dark at 11pm, and were safely at the end of the runway, I left the plane with the goods, and hid them in the grass alongside the tarmac. Meanwhile, the pilot revved the engine and, using a combination of controls, produced various bangs and pops to help convince the reception committee back at the aircraft hanger. Eventually, he taxied in and told the Customs officer what a problem the engine had been, and how he had managed to clear it once on the ground.

The following morning, a party, which did not include me, was on its way to Glaverbel in Belgium and needed to take some glass checking fixtures. As, again, these would need an en route landing for Customs, they decided they would take off, circle, and land again, after the official had left, to take on the cargo. It so happened that the officer was the same one as on the previous night, so he must have had some suspicions, because, after the plane had taken off and flown away south east, he waited on the road by the Norwich end of the test track. Soon, he was treated to the sight of the plane returning and was waiting for them as they landed to load the fixtures. One hell of a row broke out. Chapman was livid that his precious concession might be lost. Eventually it was sorted, with

My model for the Lotus Europa replacement (M70).

dire warnings from Chapman that breaking the rules would not be tolerated.

1972 was a very busy year for me, taken up with the development of the M50, Europa Special, the Italdesign Europa-based show car, and its design for the M50 interior. I was involved in all of these, although most of my time was spent on the M50. The original version used a one-piece door glass, but, when the design was first run, the glass wound up until it was inches from the top of the door, then rolled outwards onto the floor, where it smashed to pieces. On June 1, the design changed to a two-piece glass. The reason the original idea had failed was only through my ignorance of how to do the job properly.

Colin Chapman had always wanted a fixed-vent pane in the front windows, as he believed it allowed one to drive fast with the window open without draughts. One winter's evening, he lent me his personal Elan +2, with instructions that I was to drive it round Norfolk with the window open, to prove his point – which it certainly did. The other revelation that drive brought me was the magnificent abilities of that particular car. Normally, I drove our development cars, but his was virtually blueprint perfect, and was much better than a regular production car. He may never have realised how big the difference was.

Development on M50 parts was ongoing, involving many suppliers – among them was Terry Hunter Seating, at Mildenhall, whom Chapman had recommended. Terry had retired from the BMC works rally team to set up a factory making aftermarket seats. A very sociable man, he worked hard to perfect the front seats, which were designed to be very thin for packaging purposes. Sadly, he saw his business fail before the Lotus contract came to fruition.

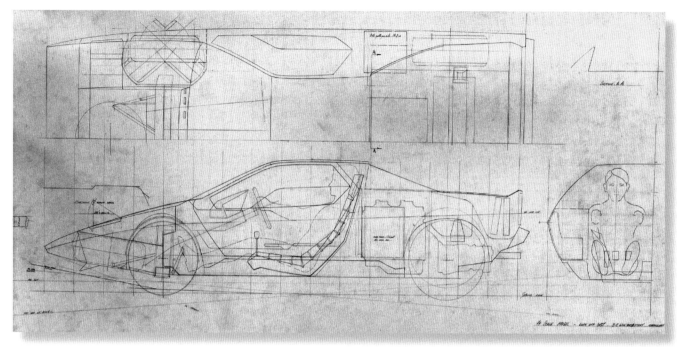

The general arrangement drawing for my Europa replacement.

Another port of call was Iralco, in Ireland, which was chosen to make the aluminium bright trim. Originally, it was all to be extruded, but the supplier eventually made 90% as rolled sections. This German-owned concern was located at Colinstown, County Westmeath, in a redundant Georgian mansion. My visits there were numerous, as the fit of the parts was crucial to the vehicle's appearance. Flying from Hethel to Dublin in a company aircraft, on one occasion we had been cleared to land, only to need a full-throttle abort at the last minute, as another plane traversed the runway.

While Italdesign was working on its show car, based on a widened and lengthened Europa chassis, I drew a design for the forthcoming M70 Europa replacement. Due to the level of activity in the Pattern Shop, Tony Rudd gave permission for the model to be built outside, and a pattern maker living outside Norwich took on the task. Working only from drawings, as I had little time to visit him frequently, he built a fifth-scale wooden model, which, on my instructions, lacked the cross-curvature on the roof and bonnet in order to simplify the job. It was expected that the model would still excite the 'Old Man' enough to allow the project to proceed. It featured an integrated front bumper painted to match the body, small dropping side window panes and a rear-mounted cooling system. Other pioneering features were electrosensitive Perspex auxiliary lighting, vertical 'beeswing' doors, and a gold film electric heated windscreen.

The dimensions dated 22 March 1972:		
OA Length	164in	4165mm
Wheelbase	96in	2438mm
OA Width	72in	1828mm
OA Height	43in	1092mm

Tony Rudd let the model go to MIRA for wind tunnel testing, where it had disappointing drag and lift performance, and initial indications that the rear-mounted cooling system didn't work very well. Colin Chapman showed some interest, but was hanging his hat on the Italian creation. I don't think there would have been much progress on a new mid-engined car if Italdesign had not been in the equation; we were all very busy with the M50 and had even done little about its coupé variant.

On 18 July 1972, Chapman made the decision to use the interior design submitted by Italdesign for the M50, which was not only a disappointment for me, because I felt it looked rather staid for my idea of an advanced Lotus product, but it also gave Hethel a lot of work to get it to production.

The adoption of the Ital interior marked a change in direction for the car. I had been working on designs not dissimilar to the Lamborghini Espada, and, indeed, Chapman had arranged for me to inspect racing driver Ulf Norrinder's car at Silverstone earlier in the year.

The Italdesign interior for the M50 Elite. The plethora of bright trim finishers cost a lot to produce.

Colin Chapman signing autographs in Ulf Norrinder's Lamborghini at Silverstone.

All my designs were based on a light and airy open feel, with a box of instruments in front of the driver. In contrast, the Italian design had a very tall centre panel, which stood like a grandfather clock in the middle of the car, with the instrument and glovebox structures each side. For example, Guigiaro had not maintained the designed seating position, which affected all the legislation geometry, and Colin required that the design had to be copied exactly. The thicker seats reduced the original spacious interior, although it was still, just, a full four-seater. There were all sorts of complex bright metal finishers and wooden inlays that added much to the cost of the car. The switchgear did not have any illumination, as demanded by USA law, but for this I had an idea. Dubbed 'the miner's lamp,' I suggested a closely focussed light to shine on the high centre console, with a sharp cut-off to prevent it illuminating anything else. It was built into the trim cover, which hid the roll-over hoop that helped give so much safety protection.

Many new details were used on the M50, including the single windscreen wiper, which I found wiped more usable area than a conventional twin system. The windshield, quarter and internal rear bulkhead glass was all bonded directly to the body using Solbit. Glass was difficult to stick things onto, so the internal bonded tailgate hinges were scrapped when their reliability became doubtful. The first attempt to open a rear window on internal hinges bonded to the glass kept the workshop floor sweeper busy. As the glass slowly rose to its full height, it exploded into a thousand pieces due to the hinge pivots not being perfectly aligned. Later, very substantial external hinges were used which did nothing to the original clean appearance.

The 1972 motor show in Turin marked the unveiling of the Italdesign Esprit Lotus, and Chapman, Kimberley, Mike Hamlin, the company pilot and I arrived a day before the show opened, to see the finished model wheeled out into the narrow Via Tepice, and loaded for its short journey to the exhibition halls in Valentino Park. The model was not a running car, although the cockpit was usable, and was displayed as an experimental prototype on a modified Europa Special chassis on the Italdesign stand.

However, for the Lotus people there was a problem, as no one had thought to book accommodation, and Turin was full for the show. Fortunately, somehow, Guigiaro had found a hotel south of the city with some vacancies, and, on arrival, we all took our luggage to our allocated rooms. When Kimberley went looking for Chapman, he found him sitting on a bed in a cupboard up in the roof; but, despite offers of swaps, he generously decided to keep it, and let the rest of us retain the more comfortable accommodation.

After Turin, Chapman invited us all to Frankfurt for the Boat Show. As we returned to Frankfurt airport afterwards, it was very cold and a bit foggy. But we took off, with every seat occupied, and John Standen from the boat company in the luggage space at the back of the cabin. Then we heard that Norwich was about to close due to fog. The problem was we didn't have a lot of fuel, and anyway we didn't want to divert, so Norwich air traffic control talked us in from over the North Sea; and, to be sure that there was no radio breakdown, it continued to talk us all the way in. We didn't see the ground until after we had landed. Someone met us with a Ford Galaxie that Chapman had won at Indianapolis, which was a pretty large car, although nine was a bit of a squash! Chapman drove us home through Norwich at high speed – the rest of us could see little in the fog. After the Turin show, Guigiaro took the Esprit to America, so it was early in the new year before the plans for production were laid.

At the same time, aerodynamic development of the M50 was showing much progress in refining its performance, and tests in the full-scale tunnel at MIRA gave it had a drag coefficient of 0.324, which I compared to some of its aerodynamic rivals.

Vehicle	Horsepower required at 100mph
Lotus Europa	37.6
Lotus M50 Cd 0.324	44.5
Maserati Ghibli	48.0
Reliant GTE	52.5
Jaguar E-Type	53.2
Ford Capri	53.5
Citroën DS	57.5
Jensen Interceptor	59.0
Mercedes 280 SL	67.2

This development work was associated with a front add-on chin spoiler, which I had tried out first, before attempting to sell it to Chapman. Remembering his instruction when working on the Europa – that there were to be no more add-on aerodynamic devices – it was with some trepidation that I told the 'Old Man' that a 2in-deep blade, mounted at 30 degrees, would cut the drag by 7hp at 100mph. I had chosen to see him on a sunny evening, and, once I had reminded him of his earlier policy, spilled the beans. He was absolutely delighted with the improvements, and delivered a lecture on how I should never take any of his remarks at face value!

More refining in the tunnel, on February 9 1973, saw the figures further improved to what was, until then,

Mike Kimberley (left) and me, with the first fully finished prototype M50.

The M50 revue car. Chapman insisted the silver-coloured washers in the rear suspension were finished in black for production.

an unattainable drag coefficient of 0.2996. This was the equivalent to 41hp at 100mph, while front and rear axle lifts were balanced at 35½lb (16kg) of positive lift. The final improvement came from Malcolm Bell's decision to shaping the front spoiler aerodynamically, rather than running a simple blade. This performance was at least ten years ahead of its time.

A press release in 1980 claimed the Matra Murena "was nothing short of sensational with a drag coefficient of 0.328"!

18 months later there was a postscript to these results, when British Leyland went to MIRA to test a borrowed production M50. It failed to get a match, and wrote a letter to say so. However, we discovered that it had 'borrowed' the frontal area measurement from the MIRA files, which had given it the original 17.9sq ft from the scale model, when MIRA's own accurate measurement of the full-sized car was in fact 20sq ft. I thought it a bit of a cheat to 'borrow' our confidential information.

Colin Chapman decided that the only way to get all the development issues with the M50 on the table was to demand that a complete finished car was built. Thanks to the late change of interior design, and the insistence that the Guigiaro design was followed to the letter, Vehicle Engineering was struggling with the details, while the complexity of the external bright trim was challenging Iralco and Lotus. Colin viewed a car, finished in Glitterflake Antique Brown, in the Directors' Garage on December 17 1972, after a week of night-and-day work. The bright trim, interior, boot space and gas struts were all rejected; although, after driving the car, Colin made a favourable comment on the lack of wind noise.

The small engineering team was dejected, having worked so hard, but it threw itself back into it, so that, when re-presented on 8 January 1973, the exterior brightwork was accepted. By then the air-conditioning was installed, but not yet working. The interior was proving a major task, and work on it, led by Colin Spooner, continued for many months. The exterior (female) moulds for the resin injection process were completed on 12 January, so work could start on the (male) inner moulds. These were made by using sheet wax of the intended moulding thickness to line the female, and then lay-up the relatively thin and flexible inner male mould on top of it. When complete, the two would be parted, and the wax removed, leaving a cavity for the glass and injected resin to be fused.

9 February 1973 was notable for the writing of a policy memo for the M70 Esprit by Tony Rudd. I quote:

"The body style and appearance can and will be changed every 2000 units when the mould tool wears out.

"The high investment running gear, such as engine, transmission, suspension, should be derived from the M50 to spread the tooling costs for this car. You must be able to completely justify any departure from this policy such as the gearbox, if it becomes necessary.

"Next, consideration should be given to M43 (Europa) components, provided the M50 component has been demonstrated to be unsuitable or inadequate. It will not be sufficient to say that a new component is preferable. The existing one must be demonstrated by experience to

be inadequate, and it will not be acceptable to say that they are unsuitable 'by virtue of their design.' "

The document then referred to the engineering sub-groups. Below, are edited highlights:

- Gearbox: Renault. Every effort should be taken to eliminate the crowbar in a coal bucket characteristic given by the gearbox itself
- Wheels and tyres: M50 rear, new front
- Electrics: Under no circumstances will we countenance another Callender's [the harness supplier] Carnival where they can advertise us as using more wire than anyone else
- Heating and ventilation: In view of the unsatisfactory performance of Delanair it may be possible to make a case for going to another supplier
- Hard (bright) trim, Soft (upholstery) trim: In view of the M50 experience, we had better start designing them now

This policy was very logical, but it did not survive – even in spirit. The chassis and suspension were all new; indeed, the whole basis of the front suspension changed to use an upright from the Opel Ascona, which became obsolete within a month of the Esprit being announced. Later, the Esprit and Excel became common. The tyre sizes and tracks differed from M50, because the show car stood on racing tyres, so much larger ones were found for production. Virtually no parts were carried over as it was developed for production. Italdesign had not built the car for such, but as a show car, with no design restrictions. The interior was a model not engineered to 'work,' and, in fact, the whole vehicle layout left something to be desired, as there was no defined location for the cooling system, spare wheel, or luggage.

On 26 February 1973, I was back at MIRA again for the model aerodynamic testing of the M70 Esprit. The session was to study the effect of having either a fastback rear window, as the show car, or an open back, like the Europa. Guigiaro and Giancarlo Perini brought a plaster modeller from Italy to attend to the changes, while Mike Kimberley and I hosted the weekend. The Italians were wedded to plaster as a modelling material, as Turin had a centuries-old reputation for fine artworks modelled in it.

Saturday lunch was taken at the Chase Hotel, in Nuneaton, where Guigiaro caused a bit of consternation by walking through the large bar carrying a handbag; the coal miners of Warwickshire were not used to that!

The testing showed that the fastback was better for drag and lift, although the front had too much upward lift force on it. The drag was 40.5hp at 100mph, but the lift was +132lb front and +76lb rear. The drag horsepower figure, although lower than the M50's, benefited from the much reduced frontal area. The biggest loser that weekend was the modeller, who spoke no English, and also lost his wallet, which was never found.

Early March was Geneva motor show time again. I travelled with Chapman, Rudd and Kimberley, and, this time we got lunch. Later that day, Mike and I joined Perini for him to drive us to Turin; we checked into the Ambasciatore Hotel, where I had been living for most of the time since the New Year started.

Turin had become my second home; I was working at the Via Tepice offices of Italdesign as the M70 Esprit project manager, tasked with ensuring that the resulting car would meet Lotus' objectives. This proved difficult, as, when I rejected something – the windshield wiper layout, for example – they just shrugged their shoulders, and said that they had only been paid to do the job once and had done it once! Lunch times were always a bore, as the Italians had a two-hour break, as described to Wendy once on the telephone: "We work the day in two halves, the morning half and the afternoon half. This is the time between the halves, so your husband is not here."

Due to the cost of long-term occupation at a hotel, Perini arranged for the company to rent an apartment. The first one I viewed was rejected for reasons unremembered, but the second viewing, of a ground floor flat on the Corso Lungo Po, was accepted. That this one happened to belong to Perini's mother could explain the rejection of the first offering.

I was already a member of the Automobile Club di Torino, so I could rent Fiat 500s very cheaply. A qualification was the need to be an Italian national, which I had to pretend to be – but I did not speak much Italian, and often wondered what they made of me as a mute rental client. The performance of these baby Fiats was little more than my old Austin Seven, and they had to be driven flat out all the time to keep up with the traffic. Turin was ferociously unforgiving to tardy drivers. At least one rental car was returned with ominous streaks of oil dripping from the engine cover louvres.

During the six or seven months I was principally living in Italy, I drove extensively around the city, and had a number of trips to Milan to pick up Colin Chapman from the airport. I was stopped for speeding (I think) on the autostrada, and apprehended driving through the Valentino Park after dark, which was apparently verboten, but I always managed to talk my way out of it.

The Italdesign Via Tepice premises were small, and the cramped workshop was busy on other work, such as the Alfa

Romeo AlfaSud Coupé, so that, although the drawing work was done in the offices upstairs, the original plaster model of the Esprit was at a sub-contractor, Forneri. Forneri had a works not far away, and it was here that the windshield restyle was done. I had been in the Lungo Po flat for some weeks on my own, and Kimberley told Chapman that I was a bit unhappy, missing Wendy. Chapman's immediate reaction was to say that Wendy should join me in Turin, and, indeed, to fly out by scheduled airline forthwith. So, leaving our eight-month-old daughter Anne with her grandparents, Wendy flew out the following Saturday on a commercial flight, despite Chapman being due in Turin a couple of days later.

A few days later, Wendy and I met Chapman, with Mike and Sylvia Kimberley, at Turin Airport. For this occasion, I had upgraded to a Fiat 124. Cutting through the city centre, I dropped the two ladies off in the Via Roma, with vague instructions that we would meet at the Ambasciatore at six o'clock that evening. We three men then continued to Forneri's, where, by the time we arrived, Chapman was in a bad mood, due to the city traffic delays. I pointed out that the windshield of the M70 was at 18 degrees to the horizontal, while the M50 and Europa were 28 degrees, which was considered at the time to be the practical limit. The full-size model was made of white plaster, and much scraping and rubbing with bastard files eventually brought the surface down to the steel frame supporting the model. Guigiaro said it was impossible to go any further, so an almost flat windshield was compromised upon. All this took hours, and it was nearly 10pm when we left for the Ambasciatore.

Chapman had done nothing to remove the brilliant white plaster dust from his clothes or shoes, and he hurried up the lobby steps to the cocktail bar leaving a trail of white footprints on the dark blue carpet. Apologising to the two girls, who, by then, had been in the bar for four hours – they shrugged off the concern that they had been kept waiting so long by announcing that they had booked all the drinks on his room account. The hotel must have been very trusting, or knew me well enough by then, as Chapman had not even booked in at that stage.

Everyone was ready to go out to a late dinner, and Guigiaro had chosen a traditional Piedmontese restaurant, which was very full when we arrived. Colin rushed ahead to take the ladies' coats, before we were all subjected to an hour's worth of hors d'ouvres of fried Brussels sprouts, amongst other delights. Bored by this time, Chapman suddenly stood up and announced he had finished, it was late, and we were leaving. He went to the enormous pile of coats and picked out the correct two without prompting; he could remember anything he wanted to – and forget what suited him. The next morning, Mike and I picked him up from the Ambasciatore, where he claimed he had no Italian money, so Mike had to use his limited currency reserves. So the girls hadn't had their drinks on Colin the evening before, after all!

My time in Italy would soon be over, because the revised Italdesign Esprit was nearing completion, using a chassis with a 2-litre Lotus engine, a Citroën gearbox, and an undertray packaged around it. The chassis/undertray had taken Lotus three-and-a-half weeks to build in the May, and once it had been shipped out, Italdesign built the second car on it. I saw the moulds being taken off the plaster model and was aghast to see Forneri nailing rough sawn timber into the model to form the mould joints. The reinforcement of the light prototype moulds was hopeless, and I tried to stop the work to allow it to be done properly, as it was doubtful it would fit back together accurately. My attempts to have the moulds taken the 'Lotus' way failed; subsequently, Lotus had a major problem aligning the body parts, and had to have a contract model house do most of the job again.

Occasionally, Italdesign would bring out an interesting car to show visitors. One of these was the Volkswagen Porsche Tapiro, a show car first seen in 1970 at the Turin motor show. A number of runs were made round central Turin in this car, accompanied by plenty of noise, and half the population trying to keep up.

Two crayon-on-Canson paper drawings for the M52, retaining as much of the M50 as possible.

Later, when I was in the apartment after lunch one day, I heard a sporty noise approaching. Being siesta time, the streets were deserted, but, by the time I had reached the front steps of the building, the source of the noise was surrounded six-deep. In the midst of the crowd was the Maserati Boomerang, the 1972 Turin show car – as sharp as a butcher's knife. I climbed in beside Perini, as he fired up the 4.7-litre Maserati V8 engine, and we moved off to the admiration of the crowd. Such traffic as there was stopped to see it go past – an extreme caricature of the future Esprit, on the road, with all the right noises, in the spring of 1973. Wow!

Towards the end of that intensive period in Italy, Guigiaro suggested to me that we went for a drive, and he led me across the Via Tepice to a small multi-level car park. On the ground floor were some lock-up garages, and he opened one up to reveal the Alfa Romeo Caimano. Another show car from Turin, this time 1971, it was built on the Alfasud platform with the wheelbase reduced. The cockpit was covered with a one-piece Perspex dome, which, for entry, was tipped forward with the half-doors. Snug inside, Guigiaro lowered the roof, which just touched my head when closed. Sliding down in the seat, I was treated to a hairy ride up and down the ramps of the parking complex, noting that the Perspex did not make a distortion-free windshield. Guigiaro's enthusiasm for his baby was a joy to witness.

To round off my exposure to exotica, Perini laid on an official ride-and-drive in a production Maserati Bora, another Guigiaro creation. The noise of the four dual Weber carburettors gasping for air when the throttle was opened, added to the V8 exhaust roar, was thrilling stuff; although its 160mph maximum speed was not exercised, great care had to be taken on Turin's streets of wet stone sets. Fortunately, I managed to keep the car on the damp road, and I was most impressed.

Meanwhile, back at Hethel, I had another car to worry about, the M52, the 2+2 version of the four-seat M50. I had sketched a three-quarter front view a year before, but realised that, while it looked okay from the front, the design would not translate from the side or rear very well. Chapman was enthusiastic, though, and a quarter-scale model was made, which I believed proved the point that the proportions were wrong. The design featured a stout rollover bar behind the front doors, which terminated with a wraparound back window. A conventional boot sloped down to rejoin the donor car at the rear bumper.

Chapman, however, wanted it to work, as it fulfilled his desire (seen again later with the M90) to have the door glass as the only side window – his definition of a sports car. In the spring of 1973, there were full-size bodies available from the M50 moulds, so Chapman asked John Frayling to translate this idea into full-size. Once he had delivered it back to Hethel, all agreed that it didn't work, so I went back to the drawing-board and drew out some fastback designs. Some had glass nearly all the way back to the tail and some rather less, and, as Colin could not decide which he liked best, a quarter-scale model was built.

Up and down the back went the bottom edge of the glass until I reached near-desperation point. There was to be yet another viewing of the model, set for two o'clock on the Friday before the works summer holiday began. That day, I and some others went down to the King's Head for a celebratory holiday lunchtime pint. Then someone remembered that Colin didn't like his staff drinking at lunchtime – and I had this presentation to make at two o'clock. I borrowed a Second World War gas mask from the landlord, and returned to the Lotus board dining room in good time to ensure the model was set up on the large dining table. There, I waited for the board of directors.

At two o'clock sharp, in they came, to be greeted by a gent wearing a gas mask. Tony Rudd reversed through the double doors into the boardroom, while Fred Bushell tried to hide under the table. Chapman asked why his presenter was wearing a gas mask, and pulling the rubber mouthpiece away, I explained that I had been for a beer, and, as I knew that it was not approved of, I was masking the odour. I then released the tensioned mouthpiece, which struck me on the mouth quite painfully. "Well, what are we here for?" asked Chapman, and I explained the latest iteration of the M52 model. Chapman quickly approved the design, asking when he could drive a finished car. "Fifth of November," I said. "Good, I look forward to it," said Chapman, and was gone. The rest of the board reappeared (including Kimberley, who had become invisible earlier), and ratified the decision. I had three months in which to build a car – and the donor vehicle was still ten months from production.

An additional responsibility for me on the M52 project was that I was made programme manager. It was typical at Lotus, in those days, to have the programme run by one of the 'working' engineers. The only serious burden was the monthly MBO, or reporting meeting. MBO (Management By Objectives) was a Ford Motor Company-inspired system, and if you were not doing too well, it increased the midnight oil consumption. The M52, however, did go to plan.

By August 1973, two of a projected 12 pilot-build M50 vehicles were ready for the interior trim. However, the trim was far from ready, and Colin Spooner was still trying to engineer designs to replicate the Italdesign model.

Meanwhile, I was preoccupied with a prototype M52, for which I had to detail design, and build to the self-imposed deadline of 5 November. Taking a full-size bodyshell from the M50 moulds, the upper rear was cut off so that Charlie Prior could model the new shape above the maximum width line and behind the doors. All the body rebates, gutters, etc, had to be designed and incorporated, and glass jigs taken for the new quarter-windows and backlight. The rear seatback angle was made steeper, in recognition of the restricted headroom towards the back of the cockpit, although this was subsequently brought back to match the four-seater Elite.

Terry Keogh was seconded to do the detail drawings. He was very thorough, and made a very good job of the boot and rear glazing details. New rear seats were designed, built on millboard bases to save money and complexity – on the sister car, we had been struggling to make complex wire frames work, incurring much additional cost and time penalties. While designs, tools and then prototype parts were being made, a complete car had to be built – yet there were no parts, in production, that could be picked out of the parts bin.

However, there were those 12 pilot cars being built under lock and key, so, in the evenings, I would ask security for the keys to 'check on the day's work.' Being a manager, I had no difficulty getting in, but the workshop supervisor had to hide round the corner and get his barrow in secretly. Slowly but surely, we got the parts we needed to get a running car built – and, for some reason, only 11 pilot M50s were ever completed!

Concurrent with the engineers trying to perfect the body manufacturing processes for the M50, there were people trying to get the interior trim to fit and be functional, the vehicle systems, such as the air-conditioning, to work, and to make a more powerful 2-litre Lotus engine and Lotus gearbox reliable. We were busy building the prototype M52, and the completed M70 Esprit prototype model was shipped from Italy that September. We were stretched to the limit.

I was able to complete the prototype M52 in time to present it to Colin Chapman, on November 5, as promised. The document stating his 'qualified approval' is interesting as it gives a clue as to where some of the ongoing problems lay in the M50. The approval document, signed by Chapman, was released on November 6. (See opposite, and shaded panel, right).

Immediately after the presentation, I took the car to Ketteringham Hall for Ron Middleton to photograph. With approval from Chapman, Terry Keogh continued to release production drawings, while a heavy moulding was taken from the prototype body moulds to prepare a

Comments on the sign-off document (see opposite):

"1. Rear Body Panel – Too plain, improve interest – try lateral flutes, texturing/finisher. Try broad 'Lotus' outset on the panel …"

This vertical panel above the bumper at the back of the car was a separate insert on the prototype only, and, in fact, could have been made part of the undertray, except that would have made it different to the M50 one. The design was altered for production, after I had left the car company, to enable the tail to come out of the upper body tool. This produced a plain rear panel. Meanwhile, various textured aluminium panels and other ideas were mocked up, but none attracted approval.

"6. Maximum Width Finisher – Phase in on M50 and M52 as soon as procurement allows."

This was a plastic strip which covered the body joint at the maximum width of the car. On the prototype M52, it also ran up over the top of the inset tail panel, helping to frame it and add interest, but as stated earlier, that part did not remain into production. The M50 originally had a plain black section, which was replaced by a chrome and black one during development; this presentation was a successful opportunity to introduce the plain black once again!

"7. Front Seats – Lower seating position 1in keeping squab as M50/52. (Headrest stays at same height)."

The seats were carried over from M50, but the development team was having a lot of difficulty getting seat foams of the correct and consistent density from the suppliers.

"8. Ride level – Lower to level approved by ACBC (Chapman) (achieved by 195lb (88.5kg) (of ballast) in the boot of the presentation car). Ensure front still gives parallel sill to ground line."

Colin Chapman always wanted his cars to sit at designed ride height, but, of course, when the vehicle was empty, it would sit higher due to the reduction in weight. All motor show cars were ballasted to achieve this, and, on this occasion, he had been able to drive the presentation car suitably ballasted. He caused some concern to me, when he left the factory with his usual gusto for lunch, with all this weight loose in the boot. However, it didn't seem to do any harm.

"9. Roof Panel – Try silver Glitterflake roof panel."

We never did. Chapman had a 'thing' about Glitterflake!

"11. Fascia Bright Trim Strip – Ensure trim strip is horizontal NOT dropping at outboard ends."

Another troubled piece carried over from the M50 interior.

"12. Blue Trim – Release for purchase after manufacturing verification."

The prototype was finished in Mid Green Metallic paint on the exterior – which was offered on the Elan and Europa models for a short time, but withdrawn as it was not popular – and a mid-blue interior. The standard colours for the M50 were a beige vinyl and a creamy beige corded nylon, made especially to match the colours Guigiaro had used on the original model. The cost of these low-volume specials was very high.

<u>M52 PRESENTATION ON 5 NOVEMBER 1973</u>

Further to Mr. Chapman's approval of the M52 today, the following areas are noted for action with re-approval where denoted thus * :-

* 1.   Rear Body Panel   – Too plain, improve interest – try lateral flutes, texturing/finisher. Try broad 'Lotus' outset on panel as per ACBC proposal as one alternative

2.   Sill Finisher (S130)   – Introduce immediately on M50 and M52.

3.   Wiper   – Matt black arm for M52 – phase in on M50.

* 4.   World Championship Badge – Position elsewhere.

5.   Tailpipes   – Lengthen tailpipes at least 2".

6.   Maximum Width Finisher   – Phase in on M50 and M52 as soon as procurement allows.

7.   Front Seats   – Lower seating position 1" keeping squab as M50/52. (Headrest stays at same height).

8.   Ride Level   – Lower to level approved by ACBC (achieved by 195lb in boot on M52 presentation car). Ensure front still gives parallel sill to ground line.

9.   Roof Panel   – Try silver glitterflake roof panel.

10.   Rear Seat Arm Rest   – Ensure section change is constant during fall to seat base.

11.   Fascia Bright Trim Strip   – Ensure trim strip is horizontal <u>NOT</u> dropping at outboard ends.

12.   Blue Trim   – Release for purchase after manufacturing verification.

Signed ..... *A.C.B. Chapman* ....
A C B Chapman

Dated ..... **5-11-73** ....

MJK/HAJ 5.11.73.

The M52 sign-off document.

Standing alongside the M52 prototype the evening after its completion.

The rear panel was inset, but, although there were manufacturing methods to do this, it was abandoned for production.

tooling master. However, as the M50 body was attracting all the effort in the Body Process Department, progress ground to a halt. On 18 November 1973, I took both the M52 and the M70 Esprit to the MIRA wind tunnel for full-size testing. No results survive, but there were no modifications to either vehicle as a result of the tests. However, I can remember that the M52 had a worse drag coefficient by some 0.03 or so over the M50.

Outside the factory gates at Hethel, the world was facing a major change. From 6 October 1973, Israel was at war with Egypt and Syria; OPEC began to limit oil supplies, and greatly increase its prices. At home, the unions declared war on the government; on 12 November, the coal miners announced an overtime ban, capitalising on the nation's energy shortage. The following day, the government declared a state of emergency, and, a week later, announced that deliveries of petrol and oil would be cut by 10% to help conserve supplies. Motorists were asked to keep to 50mph or less, and not to make unnecessary journeys.

December arrived, and the speed limit became law, while a temperature limit of 17°C (63°F) was imposed on business premises. On 13 December, the government announced that, in the new year, business and industry would only get 65% of their electricity. Floodlit football

was affected, and TV finished at 10:30pm. Coupons for petrol rationing were issued, but fortunately never used. Lotus needed none of this, as it tried to get three new models prepared for public announcement.

One of the last jobs in 1973 had been to ship the checking jigs to Ireland, so that Iralco could proceed on the bright trim for the M52. An Irish transport company was to do the job, but it refused to come to Norfolk, unless Lotus could guarantee a full diesel tank on its truck for the return trip. Garages either restricted the quantity available to their customers, or they ran out completely. Somebody in the Powertrain Department said that the factory heating oil would work, so some drums were filled, and the truck was duly sent on its way. We acknowledged this was highly illegal, but the job had to be done. It was a pretty cold night, and the truck only got a few miles before failing to enjoy its new diet of heating oil, and broke down. Lotus had to arrange a tow to a 'friendly' garage, where the truck was replenished with far more than the usual allowance, after the tank had been cleaned. What happened to the heating oil was never known. The jigs had to get to Ireland to stay on programme.

Early one morning in the middle of January 1974, I set off in the prototype M52 with Terry Keogh on our way to Liverpool and the Dublin ferry. The 50mph

A production M50 Elite, at Portmerrion, for an Aramis cosmetics promotion.

speed limit was not just enforced by the police, but the general public would shake a fist and show displeasure at anyone exceeding the magic figure. Eventually we reached Liverpool docks at six o'clock in the evening. The car was a big hit at Iralco's factory, as the staff there was not used to being involved in the development stage of the actual vehicle, and, anyway, that type of car was rare in rural Ireland.

From January to March 1974, virtually all work on the M70 Esprit and the M52 halted, as everyone pitched in to get the M50 to market, while the miners and the Arabs did their best to prevent it.

Lotus was planning to launch the new Elite, as the M50 was named, in late March 1994, and had taken the back page of the *Weekend Telegraph* colour magazine for a magnificent full-colour advertisement. Due to the ongoing industrial strife, the launch had to be delayed until May, but, as the colour supplement was printed ten weeks ahead of publication, all attempts to prevent the premature public launch failed. There was just the one advertisement, but it took the edge off the launch; however, the press did not scoop much in those days, so, to most people, the car remained a secret.

The body process was the biggest issue at the end of the Elite development period, and the idea of self-colour instead of paint was abandoned (temporarily, as Chapman continued to press for it up to his death). There were difficulties with the resin, generating bubbles when under vacuum, and with the dry glass mat, which would slide down the mould when it was being closed, so it would all end up at the bottom. Foam beams would get displaced, and mouldings would come out far too thick.

Much work was done to made a preformed shape of dry glass fibres to fit the mould, with attempts to 'spray' continuous filaments over a former bound with size. Huge blankets of glass fibres were knitted to form a 'pullover,' but that stretched too much. Eventually the problems were solved, and production started, although the bodies were always heavier than the hand-laminated prototypes, with a consequent loss of vehicle performance.

With Lotus on its knees, the Elite was launched to the dealers, at Hethel, on 2 May 1974, and to the press the following day. When times had been better, plans had been made to launch the car in Monaco. I became a guide passenger on the test track drive for the press. Just three laps of the Hethel track were allowed per journalist, as there were only two cars available. Chapman had a personal car, which he brought into service to help out mid-way through the afternoon session, but it disgraced itself by shedding the windscreen trim strip, as it did not have the production attachment clips. I found myself

with a journalist from a well-known magazine late in the afternoon. He and Chapman were not the best of pals, as he would try to catch Chapman out technically, and usually lost! However, he managed to get third gear to jump out of engagement, and he made a big fuss about this. I was convinced that he was not putting the lever fully in gear, although the journalist concerned denied it. No one else had suffered from the problem in the same car, but he duly reported it in the press as a negative, anyway.

On Wednesday, 15 May 1974, the Norwich-based *Eastern Daily Press* carried the headline: 'THE NEW ELITE' and went on to describe it as "The most luxurious and expensive Lotus road car ever built goes on sale in UK showrooms today …" A beautiful colour picture of a blue Elite in front of a daffodil-bedecked main office entrance dominated the front page – many years before colour was used in newspapers with any frequency. More information, on page 20, revealed: "The nose is as low as the law permits, and its high fashion wedge shape is the work of styling manager Oliver Winterbottom, of Ketteringham Hall." Well, the address was nearly correct! (I lived in the Garden Cottage). Incidentally, Colin Chapman did not permit anyone to speak to the press, except with his and the PR man's permission.

The motoring press welcomed the newcomer, with some reservations over the cost, which was £5445 for the basic model. *The Motor* suggested that it had expected a figure of £4500, and, in its driving impressions, took delight in reporting the gearbox and windscreen trim misdemeanours. Even so, it finished the article: "In sum the new Elite seems a very fine car and we can't wait to put it through a full road test." The motoring magazines in general went to great lengths to describe the innovations of the car. The advanced specifications, which were highlighted, included three major components which were way ahead of their time:

1) "A high-speed luxury car with low specific fuel consumption." It was lucky that the oil crisis had been so recent, but fuel economy was not a major feature for another four years.

2) Aerodynamic, with low drag and lift. The Motor said: "… its 0.3 drag factor, almost certainly the lowest of any car now in production …" Low drag around this figure didn't become fashionable until 1982, when the Audi 100 CD was announced, and it was two or three more years before the others caught it up.

3) Safety. "The Elite meets Federal (USA) and European safety requirements with generous margins. Roof crush deflection 60% of allowed, door beam resistance nearly double the minimum and the steering wheel

displacement in the 30mph barrier crash was half an inch of the 5in permitted." It was not until the 1990s that safety became a factor in the automobile business, by which time Lotus was leading the introduction of airbags in sports cars. (Shortly after its launch, the Elite won the Don Safety Trophy, for which the company and I were very proud.)

Like most new Lotus products, the car bristled with new technical features, which included:

- Lotus-built aluminium 16-valve 2-litre engine
- Lotus five-speed gearbox – five gears were not common then
- Matched mould-injected resin body
- Integral foam body reinforcing box-sections
- Steel rollover hoop and door beams
- Super-thin Glaverbel windscreen, which reduced weight and laceration injuries in accidents
- The huge single windshield wiper, which cleared virtually all the steeply raked glass
- Accommodation for a 6ft 2in (1.88m) male, in the rear seat of a car only 47½in (1.2m) high
- Halogen headlamps in retractable pods, still a novelty
- Energy-absorbing (USA only) bumpers
- Aluminium radiator
- First car with 60-profile 205-section steel-breaker radial tyres
- Dashboard-focused floodlight
- Rear radio speakers' reverse mounting, working on the 'reflected sound' principle
- Glass rear bulkhead to shield the interior from the weather, when the tailgate was open
- The use of the then-novel gas struts to support the tailgate, when open
- Off-glass parking of the rear wiper, which was itself, an uncommon feature

The road tests followed, and the testers found that the legendary Lotus ride and handling went to new levels; the accommodation and lack of wind noise were commendable, as was the fuel consumption, but the interior was noisy, and the car lacked low-down power. Both these issues were addressed shortly afterwards, although one wonders what would have been its subsequent history, if the projected M51 4-litre V8 had ever matured.

The 2-litre gave a maximum speed of 128-130mph, with acceleration to 60mph taking 7.1sec. For comparison, the Alfa Romeo 2000 GTV only 120mph and 9.2sec. As for

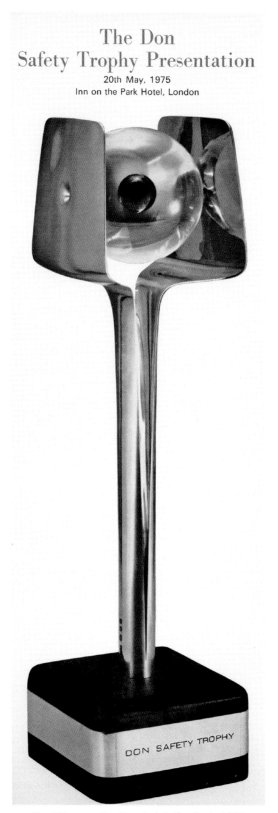

The Don
Safety Trophy Presentation
20th May, 1975
Inn on the Park Hotel, London

The Elite won the Don Safety Trophy in 1975.

The special luggage available for the Elite.

the targets that had been set for the project, it comfortably exceeded the performance, but failed to meet the weight objectives by a massive 571lb (259kg), with a kerb weight of 1097kg. However, the car was equipped with such new luxuries as air-conditioning, and the body process undoubtedly contributed significantly. It should also be noted that, today, despite the advent of computer-aided design, most medium sporty cars weigh about 300kg more than the Elite, so it upheld Lotus philosophies more than some people will admit today.

On the evening of announcement day (15 May), the local television station ran an early evening special programme covering the design and development, as well as the production, of the Elite. The cameras came to Hethel a few weeks before the release, and we had to try to recreate the early part of the project. The conference room was made the design office, and I had to stand at a drawing board and sketch the shape for Colin Chapman, Tony Rudd and Mike Kimberley to 'approve' – before their very eyes! I drew out the shape in advance and covered it with tracing paper – under the strong lighting, the drawing beneath was not visible on camera. Then, on receiving the command, I drew over the tracing paper with a thick black pen, thereby appearing to be a more accurate artist than I really was!

The factory had to get the production rate of the Elite up and labour time down. The original plan was 100 cars per week, and, had the company been able to achieve it, had the customers been there, and had world events been easier, then the Lotus story could have been very different. In practice, I think the maximum produced was 29 in a week. The problem was that, to make way for the Elite, the Elan +2 and its two-seat sister had stopped production. This meant that the Europa and Elite had to

cover all the Hethel site costs. There were difficulties with some suppliers – for instance, quite early in the life of the car, Lotus started to make the air-conditioning units itself, as the supplier had failed to perform.

While the country had been in chaos, the Esprit had also come to a halt. The Italdesign full-size model had arrived at Hethel the previous September, but the Elite work had prevented much activity on it. Although Colin Spooner was made project engineer for it in the October, most of his time was still occupied with getting the Elite interior completed satisfactorily. Ital completed the Esprit as a fully representative, non-running car, resplendent in an orange/red paint with tartan trim. Now, as the Elite went into production in the summer of 1974, so the Esprit project got going again, with Tony Rudd taking Colin Spooner down to the stables at Ketteringham Hall, where a very small team, working on a very tight budget, set about preparing the car for production.

The previous December, Charlie Reynolds' independent glass fibre workshop, at Barnham Broom, had assembled the moulds produced in Italy. Colin Spooner and I had explained to them how the moulds went together, and that a heavyweight body for use as a tooling master was required, as well as a 4oz hand lay shell for the first running prototype. They had a difficult time trying to get the moulds to align without a twist, and, in the end, the master was completely rebuilt. This was ready for the Esprit project team to accelerate its efforts, once the Elite was announced.

Also at this time, Mike Kimberley became Chief Engineer for Lotus Cars, while Jack Phillips came from Rolls-Royce to get Tony Rudd's 4-litre V8 engine ready for production.

Meanwhile, the M52 was barely moving, as the Body Toolroom and the Purchasing Department were both tied up with Elite matters. The loss of revenue from the cheaper Elan was obvious straight away. Mike Kimberley and I had discussed this with Colin Chapman, suggesting that a cheap two-seater on a modified M50 platform could fill that sector. Chapman was very keen, but knew that money was in exceedingly short supply. He had issued an edict in early 1974 that any work done on it must be in unpaid overtime, to keep Finance Director Fred Bushell happy, so slow progress was made on the idea, which carried the project number 'M80.' This work continued on a part-time basis for a year.

The idea for a replacement Elan was hatched in mid-March 1974, with a drawing numbered M80-0001Z. Known as the 'Two Seater Project,' its appearance was a development of the M52 I had done, with a shorter tail and lower roof. The backbone, however, was shortened by 8in

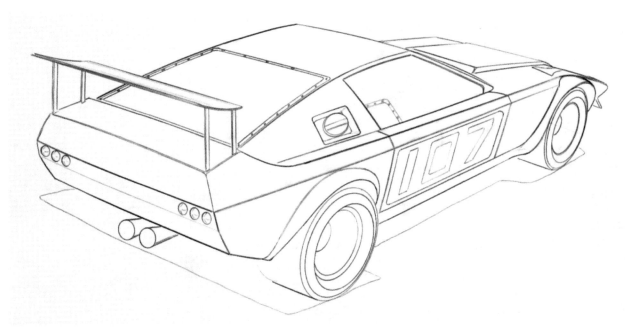

A sketch for M80 without a rear quarter window as Chapman decreed.

How the Lotus M80 might have looked had it gone ahead.

(203.2mm), which brought the rear suspension radius arm forward as far as it could go, to the back of the front seats. There was no rear seat, so twin fuel tanks were located above the radius arms and under a flat platform. The tanks had a capacity of 12 gallons. The vehicle specification was reduced, with no air-conditioning and a simple interior.

The height was down to 46.25in (1175mm), as the front seats were lower, but Chapman was critical of the concept. He decided it was too high, too heavy, had too much frontal area, and therefore drag, and that it should have had a less powerful engine – the proposal embodied the 2-litre Lotus, with either four- or five-speed transmission.

My handwritten notes with comparisons to the original Elan and the Jensen-Healey suggested that the M80 would lose 120lb (55kg), and the frontal area was reduced by 2.5sq ft, as the side windows were pulled in from the M50 location. As a result, the drag horsepower at 100mph would go down to 35hp to give a maximum of 133mph. It estimated the Elan at 42-45hp, and a maximum speed possibility of 128mph. The Elan was credited with a 0-60mph acceleration of 6.6 seconds. Acceleration for the M80 should have seen a 0-60mph time around 6.5 seconds. The Healey is credited with 8.3 seconds 0-60 acceleration – more than the base Elite – and with over 130mph maximum speed, the new car would have left the Healey far behind.

As the 'unofficial' work progressed, Chapman debated 'What is a sports car?' The question would present itself to him a number of times in the future, but it was never defined to everyone's satisfaction. Chapman decided that a sports car should have no side windows behind the doors, just like the Elan and the original Type 14 Elite. This, however, would have eliminated cars such as the Jaguar E-Type, MGB GT and Ferrari Daytona, amongst others. I thought that the term could be defined as 'a car whose wheels only just fitted into the body.' Chapman, however, requested that the car be designed with his discriminator in mind, and I drew a sketch with simple soft lines and a short rear without side glazing.

Chapman was very keen to develop this, but Fred Bushell got it stopped, as there were barely enough funds to keep the company running, let alone any for more new products. The code number M80 resurfaced in the future as a four-seat luxury high-performance limousine, first as drawings and models by Italdesign in 1980, and later as a Harris Mann drawing for the London Motor Show, named the Eminence.

In the autumn of 1974, Colin Chapman asked me to help with the new boat he was building, the JCL Marine Mamba. He had got into the marine business in 1971, and, as time went by, he expanded the range considerably. The next chapter will cover this in more detail.

I had already been involved with his boats in a small way, laying out the multi-tapered conical windscreens for the Marauder, but, in this case, I was a bit reluctant, as Richard Morley had just informed me that Lotus would not require my services once my contract had expired on 31 December 1974. When I explained this to Chapman, he just said that he would discuss the possibility of a

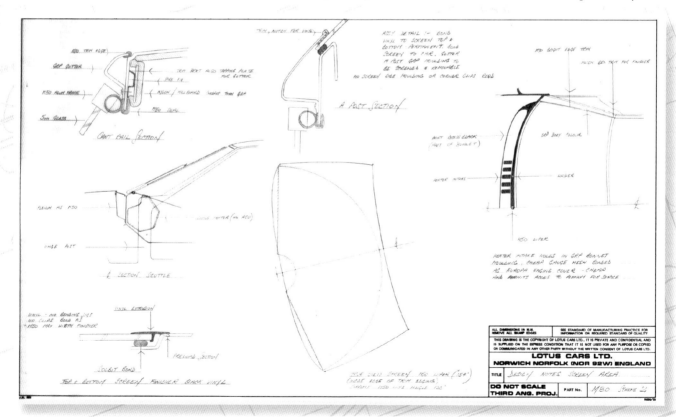

Above and opposite: The M80 was researched in some detail.

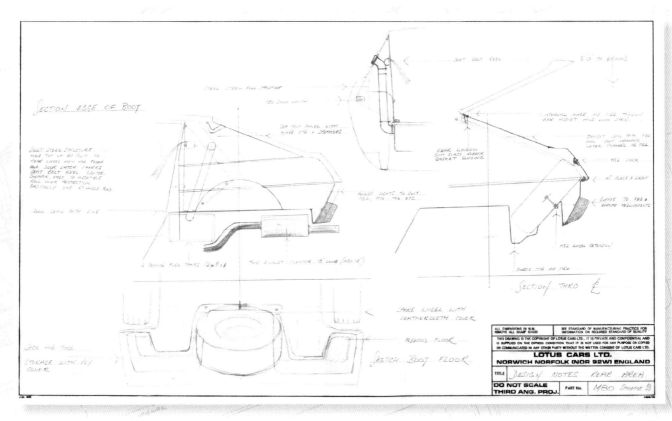

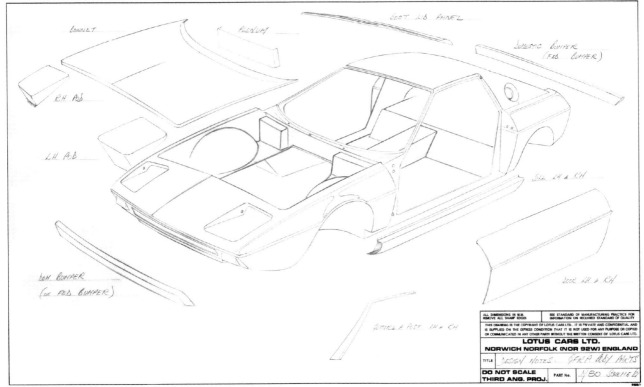

job, once I had readied the Mamba for the Boat Show, which was scheduled to open on 1 January 1975. With an ultimatum like that, I headed for the boat-building factory at the end of the Hethel site, and went nautical.

Later that year, the 1975 Earls Court motor show opened in London in the October, with the Lotus stand launching the coupé version of the Elite, named the Eclat, and the Esprit. The Eclat 520 was priced at £5729 against the Elite 501 at £6483.

In my absence, the rear of the M52 had been simplified without the inset rear panel – which I felt made that aspect weak and dull. However, the Eclat went on to outlive the Elite, and become the Excel, remaining in production to the end of the 1980s. The Esprit was also shown at London to end the continuous speculation that Lotus would produce the Guigiaro show car that had been rumoured since its showing in Turin three years earlier, but it was far from production-ready.

The M52 was launched in 1975 as the Lotus Eclat.

www.velocebooks.com / www.veloce.co.uk
Details of all current books • New book news • Special offers • Gift vouchers • Forum

62

Chapter 5
The Chapman boats

Colin Chapman acquired Moonraker Motor Yachts in 1971, and expanded his interests by creating his own – very technically advanced – products at JCL Marine. He retained the Moonraker boatyard, at Brundall on the River Yare, close to Norwich, and set up JCL Marine in unused buildings at Hethel. He was becoming increasingly frustrated by the imposition of rules on both racing and road cars, and he saw a technical challenge in the marine environment. He was not fond of traditional methods, unchanged for years, so every aspect of design examined ways to reduce weight and cost. The Chapman boat model line-up eventually comprised the following:

Moonraker 36

36ft (11m) seagoing cabin cruiser, built at Brundall. Traditional northern European design with accommodation for eight. It was powered by twin mid-mounted diesels, and was good for around 24 knots. Built on a hand-laid glass fibre hull, at its peak, it was produced at four per month.

Marauder 46

46ft (14m) seagoing cabin cruiser, with the hull designed by the offshore powerboat designer Don Shead, to Chapman's requirements. The prototype, built in wood, was conventional, but the production glass fibre model bristled with innovations. Powered by two Ford Sabre diesels, rubber-mounted in the middle of the injection-moulded hull, one engine was modified to run 'silently' as an electrical generator. The fuel and water tanks were moulded integrally into the hull, which also had locators for the bulkheads on its inside surface. Intended for mass production, by building the interior as modules, off the

boat. They would then be dropped in from a mezzanine floor, in the factory at Hethel. She was intended to weigh 8½ tons (8636kg), when the typical weight for that class was over twice as much. The complex systems gave endless development problems. The light weight gave a maximum speed of some 28 knots.

Mystere 43

42ft (12.8m) Mediterranean-style boat, built in glass fibre under licence from Versilcraft, which built wooden versions at the rate of three or four per year. Moulds were taken from a finished Italian craft, and the fittings and finishes copied, to permit the build of around 25 per year. Powered by twin mid-mounted Ford Sabres, the interior was spacious for four, plus a crew of one. The stern was open-decked, and there was a flying bridge over the saloon and main helm.

Mamba Mk 1

33ft (10m) high-speed, seagoing motor yacht, built on a mathematically reduced version of the Don Shead Marauder hull design. The original Mamba of 1974/5 had two Mercruiser Chevrolet V8 petrol engines with Z drives projecting from the stern. The superstructure was styled by Chapman, and featured a wraparound helm window similar to the Marauder's. Weighing in at less than four tons with a combined horsepower of approximately 700hp, top speed was estimated at 40+ knots. Only one of these was built.

Streaker

An open-decked, high-performance seagoing speedboat, with a double-berth forward cabin, plus bathroom and galley. Powered by two GM V8 petrol engines, the hull height was cut down from the Mamba 33. A full-size mock-up, built in 1975, was never completed.

Mamba

Mark II version of 1976, also built on the 33ft hull – actual length 34.5ft (10.5m) – but with the hull knuckle cantilevered out to give more deck width. Completely new superstructure, which I styled and packaged. A pair of Ford-based Mercraft six-cylinder diesels provided a total of 360hp in the stern, using V drives to the propellers. Planned top speed was 30 plus knots.

Mistral

42ft (12.8m) six-berth redesigned Mystere with the twin 212hp Sabre diesels mounted in the stern facing forward and propelling the craft through V drives similar to the Mamba. The superstructure was all new which I styled alongside the Mamba in 1976 and incorporated an extra midship cabin where the original engines had been. Colin Gething took over the detail layout from me once the basic shape had been established.

Mangusta

60ft (18.3m) three-deck super luxury motor yacht, which I had two hours to draw up in early 1977, for Chapman to show Chris Craft Boats of America. Never built.

My employment contract with Lotus expired at the end of 1974. At the beginning of December, Colin Chapman had asked me to work on his latest boat, the JCL Mamba. There was no promise of long-term employment, but I had much to do in a short time. The Mamba had run in the water, but had no interior at all – in fact, the lightweight saloon floor had collapsed, while Chapman was 'testing' on Breydon Water, so that had to be rebuilt before anything could proceed inside. All the electrical and plumbing systems had to be made and fitted, and the galley equipment designed and built. Outside, all the deck fittings had to be built, and there was very little time till the opening of the London Boat Show. I soon found out why progress was slow – there wasn't anyone to do the work, as the JCL boat business was suffering from too much work and not enough money.

I worked hard designing and getting the Mamba ready for the Boat Show, which opened in London on 1 January 1975. With next to no labour available, I had to resort to trimming much of the boat myself. Working late on Christmas Eve, and taking the family to the factory to clean the interior on Boxing Day, we got the job done. I found Chapman in his office and gave him the news of the completion, and asked if I should then return to work in January. Colin told me that, of course, I should, and appeared surprised by the question. When I reminded him that my contract with Lotus had expired, he just said

From the left: The original JCL Mamba, Marauder, Mystere and Moonraker at the Brundall yard.

Mystere in the foreground, by the houseboat offices at Brundall.

The prize-winner declined to accept the hardware, preferring to take money in lieu. Some months went by before a buyer was found. The boat had a combination of petrol for the engines, and gas for the cooking, which, should a mixture of the fumes occur, produces a bang akin to dynamite. Ten years later, the Mamba blew up, fortunately without serious injury, and now resides on the bed of Lake Geneva.

With the Mamba out of the factory, work started on the Streaker. I designed a very racy, aggressive-looking open powerboat, with a luxurious forward cabin. This contained a large sleeping berth, galley and bathroom. The remainder of the vessel was open decked, and featured a military-looking tripod mast, which I replicated on later boats. Designed on the Mamba hull, a plywood mock-up was built, which could have formed the basis of production moulds. Chapman wanted the open main deck to be dominated by a table, which could either be raised for meals, or lowered flush with the deck for unobstructed sunbathing. As the freeboard of the hull had been lowered, there was little space between the deck and the fuel tanks under it. Around that point, the project stopped, as Marauder still occupied most of the resources.

Working for Chapman could be taxing at times: one Saturday morning, as autumn approached, I was in Factory Three at Hethel, when Chapman arrived. He started to criticise me for just about everything that was going wrong, and become very angry. I tried to explain that many of the subjects he was complaining about were nothing to do with me, but Chapman became even more vociferous, telling me that, as a senior company manager, I was responsible.

I was very shaken when he left, so I called Peter Wright, and arranged to meet, so that he could explain the reason for the 'Old Man's' temper. It transpired that, early that morning, the company Piper Navajo had taken off from Hethel in fog. The pilot was confident that, if he

that I should carry on as before, so on 1 January 1975, I officially joined JCL Marine, and took up residence in the Boat Workshop in Factory Three at Hethel. The Mamba did not go to the Boat Show, so the first job was to complete it, in full working order, as it had been sold to a customer.

Chapman had manned his marine companies with a number of hand-picked Lotus personnel. John Pettifer moved from his job as Assembly Line Manager of the car company; Tony Rudd became involved in various technical adventures with some of the more advanced boat systems, before – kicking and struggling – being made Chief Executive; John Kelly left Lotus Service to run Moonraker; and Peter Wright (brought into Technocraft, the moulding company) became my boss for a time.

The Mamba was first prize in a competition run by Martini, the drinks company, and the winner was due to collect the prize in the spring of 1975. Martini had recently become the main sponsor of the Lotus Formula One team. The boat was far from finished: it had no working systems for the electrical, water or drainage functions, and the detail finish of my amateur-built furnishings and exterior detail needed rebuilding. Again, there was a staff shortage, as the Marauder had continual challenges with her novel systems, and consumed the attention of most of the workforce.

gave the plane full throttle and took off normally, all would be well. However, the nearby trees had grown, and were taller than he realised; the aircraft hit the tops, sustaining serious damage. RAF Honington laid a carpet of foam on its runway as the Piper landed, minus undercarriage, and with major damage to the tail. Chapman had rushed over to the landing site to bring the passengers back to Wymondham, and seen the wrecked plane. Worse, he had the bill from the RAF for the foam and the clearing up. He had come to the boat hanger upon his return to Hethel, where I had been the innocent target for his frustration.

The first Moonraker F350, photographed on the night before departure to the Boat Show.

As previously recounted, Chapman had the Moonraker 36 updated by Specialised Mouldings in Huntingdon, in 1971, with a flying bridge over the wheelhouse, under Ian Jones direction. This was shortly after he had purchased the firm. A good seller, the boat's sales were hit by the economic disasters of the '70s and, after three good years, instead of four boats per month, they had no sales at all for the last two months of 1975. Colin Chapman asked me if I could update the product in time for the 1976 London Boat Show. He also wanted his wife, Hazel, to be involved in designing the interior decor.

I moved over to the Brundall boatyard to take a desk space in the office there, and made myself familiar with the product. Using A4 plain paper and a biro and ruler – there was no space for a drawing board and, anyway, the there were no layout drawings for the boat available – I started to revise the whole interior layout. In this I was helped when the company buyer, Mr Warner, got hold of some pocket calculators from Casio, which he sold at some £15 each. Expensive then (equivalent to over £140 in 2015), mine more than provided its worth. This was my first calculator, and it made the work much, much quicker. Until then, all scaling up or down had to be done with long-hand mathematics.

The colour scheme chosen for the Show Moonraker F350 featured a red hull. The superstructure was finished in white, with the flying bridge in red to match the hull. It took about a week to mould and release the hull, which was then put in the fitting-out factory. Here the bulkheads, tanks and engines were fitted, prior to the superstructure being lowered and bonded to the hull and the bulkheads.

The interior was all new; the main saloon featured a continuous piece of furniture along the starboard side, housing the hi-fi, cooker, sink and fridge, as well as all the food and household storage. Opposite, there was an L-shaped settee, which converted into a double bed, and a table, which plugged into the floor. I had a chair made to plug into the floor, too, but Chapman had it taken out, and gave it to me as a gift, which I still possess.

The main bathroom was midships, and featured a bulkhead covered in plastic mirror. The decor throughout the craft was the same: dark brown carpet, with a pale off-white woven fabric for the upholstery. The sapele-veneered timber was set off with a Formica leather surface and tabletop.

The helm position was new, with a black-trimmed housing holding the instruments and switchgear. The controls were illuminated at night by a soft red light, which came from a single source overhead made up from a large red warning light shrouded by a length of stainless steel tube. The twin 175hp turbo diesels (hence the 350 in the name) lay under the helm.

The aft cabin had single bunks, with a double option. The curtains were either bright red, or a rich brown, throughout the boat, pillows white, and duvet covers in a brown-and-white patterned fabric.

Working with Hazel Chapman on the decor, I would often call at East Carleton Manor first thing in the morning to discuss this and get approvals. Time was desperately short to meet the Boat Show deadline, so rapid decisions were vital. Colin once remarked that I saw more of his wife than he did!

The fittings on the outside of the vessel were tidied, with new handrails, and the appearance finished off with a new 'Moonraker' script logo.

The factory at Brundall worked round the clock to manufacture the furniture and fittings, and make the jigs necessary to support further production, while I had to keep up the supply of drawings and specifications.

Warner had to get the new equipment, such as the cooker, fabrics, laminates, and the spot lights which replaced the utilitarian strip lighting, while the stores were building up the parts list to provide us with a the final cost The vessel was brought out and gently lowered into the water, three weeks after the hull was moulded. The stores staff excelled themselves by providing the bill of materials and costs three hours later. The Chapmans were very pleased with the result.

The night that the F350 was launched, Ron Middleton came to take the interior photographs for the brochure. Don McLauchlan, the Lotus PRO, brought the props. These consisted of bread, cheese, wine and fruit to 'decorate' the galley and saloon, so, when all work was done, Don and I ate and drank them. The 'on water' shots were taken at first light the next morning, before the boat was lifted out onto the Abbey Transport trailer for its journey to the Boat Show at Earls Court. The only time a boat that I was involved with left for London on time.

On reaching London, she was placed on a show stand, that I had devised, in the Pembroke Hall at the back of the Earls Court exhibition complex. The plan was to get away from the acres of expensive carpet, so I specified a carpeted walkway through a beach of washed pebbles. The plan had to be hastily modified when a truck arrived with tons of Thames Valley stone, as the authorities pointed out that the display was over the railway line,

so the floor had a weight limit. A few pebbles were interspersed with some plants, and the stand remained at street level. This was the third exhibition stand that I had done, following the two for Lotus Cars Motor Shows there. These had been very successful, and so, happily, was the Moonraker one, with boats sold, and the business back to a satisfactory level.

I was tidying up the paperwork, and sorting out the optional parts of the specification for the F350, when an opportunity came up to go out on sea trials. Our run down the River Yare from Brundall to Breydon Water was slow, due to river speed limits. Arriving at the Haven Bridge in Yarmouth, we moored, to wait for the tide to drop before the bridge was raised. The sea was very rough, and the trials restricted to running close to the harbour mouth. The Moonraker weighed about nine tons as she was tested, and the waves were enough to get her completely out of the water. Despite precautions for storing household chattels, they were strewn all around the main cabin. I remember standing in the centre of the helm and having my knees thrown up into the roof, while I hung onto the handholds by the saloon entrance. The boat seemed more than capable of taking the punishment, but it was a very important lesson to the designer on how the vessel would be asked to perform in bad weather. Shortly after, I was summoned to Ketteringham Hall by Chapman, and asked to redesign the Mamba. I left Moonraker with regret, as it had been a happy project.

February 1976, as I reached the age of 32, saw me move into the chapel at Ketteringham Hall, where I had but a grand piano and three old drawing chests to keep me company. Always known as 'The Chapel,' it was actually built as a dining hall. The Hall dated from Tudor times, and was requisitioned for the American Airforce in WW2. Later, it became a boarding school, and, when that left, Colin Chapman bought it. He started to renovate it as his corporate headquarters. By the time I arrived there, Team Lotus had joined Chapman, Bushell and Rudd.

The 'Chapel' was lit by three 60 watt bulbs hanging from the lofty ceiling, while daylight came from the huge, but high,

The front of Ketteringham Hall,:'Chapel' on the right.

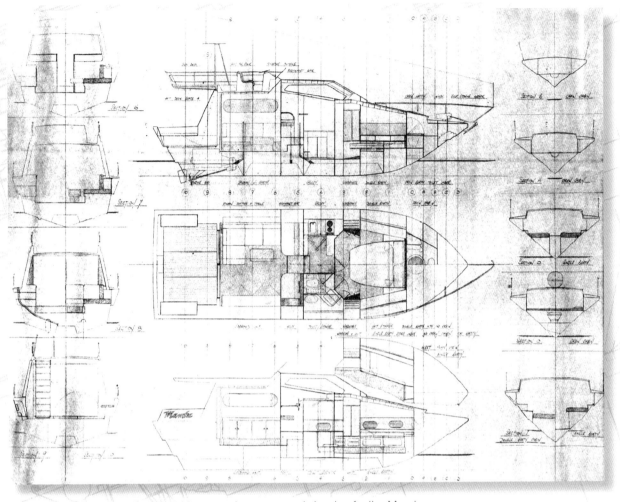

My general arrangement drawing for the Mamba.

gothic east window. With long dark evenings, the lighting was so poor, I could barely see my work on the drawing board, so I modernised by fitting a 150 watt bulb in the nearest socket.

The Orangery housed the Team Lotus designers, where Ralph Bellamy was working on the ground effect Type 78. The aerodynamic development model was to be covered at all times it was not in use, to maintain strict secrecy. Chapman thought Ken Tyrrell was hidden in the grounds with a camera! It was through the window of this 'secure' office that I had to climb in the mornings, having released the latch with my credit card, as the janitor usually failed to unlock the more conventional entrances in time.

Tony Rudd and Peter Wright had offices there, and it was in the spring and summer of 1976 that they developed their radical ideas, in collaboration with Chapman, into a world-beating ground-effect racing car. The secretarial staff worked in a central office, alongside a technical

library. The stables were renovated and equipped for use by Team Lotus as workshops, and my old friend Charlie Prior had a turret in the stable yard as a model shop, with his assistant Roger Pestell.

The Mamba was to be the pièce de résistance of the Chapman marine design influence, and it all started with an ordinary white envelope on which Colin drew a tidy side view arrangement, marking the basic dimensions of his requirements.

The layout of the craft had a crew cabin, forward double berth and shower/wc, midships main saloon with the helm on the starboard and galley to port. The aft well-deck gave access to the ladder up to the flying bridge, which had to provide sunbathing space for the passengers, as well as room for the upper helmsman. The styling objective was to make the boat appear much larger than it really was, when moored away from a jetty – where scale would be hard to determine. The weight

An artist's impression of the Mamba for brochures, made before the boat was finished.

was to be as low as possible, and it was all to be built on the original Mamba hull, with a major change to the knuckle line.

Although the hull had already been used for the one-off Martini prize boat, Chapman had the idea of greatly increasing the step out at the knuckle, and cantilevering the upper hull out to support a wider side deck. Its second attribute was to stiffen the sides of the hull, which were to be laminated in 6oz/sq ft glass fibre, while the parts below the chine were to be moulded in 10oz. The boat would be stiffened along the keel line by three tanks, integrally moulded into the bottom of the hull, one for drinking water and two for diesel fuel, while further stiffness was gained from the vee-shaped longitudinal spray rails.

Once these details were settled, the full-size model of the original Mamba hull was modified, and a mould taken off by Aquafibre in Rackheath, reinforced with resin and sand 'cement.' Meanwhile, I was drawing up the superstructure ready for Leslie Landamore to start building the full-size model in timber, at his long-established Wroxham boatyard. The drawing was very complex, as the flying bridge and side decks were to have veneered plywood decking, bonded with vacuum assistance onto a ribbed understructure, which created a very stiff hollow double-skinned structure. The spaces under the deck all

had to interconnect, in order that the vacuum would pull all the timber down evenly. This meant that the drawing and its dimensions were very different, and more complex, than the general arrangement drawings of the style and layout approved by Chapman. It was while I drew these that I quietly increased the Saloon headroom – of which more later in the story.

The original intention was to make the superstructure a 'simple to draw' moulding, with no undercuts or plugs, so that it could be manufactured by the Vacuum Assisted Resin Injection process. But Colin wanted the undercut toe line where the deck meets the superstructure, for both style, and the practical addition of more deck surface. He therefore allowed it to be hand lay-up. Nevertheless, he was acutely aware of the cost of cleaning up the flash left from mould joins, so a number of exercises were done to ascertain the shortest mould joint patterns. As these measured many metres, the correct choice had a major influence on production labour cost.

In May 1976, work started at Landamore's on the wooden master of the superstructure, a daunting job due to its size, as I was more familiar with full-size car models. As it was the size of a large house, I was quite uneasy as the main framing came into place. Landamore's soon had the basic framework done, and started to sheet-in the main surfaces, but a lot more time was spent on the convolutions in the decks – which mystified the Landamore's team, as no other boatbuilder would have had corrugated them!

Another curiosity that interested Landamore's was the very slender overhanging aft part of the flying bridge. At first sight this would not obviously take the weight of a number of people, but the structure was to be reinforced by a pair of steel cables, in tension, hidden inside the edge of the deck. They did their job, which helped disguise the scale of the finished design. This was a typical Chapman solution!

Once all the woodwork was finished, it had to be filled, flatted and painted, to get a good finish for the mould. Once again, Aquafibre made the moulds, but this time there was a hitch. Before it would release the work, it wanted paying for the hull mould, which was long overdue. I needed the first superstructure moulding as quickly as possible, as the new boat had to be completed for the Boat Show debut at the end of the year. Much shouting, message-carrying and promising was done, before delivery took place.

The chronic lack of cash was a perpetual problem in JCL Marine, illustrated by the following events. I had retained my Lotus company car when I went to the boat division, and had continued to use the Lotus company petrol pump. The procedure was that Lotus would bill JCL for the money. As JCL never paid, Lotus put a stop to it, and I was instructed to open an account at a local garage. I chose one and it was pleased to take on a new

account. About three months after the arrangement had started, I pulled up at the pumps to be told that, as the account had never been paid, there was to be no more credit. Unfortunately, I had no cash, nor did the car have any petrol, so I had to walk to the local pub, and borrow £10, to be able to fill up.

Not only was JCL short of money, but so was I, and, during an interview with my bank manager, I asked for some advice on how to make ends meet. He suggested talking to a builder, property developer and racing car manufacturer, in nearby Watton. An interview was arranged, and I went over to its headquarters, where the discussion opened with, "I am a friend of Colin Chapman, you know, and he doesn't want you to leave." The interview went on for half an hour, but the cause was lost.

When I got back to Ketteringham Hall later that day, Chapman asked me why I had gone for an interview. Explaining that I was broke, after two years of very high inflation, with no pay increases, Chapman replied, "you and me both, mate." Later in 1976, the builder went bust.

The interior of the Mamba provided the challenge of making all the furniture – beds, cabinets, structural members, etc. This greatly improved the stiffness of the boat, and much was finished in 'soft' trim. This was a suede-like material, called Marcasite. As to the Chapman edict, no attachment fixings were to be seen.

Before the boats were built in full-size, models were made – not only to show the styling, but also built with

The JCL Mistral, which I designed to be similar to the Mamba.

a lift-off superstructure, to show the interior layout. Charlie Prior and Roger Pestell provided these, alongside their Team Lotus wind tunnel model commitments. In the summer of 1976, they also constructed the model of the Mistral for me, with work continuing on both boats during autumn 1976.

The Mistral had a completely redesigned layout and superstructure, built on a revised Mystere hull. However, on Chapman's instructions, I carried over the design themes from the Mamba.

Once I had drawn up the exterior styling for the Mistral, the whole project was detailed and managed by Colin Gething. The craft had completely new powertrain layout and interior, with a midships lower cabin. This was located in the old engine room, as the engines were now relocated at the stern, powering the propellers through vee-drives. By the summer, Gething moved into the chapel to join me, followed shortly afterwards by Malcolm Leeds, who did much of the mechanical work on the Mamba.

Back at work on the Mamba, in order that it could maintain the illusion of being bigger than it really was, it was necessary to keep the aft deck as low as possible. Chapman asked Tony Rudd to work with Mercraft on a lower and lighter power unit for the boat. A Ford truck engine was chosen, but instead of standing it upright as other boatbuilders did, they were to retain the 45 degree inclination of the original. The weight was reduced by using aluminium exhaust manifolds, saving 30kg, and the pair of 180hp engines allowed the aft deck to be only 1m above the bottom of the hull.

After all the problems on the Marauder, where the propeller shaft was supported by the rudder pintle to avoid using conventional P-brackets, the Mamba was allowed them. However, the engine cooling water was taken in through a series of holes in the leading edge of the rudder, to remove the need for high drag underwater scoops.

Progress on building the Mamba was painfully slow. As usual, cash was a problem, and this strained the organisation, as essential parts were not forthcoming when needed. One stalwart sufferer was an ex-BRM mechanic, Dobbin, as Alan Challis was known, who found himself building a boat with no finance – instead of a racing car with no finance. He did a first class job, within these restrictions, to ensure the craft reached the London Show at all. Later, Alan became the very successful Chief Mechanic for Williams Formula 1.

As Christmas 1976 loomed, the Mamba and the Mistral were far from ready, so, to help speed up the build, a Ford Granada estate car was dispatched to Italy, with two staff carrying a bag of money. Within ten days, they were back in Norfolk, with a treasure trove of winches, bathroom and galley fittings, lights, window frames, and various other essentials, procured from the artisan Italian marine industry. The JCL boats demanded more avant garde designs for these than supplied by traditional British marine industry. We were forced therefore to look elsewhere for these parts, and Italy had a bespoke industry ready to help.

The Mamba got to Earls Court just in time – there was a schedule imposed, to get the big boats in place in the right order, otherwise they would not have room in the isles to reach their stands. It demanded a timetable of military precision, the penalty for lateness being an empty show stand. However, various craftsmen were dispatched, armed with sewing machines and tools, to complete the finishing touches to the Mamba on the exhibition stand. This demanded some delicate negotiation with the Earls Court unions, and not a little subterfuge.

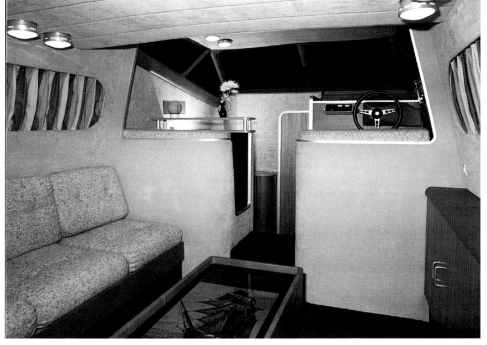

Interior of the Mamba.

The Lotus Eclat Sprint.

Meanwhile, throughout my time at Ketteringham Hall, Chapman would divert me to attend to other areas of his business interests. For instance, Lotus Cars had built some 36 white-painted Eclats with cheaper off-the-shelf wheels, a four-speed gearbox, and a low axle ratio, to try and get a 'loss leader' into the showrooms. The dealers weren't interested, and the cars remained homeless, so I spent a Saturday morning 'tarting up' the cars, with black stripes and a Union Jack 'Sprint' logo on the rear. The cars were all sold by the Tuesday, so that was a success. They never made any more, however.

Another job was to design a replacement for the proprietary Wolfrace alloy wheels on the Lotus Esprit. I had just a morning to create those, featuring large ducted spokes – they were eventually used on the Eclat, as well.

A less successful job was the introduction of the mock suede trim, used on the boats, into the cars. It was often used for shop window dressing and other indoor applications, but, when the top of the dashboard was subjected to the intense sun of North America, the material rapidly disintegrated. The cars looked good with the interior of suede, set off with a special knitted nylon, which had a bright sparkle, but this mistake was to cost Lotus Cars a lot of money, and was a sharp reminder of the need to test materials in their final environment. Later, suede successfully re-emerged in the automobile world as Alcantara.

In the course of the year, Chapman asked me to "JPS gold line" the wind tunnel model of the Type 78 Formula 1 car, as he thought it looked so ugly that no one would photograph it! With its large side ducts, it was certainly a major change – one which has since become commonplace. Ralph Bellamy had little time for aesthetics, but Chapman was genuinely concerned that sponsors would be put off, if the Press failed to photograph it. I applied the lines to the model, hopefully flattering it. I don't know if it helped

Marcasite suede and nylon interior of the Lotus Elite.

JCL Mamba on Breydon Water.

JCL Mamba Fore cabin.

very much, but at least I could claim to be a (partial) Formula 1 designer!

The 1977 London Boat Show brought a major opportunity for JCL Marine. The American boat company, Chris Craft, arrived to do a deal to buy 50 boats, and a licence for the injection-moulded glass fibre process. Shortly after its arrival at Ketteringham Hall that January, Colin Chapman asked me to draw up a 60ft (18.3m), three-decked boat. The plan was for Chris Craft and JCL to joint-fund the development, 50% each.

Having to seize the opportunity instantly, the Mangusta was 'sold' as being already in existence. I only had two hours on the drawing board, and yet it emerged with a grand state cabin midships on the lower deck, with a grand saloon above. The two cabins were about 18ft sq (5.5m), and, at that early stage, had a cellular floor thickness between them of only 200mm. With no other signs of support, the structural strength in a heavy sea was doubtful! The atmosphere at the Hall, with Chris Craft's Jim Rochlis, Herbie Siegl and financial specialists, was strained. They would arrive with hoards of lawyers, which made open speech a dangerous commodity, as they would appear round every corner. I was looking forward to working up designs on the Mangusta, but at the end of January, everything changed.

Colin Chapman called me into his office and asked why there was not sufficient headroom to stand comfortably in the saloon of the Mamba. I responded by reminding him that the ceiling height was higher than the dimension in the original sketch on the envelope of a year before. Chapman had specified 1875mm (73.8in), which I had thought a bit tight and had increased the finished height to 1900mm (74.8in).

Chapman was a stickler for requiring his 'golden dimensions' to be obeyed, and, while I was preparing the drawings of the superstructure, I was in fear of having to explain the far greater dimensions from floor to roof to allow for its trim panels and, of course, the deck floor carpet. Chapman hadn't noticed this, which was unusual, as he had made numerous daily visits to my drawing board.

To support my case, I fetched the original white envelope and showed it to Chapman, with the information that the centre of the ceiling was 25mm higher than his requirements. Chapman was now getting very angry, and said that the roof height he had put on the drawing was the minimum at "any part of the ceiling." I retorted that in a side view drawing, it would be conventional to show centreline dimensions only (as all the others did), as the changing width of the curved cabin roof gave varying height dimensions. Chapman then said he would have to add to the height of the hull to increase

the interior dimensions, and that I was incompetent. It was no surprise when Chapman's P/A and doer of his less pleasant work, Tim Enright, summoned me to his office, and said I was fired.

I didn't accept that, and explained I had in fact exceeded Chapman's requirements on the Mamba, as the minimum specified height was available at the widest standing position in the saloon anyway. Enright took the point, but said that Chapman had demanded that I should go; it wasn't negotiable. I returned home, shocked and bewildered, as I failed to understand why this issue had taken so long to emerge (the Mamba had its superstructure in place and the cabin floor built by August '76).

Later, I learnt of some of the events which may have coloured that unfortunate January. It was quite likely that it was the Chris Craft entourage who wanted the Mamba saloon to be more spacious, as it had a long list of changes to the detail of the Mystere and the Mistral (the Mirage in the USA). Chapman was fully aware that the whole design was pared to the dimensional bone, in order to get the required proportions, and keep the weight down.

According to Tony Rudd's excellent book *It Was Fun* (Patrick Stephens Ltd, 1993), by the time Chapman had concluded a successful agreement with the Americans for the 50 boat sales, which JCL so badly needed, he refused to sign it, as he felt there was no longer a profit in it. It took Fred Bushell two years to extricate the company from the deal, and destroyed the boat companies financially.

The book also suggests that the Mamba could not get up on the plane, and perform to the high speed as planned. This was undoubtedly the case on the first trials, but once Malcolm Leeds had retuned the propeller specification, it certainly could, with a tested maximum speed of thirty knots. What I do remember, however, was that when she was launched immediately after the boat show, stability was a problem. This was caused by the narrow wetted area of the hull, compared with the width of the deck, caused by the cantilevered knuckle. When a person walked along the side deck, the boat would roll more than usual, as their weight was out over the water, and the craft would also roll more than normal on high speed turns.

Motor Boat and Yachting published a report on the Mamba in the summer of 1977.

It quotes 'points for': style; excellent engineering; smooth engines; good handling; comfortable accommodation.

'Points against': poor generating system; lack of grab rails; poor deck material; not enough gear stowage.

The magazine was "… particularly interested to see how Colin Chapman's first design performed as a whole." The conclusion was that "Colin Chapman and Colin Gething have done a remarkable job with the design of this boat and even if the concept is, for most of us, rather impractical, some of the ideas and solutions to common problems are worthy of great praise." I noted that I had apparently not contributed to this!

The test showed a maximum speed of 30 knots, with a range of 280 sea miles at 28 knots. The data panel gives the displacement as 11,043lb – 4.9 tons (5023kg). She carried 200 gallons (900l) of diesel and 100 gallons (454l) of water. The 1977 price, as tested, was £79,690 (about £518,000 in 2015), excluding sales tax.

Despite the financial frustrations, I had thoroughly enjoyed my marine saga. The styling was influenced by fabulous Italian bespoke designs of the day. Working for Chapman, and being involved with his far-reaching ideas, had been invigorating. The massive change of product size from a motor vehicle had taken some getting used to. I had found it interesting and a challenge. And the change in finished boat weight – being approximately 50% less than contemporary similar-sized vessels – was a leap forward, I was privileged to experience.

JCL Mamba at full speed.

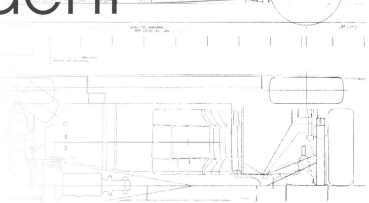

Chapter 6
Independent

So I was redundant, without any form of income; not a situation for which I had prepared. I had a wife, two young daughters, and a house to maintain. I signed on at the Labour Exchange, and was entered on the Executive Register. This was for professional people, and was specialised to suit their needs, but, despite me putting no restrictions on job location, it didn't produce a single idea in seven months.

However, Tony Rudd was more help, and he arranged an interview with Rolls-Royce, which was seeking someone to work with its body styling. I met the interviewer at the company's London showroom, where he explained that I was probably the wrong material for Rolls-Royce, as I had apparently designed about 12 cars and boats in five years, whereas Rolls-Royce would need one new product every 15 to 20!

Two weeks after I left, Lotus asked me to do some drawings to show compliance to Australian Design Rules for the Esprit. Payment was to be my drawing board, delivered in advance. This was most valuable as it was oversize, which allowed space for typical car and boat layouts in the normally-used scales.

I cleaned out the garden shed at home, painted the walls white, and ran an electrical supply from the house, although the telephone never made it, and within three weeks of leaving, I was working for Chapman again: various small drafting jobs came from Lotus, and I carried out the body styling modifications to the S2 Esprit. This included presenting them to Chapman, who was obviously instrumental in allowing the work to come to me. He also gave me some Moonraker styling work for face-lifts.

At the same time that I was 'made redundant,' so, too, were John Kelly, the Managing Director, and John Newman, Sales Chief of Moonraker Marine. I used to meet Kelly once a week for a beer. From those evenings grew the idea of building our own boats. Newman was to arrange finance and marketing, and Kelly would run the business, while I was to be the designer. The first boat was to be the Kelly Newman 44 seagoing motor yacht.

We hoped to combine some of the Chapman flair with traditional (hopefully, reliable) technology. The plan was to reduce the burden of overheads – avoiding the need for our own factory by getting the boats built by established companies under contract. They would need stage payments, as was normal in the industry. These would be passed on from the customer to the builder, with the new company retaining a percentage of the profit.

We needed finance in order to get the patterns and moulds made for the superstructure, and we were going to use a 44ft (13.4m) Tremlett hull, although I wanted the sheer line straightened out. Discussions on that, and a suitably reduced weight glass fibre layup, were in progress.

The design included a forward double 'stateroom' with shower, two midships twin bunk cabins, and a large saloon with double bed capability. Twin Volvo Penta diesel engines had Vee-drives to the twin propellers at the stern. An unusual feature was slotted window openings, with a sliding rigid blind, to remove the need for curtains.

The strategy was 'style and luxury with reliability and minimal financial exposure.' John Newman's backer (who was never revealed to me) wanted Kelly and Newman to tour America with my drawings, and obtain orders with

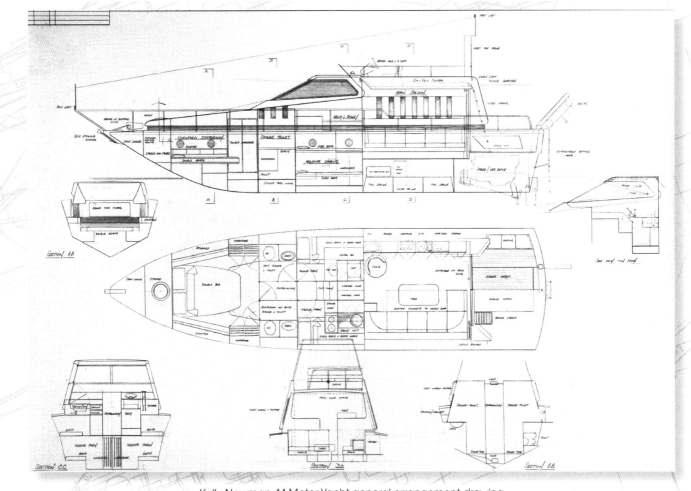

Kelly Newman 44 Motor Yacht general arrangement drawing.

deposits, which would launch the finance for the venture. After much discussion, we all agreed that the Americans would show lots of interest, but would be unlikely to commit to an unknown company; and, anyway, we had little cash to finance the trip. At this point, the venture fizzled out.

About six weeks after I left Lotus, Albert Cole of IDAT, a body pattern company we had used, told me that he was going up to TVR Sports Cars in Blackpool, as it had some work coming up which might hold an opportunity for me. Despite suggesting that we went up to visit together, Albert went alone, and, indeed, after the trip, was not forthcoming with any helpful information, beyond the fact that TVR was thinking of doing "something."

At about the same time, I got a call from Mike Rawlings, who suggested a meeting at his office at Norwich Airport. I drove over to the home of Topelec Ltd to find that the office was the old airport water tower, and the workshop the huge concrete distribution tank

underneath. Mike said he had heard that I was at a loose end, and wondered if there was perhaps something which could be a business opportunity, as he had a glass fibre business under the wing of Norwich Coachworks. He had a contact in Bristol, at the Lotus dealers from which the William Towns' re-bodied Europa had come, and we made a visit to it without success. Shortly after that, the TVR incident happened, and I mentioned it to Rawlings. Mike immediately said that he knew Martin Lilley, the owner, and gave him a call. A couple of days later, we were both heading North to talk to TVR.

Reaching the Bristol Avenue works, I was excited not only for the automotive opportunity, but also as it was my first visit to Blackpool – an icon of the British way of leisure. Martin Lilley explained that TVR was looking for a new car, as the existing 3000 model was facing obsolescence of many of its parts. It proposed to lengthen and widen the existing body and fit it to a new tubular frame which would be inside the body. Putting the frame inside the body could have created some challenges! I suggested that I should go home and work up some ideas for Martin's consideration, and get back to him.

In recent years, I have seen comments that suggest that Martin was wrong to drop the M series cars. The reality, at the time, was that he had no choice, as the number of components going obsolete meant that a new car was the only course open to him. USA regulations were still expanding, and, as the new car was to be sold there, these needed to be incorporated.

Mike Rawlings and I had returned to Blackpool, and began to have work awarded to us. I persuaded Martin Lilley that the new TVR should be of contemporary design – and not be a copy of the existing 3000M series – or his company would never move forward, but stagnate and get into a rut. As a result, I started to lay out a new design, and suggested that Ian Jones, the ex-Lotus designer who was now an independent consultant, should do the chassis. Many years later, I have read that Stewart Halstead, Martin's Sales Director was never happy with this change of direction, a fact which may have proved to be unfortunate.

Ian drew up a well-braced backbone chassis frame from one-and-a-half inch (39mm) diameter 16swg seamless steel tube. Fitted with twin wishbone front suspension, it used a mixture of Ford parts for the uprights, brakes and steering rack. The 2.8-litre Ford V6 fuel-injected engine was well back in the frame, and drove a Salisbury Jaguar final drive, with inboard brakes at the rear. The rear suspension was similar to the Lotus Elite, with stressed driveshafts, a lower link and a radius arm. The backbone supported an outrigger structure in steel tube, and the finished article proved rugged, adequately stiff for a convertible, and simple to manufacture.

On the way home from our first TVR visit, I learnt that Mike Rawlings had got involved with the proposed TVR 3000M convertible, which Lilley had at the prototype stage with Jensen. They had skilfully incorporated the Jensen Healey windscreen and modified soft top to the TVR. This kept me busy, fine tuning the body surfaces, which was done in the 'water tank' at Norwich Airport, and, when complete, Rawlings made the moulds.

A contractor was making the hatchback for the TVR Taimar coupé, and the factory was having a lot of trouble getting mouldings to fit the bodies. Rawlings took over the manufacture, and it formed an increasingly important part of his business.

In the spring of 1977, Don McLauchlan, the Public Relations manager at Lotus and a good friend, arranged an opportunity which was unusual for someone no longer employed by the company. The Design Centre in Haymarket, London, had an exhibition showing the best of British design and, among those featured, was Lotus. The Elite had been 'approved by the Design Council,' and the wind tunnel model of the car was on display. Its magazine, *Design,* wanted to publish an article on the design process at Lotus, and I received an invitation to participate. The story covered four pages of the magazine, and Lotus featured on the front cover, in August 1977.

I also spent a little time doing nautical work, supplying Moonraker with ideas for alternative colour schemes for the exterior of the F350. Colin Chapman and, later, Mike Kimberley were always hopeful that a new paint or decal design could dramatically change the appearance of a product, without the costs associated with retooling panels, or other expensive design changes.

As most of this work involved substantial sums of

Assessing the TVR MAL100 cockpit, in the basic seating buck, at Topelec, Norwich.

money, I removed myself from the unemployed, and set up my own 'Sole Trader' company. On 11 August 1977, the name Concept Design was registered. I was elected to the Institute of British Carriage and Automobile Manufacturers, and was also elected as a Royal Chartered Designer by the MSIAD.

I quickly completed a general layout of the new TVR, and supplied a coloured rear-three-quarter sketch, alongside the general arrangement drawings, to Martin Lilley, who approved them; and detail design work on the project, codenamed MAL 100, began.

My concept for the MAL 100 (later to be called the Tasmin) was to extend the wheelbase four inches from the M Series to 94.0in (2388mm), allowing the engine to be placed well back in the frame, but also to increase the cockpit space. With the engine behind the front axle, the bonnet height could be nearly parallel with the ground. To get a low nose – based on the American bumper height requirements – the front wing line had a pronounced break over the front wheel. This feature was the subject of some controversy, but had the lines been smoothed, the front would have gained a lot of visual bulk.

The tail was made as short as possible, to maintain a TVR trademark that stretched back to its earliest models. The roof of the fastback coupé featured a large, one-piece opening glass, which lay at a very flat angle to maintain a wedge profile. Experience with the Lotus Eclat back window suggested that the visibility would be poor, so the tail panel featured a vertical window. This was later the subject of discussion with members of Cambridgeshire Constabulary who, when following a production Tasmin, were dazzled by their own headlights. I had to write to them explaining that there was no regulation on the angle of back windows, so it wouldn't be changed.

The convertible was drawn up in a basic form, at the same time, to ensure that it could be built from the same base model. Martin Lilley put me in contact with a consultant, who proposed a very heavy, expensive and complex folding roof. I felt that a new approach was needed, so the removable-solid-centre-panel-with-folding-rear-section concept was born. Care had to be taken to ensure the centre section would stow in the top of the boot, without significantly reducing the luggage capacity.

While the vehicle was being laid out to ensure all parts were packaged satisfactorily, the body manufacturing process was thought out. I was impressed by the advantages of the Lotus two-piece mould system, but not by the problems encountered in the body engineering. I designed the MAL 100 in two halves, top and bottom, joined in the mould. The recess for the side doors and the inset tail window were removable plugs, which remained

in place when the mould was released. The sills were 'add-on' parts, to allow an integral part of the chassis to be a perimeter frame.

The first job in Norwich was to build an interior seating buck, from which I could finalise the layout drawings. This replicated the floor, transmission tunnel and sills. Into this, the pedals, steering column and seat were mounted, and the comfort of the driving position assessed. As usual, I found that there were some small adjustments needed. Another exercise was to establish the vision areas for the instruments, by laying a piece of paper where the dials would be located, and sketching the areas hidden by the steering wheel. In these days of 'intelligent CAD,' these techniques may seem crude (which they were), but it was cheap and effective. I don't believe that seating and posture can be specified any other way!

For reasons long forgotten, we did not make a scale model of the car. I now believe this was a serious error, as it meant that Martin had to make his decision based only on drawings. It would also have contributed to both visual and, possibly some aerodynamic, development. By the time the body pattern was complete, it was too late to make any changes at a sensible cost.

The first major pattern job was to build the floor/undertray of the body. Once this was complete, using mainly substantial plywood, the main outer body was built over it. This produced an exact replica of the whole body, ready for mould-making. I had to keep up with the workshop in producing all the body drawings, complete with every detail of the gutters, glazing flanges, etc, which I did in my garden shed. Everything was drawn full-size, with the exception of the transverse sections on the top of the bonnet and roof. These, I drew at half-scale, due to the restricted space in the 'drawing office.' The pattern went together with few hitches, mainly due to the craftsmanship of the ex-Bristol Aircraft pattern maker, Brian Johnson.

TVR had only one member in its Engineering Department, John Southall, who was charged by Martin with keeping on top of the MAL 100, so meetings were arranged between Mike Rawlings, Ian Jones, John and me. Many sessions were held at the Buckinghamshire Arms, Blickling, in Norfolk, but these came to an end, following the occasion when John Southall failed to arrive in time, and missed the lunch altogether. As the host, he was a bit upset to get the bill without the goods.

Soon after I started on the MAL 100, I needed to find suitable components for production. John Southall had the Ford parts under control, through Williams Power Products of Manchester, which also supplied the Powertrain; but, for the rest, Roy Wood, the TVR buyer, was responsible. Roy ran the whole of the purchasing operation with just a clerk to help. Roy and I would meet in various parts of the country, as we negotiated parts from Lucas (electrical), Wilmot Bredon (body hardware), Triplex (glass), Tysley Handbrakes, Smiths Industries (heater fans), and many others.

While the TVR work progressed, other jobs also filled my time. Late in 1977, I was contacted by an ex-Lotus employee, Tony Divey who was working in Munich. He worked for an Austrian based in Graz, who had contacts within the Austrian government, which wanted to build a sports car to enhance employment. After much discussion in England, I got in touch with Mike Kimberley to arrange for the supply of the Lotus 2-litre engine. This was agreed in principle, so design work started for a modular range of cars – open and closed two-seaters and a longer 2+2. I took these drawings to Munich, in early 1978, where they were approved. I had an interesting time reclaiming the obligatory VAT (Sales Tax) in the UK, as I had failed to submit the 'goods' to Customs upon departure. They paid up, after I suggested the 'goods' were in my head!

A fifth-scale model was built and dispatched to Munich. Thereafter, communications with Tony Divey kept going on an upbeat note, but it came to nothing, and faded out late that summer.

Ironically, the base vehicle was similar to the stillborn Lotus M80 Elan replacement, right down to the Lotus engine. The Porsche 924 was used as a dimensional comparator, on a document of 15 February 1978.

	Austro Lotus	Porsche 924
OA Length mm	3731	4216
Wheelbase mm	2286	2400
Height mm	1128	1270
Max speed mph	130	121
0-60mph/sec	7.0	8.2

Another project that demanded attention at that time was the Salamander. Mike Rawlings found this one lurking in the Art College that is tucked under the flyover outside the University of Manchester – UMIST – which sounded like a roll-on deodorant to me. Here, two mature students were trying to build a car for the wheelchair-disabled, following the demise of the AC Cars single-seater. They had made a lifting device which loaded the occupied wheelchair, and located it for driving. They had also built a full-size clay model body onto a Reliant Kitten four-wheel chassis.

The project was receiving attention from nearby Salford City Council, as the Member of Parliament for Salford, Stan Orme, wanted to make a political splash out of providing a replacement for the old AC. A committee was set up under Wire and Soap, as Mike and I called them – a Mr Goldstein, the Chairman of Ward & Goldstone, the automotive wiring company, and Mr Cussons, from the famous Imperial Leather soap company. The plan was to put the vehicle into production in a factory in the area, and Mike and I were to help them achieve it.

The first visit to the Art College showed that the full-size model was not symmetrical, and, not surprisingly, didn't have any engineering applied to it; so I took all the information home, and laid out a complete general arrangement drawing, which Mike Rawlings could use to build up a proper body model in his Norwich works. This hit a lot of resistance from the 'students,' who only wanted minimal changes to their clay.

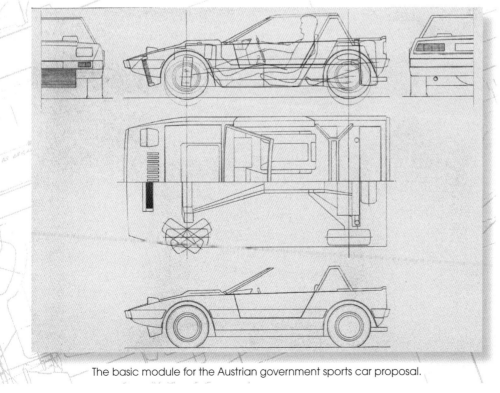

The basic module for the Austrian government sports car proposal.

Another visit to Manchester coincided with the students exhibiting their wheelchair lifter to Manchester and Salford City Councils, but, as they had overdone the advance demonstrations, the main event was as flat as a totally flat battery, which upset some of the dignitaries. Another visit to attend a meeting at Salford City Council was notable for the presence of a councillor smoking continuously throughout the meeting, while sitting under a very large 'No Smoking' sign. The meeting went round in circles all day and arrived nowhere, trying our patience, as well as that of some of the other participants, and there was little significant progress at a later meeting with 'Wire and Soap.' The project progressed slowly, as the many participants were ignorant of the complexities of the motor business.

When I later closed Concept Design and moved up to Lancashire, I naturally submitted the bill for all my work on the Salamander project, which was contested, until I rolled up every drawing, sketch and document, and delivered it all as evidence of the work – which included factory production layouts and plans. It was of quite considerable size. About 18 months later, I saw a brief local television news report, with a Salamander car in a Manchester park, supposedly representing the first of many. Nothing was heard of it again.

Work progressed to plan with the MAL 100, and Mike Rawlings moved to an industrial unit, in Weston Road, Norwich. Brian Johnson was joined by Mike McIssacs, an ex-Lotus model maker, and Roger Constable, who left Lotus to come and build the prototype. The wooden pattern was completed, the moulds taken, and the glass jigs built for the supplier. All the inner panels were modelled, prior to making moulds for the door inners, heater casing and plenum, bumpers, bonnet and door panels.

Throughout this phase, TVR relied upon John Southall for progress reports, and through my fortnightly visits to Blackpool. Martin Lilley only came to Norwich once, and Stuart Halstead later, when the prototype was being built. Martin flew from Blackpool: a sensible decision, as the road journey was at least five hours each way.

Concurrently, the chassis and suspension components were being made at Formula Fabrications, in Wymondham, another ex-Lotus employee business, while Slough Metals cast the rear hub carriers. Gradually, all the components were delivered to construct the first running prototype. TVR sent a complete set of Ford parts from Blackpool. In Norwich, we were accumulating all the other parts, from heater radiators to handbrakes.

As soon as the exterior body parts were ready for mould-making, work began on the interior trim parts – dashboard, console, etc. Once the models had moulds, the components were trimmed by the ex-Lotus development trimmer, Nick Fulcher, in his workshops, in Hethersett. During the latter part of 1978, Roger Constable built up the prototype, while TVR sent its electricians to install the wiring. Nick Fulcher trimmed out the interior, while Mike Rawlings applied a coat of red paint to the exterior. I maintained a small office at Topelec, and the vehicle was completed within the planned timescale. When finished, it was loaded onto a trailer and delivered to Blackpool. Meanwhile, the pattern makers constructed full-size models for the convertible rear body and doors. Stewart Halstead has since suggested that this phase was notable for much 'buggering about.' The progress this tiny team made would have put many to shame.

The TVR was consuming nearly all my time, with fortnightly trips to Blackpool, but there was also some

Stewart Halstead of TVR (left), me, and Roger Constable, with the first body and chassis (foreground) during the prototype build in Norwich.

work for the proprietor of a local Winery. He had a business renting camper vans, based on the Bedford CF, onto which a glass fibre roof extension was grafted, to accommodate two bunks. I designed, and Mike Rawlings built, a number of these; and it led to the idea of building a complete motor home on the long-wheelbase Bedford CF chassis. Lotus was pencilled in to supply the engine (it had run its own rapid CF during the development of the 907 engine). We built a scale model to try and get the project to move, but it faded, and no further work was done.

As the TVR was approaching road development stage, at Martin Lilley's suggestion, I discussed the possibility of moving to Lancashire, so that this could be run with his and Stewart Halstead's direct involvement. It would have been impractical to continue development at such a long distance. So I negotiated the position of TVR Chief Engineer; I would close down Concept Design, and go North.

TVR was using its Bristol Road premises in Blackpool to the full, and maintaining secrecy for the new model would be difficult. It was vital that sales of the existing models were maintained, to provide the funds for the new car. Therefore, Lilley sought additional premises to house the new TVR Research and Development Centre, and found a suitable place in the White Lund estate in Morecambe. I looked for housing around that area, and settled on a home 20 miles from Lancaster.

Further research, however, revealed that, when flood tides came up the River Lune (which entered the sea close by), the White Lund estate went under water – hardly ideal for a vehicle design and development centre. Lilley found an alternative at Bamber Bridge, where the Central Lancashire New Town had built an industrial estate. Although this doubled my commute to work, at least it was a scenic drive. So, in the first week of December 1978, we departed Norfolk, and set up home in Ingleton, North Yorkshire.

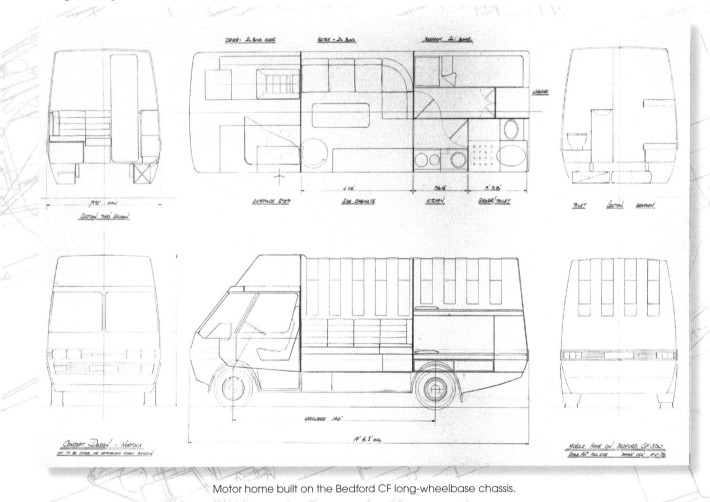

Motor home built on the Bedford CF long-wheelbase chassis.

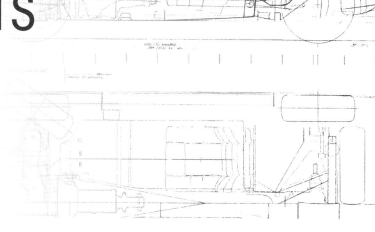

Chapter 7
TVR sports cars

My first task as TVR Chief Engineer was to equip the new Research and Development centre, in Bamber Bridge, near Preston. Martin Lilley had owned TVR since 1965 – it was founded 18 years earlier – and he took personal control of expenditure for everything, from office furniture to workshop machinery, for the brand new industrial unit. Stewart Halstead has later suggested that this was an extravagance, but it would have been impossible to develop MAL 100 Tasmin without adequate facilities.

Unit 466, Walton Summit had an area of about 6500sq ft, which we divided to give one third for glass fibre work. To provide a fire and dust break a partition was erected by the New Town landlord and a small additional office for John Southall was built. The need for welding and machining equipment required it to have three-phase electricity. A vehicle hoist was installed and some industrial shelving to form a parts store.

The purchase of one machine tool, which caused some controversy, was that of a Colchester lathe. A dealer who distributed these lathes was offering an exceptionally low price, but Martin Lilley would not accept any offer without a discount, so I had to add a few per cent to the original bargain price, to allow it to be subsequently removed as 'discount'!

The offices had desks for John Southall, my secretary Vicky, and me, and I provided my own drawing board. A large storage cabinet and chest were soon filling with drawings. All TVR exclusive parts had to be drawn and specified, to enable the suppliers to manufacture parts.

The staff was hand-picked by Martin, and either came from the Bristol Avenue site, or had worked there previously. This helped enormously with the settling-

in period, and reduced the risk of getting duffers. My secretary Vicky ably assisted me, and we quickly settled in. We had about ten people who were good-humouredly committed to developing the car, and preparing it for production.

In late 1978, the prototype duly arrived on a trailer, from Norwich. This was the first time Martin Lilley or Stewart Halstead had seen the finished car. Their first impression, on driving it, was that its outright performance seemed rather weak, after the 3-litre Ford torque available in the existing 3000 Series cars. Despite the design allowing for later conversion to meet USA legislation, the car was little different in weight, at 25kg heavier, so the more powerful engine had been expected to be somewhat faster. The Tasmin was 10mph faster than the existing Taimar, but the 0-60mph acceleration increased from 7.7 seconds to

The TVR Research & Development Workshops, at Bamber Bridge.

8.0. With the torque reduced by 30lb ft to 162lb ft, we should have perhaps expected it. The power issue was to resurface later.

The prototype had been completed with a number of systems in temporary form. This was agreed to reduce the cost and the time needed to get a vehicle on the road. The fuel system, designed with twin tanks forward of the rear axle, was simplified by having a single tank over the axle. Later, when the correct fuel system was installed, problems arose under heavy acceleration, when, despite a forward draining design, the fuel would retreat rearwards, cutting the engine. Modifying the return system from the engine cured this.

The car was not quite 100% reliable, and one of its first transgressions happened shortly after the car was completed: Martin and Stewart were returning from a quick trip to Scotland on a Sunday afternoon. They were travelling south on the M6 at a considerable speed, when the bonnet decided to part company with the car. Its pivot bolts had loosened, and it flew across all three northbound lanes, landing in a field. The next day, I retrieved it from the Motorway Maintenance depot, finding it undamaged, and it was reunited with the car. The pivots were bolts running in threaded bobbins laminated to the body. The mishap was unexpected, as it meant both bolts had undone simultaneously – an established design, being the same as that used by Lotus. It was very lucky that the flying body panel did not collect a northbound traveller. We added lock washers to the bolts to cure the potential problem.

And then it snowed. It snowed a lot over the winter of 1978-79. The prototype was well-equipped to cope, having a non-standard limited-slip differential in its Salisbury final drive, which pushed a very stable car through thick snow with little drama. Unfortunately, that was not the case for most other road users. A day trip to Ford, in Daventry, became a nightmare, as long stretches of the M6 motorway were closed due to accidents. The old road system became jammed, and what should have been a comfortable day became much extended. When the road was clear, the car could cruise through the snow surprising quickly.

Late in the winter of 1979, John Southall left the company, and was duly replaced by an ex-British Leyland engineer, Adrian Morrall. Adrian took over the type approval work, and kept the drawings up-to-date.

The development of the TVR MAL 100 was centred on a few vital areas. First, the vehicle had to get UK Type Approval, before it could be sold on the British market. Various tests had to be carried out to satisfy government officials that it complied with their requirements. Some of these were simple to do, for instance, the location of all the lighting. The prototype was subjected to successful exhaust emission tests, required because the vehicle weight, transmission and gearing were different to the powertrain donor vehicles (Ford Capri and Granada).

The door latch and release system were assessed, to ensure it would not allow the system to open in a frontal crash. The seat mounts were tested for strength, as were the seatbelt mountings. This latter physical test was carried out at MIRA, and revealed a problem.

The test entailed securing heavy chains to the seatbelt mountings, and applying load with a set of hydraulic rams. A vehicle body was secured to a baseplate. When

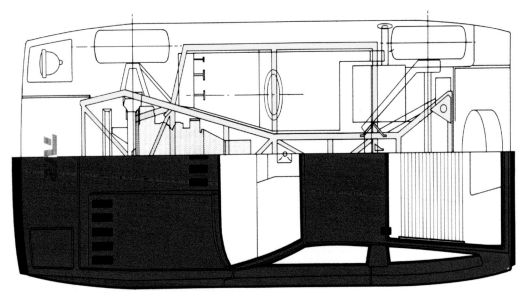

The brochure diagram of the MAL 100 Tasmin layout.

the load was applied, it had to be maintained for a given period without deformation. On the first test, one of the shoulder mounts in the roll-over structure deformed. I had specified the mounting boss with too large a diameter for the structural tube to which it was welded. A small reduction in the diameter allowed the system to exceed all requirements in the re-test a week later. This was, fortunately, the only Approval test failure.

Bamber Bridge had to build another complete car for the 30mph (48kph) crash test, also done at MIRA, in May 1979. The test was to satisfy both European, and United States, requirements, so was done to the 'worst case' for the respective legislation. A prototype was specially built for the test, and weighed 1081kg (2377lb). It carried an instrumented passenger dummy, and had 67 litres (14.8 gallons) of fuel substitute aboard. Naturally, it was painted in the usual matt yellow emulsion paint, to permit later study of the body from the high speed cameras.

The impact with the rigid barrier was at 30.6mph (49.2kph), and was recorded on seven high speed cameras. The long nose performed exceptionally well, absorbing the energy by crushing 800mm, coming to a complete halt in 121 milliseconds. This compared very well with many front-wheel drive cars, which stop around 40% quicker than this. The belted dummy appreciated this, recording less than 25% of the permitted head injury for the USA standards, well under half the permitted chest acceleration, and 20% of the allowed leg impact force. The test covered a total of seven international requirements, and excelled in all of them. The steering column moved over 30mm forward, where the limitation was to be no more than 130mm rearward, while the fuel system had zero leakage.

The Department of Transport inspector was more than satisfied with the performance, with one exception: the battery was mounted on a platform alongside the pedal box, on the right side of the engine bay. It was secured with a rubber strap which had given no problems over the high mileage of the prototype. Under impact, the strap broke, and the battery moved forward, launched upward by the shapely, curved wheelhouse just in front of it.

It sheared its electrical leads, and hit the crash barrier about ten feet from the ground, doing about 25 miles per hour. The inspector suggested that this would be a bit of a hazard to other vehicles in a crash, and something must be done. In total agreement, I altered the attachment on the production design to a more substantial one.

The hard-worked prototype also spent a night in the MIRA wind tunnel. Its performance was not revolutionary, as the Lotus Elite had been – the drag coefficient being 0.36. With a frontal area some 2sq ft less than the Lotus Elite and Eclat, the drag horsepower fell between them at 44.2hp at 100mph. The front lift needed controlling with a lip air dam, which we developed at Bamber Bridge, and which was effective. The tests were done on the night shift to save money, so it made for a long day, including the travel.

The prototype was never run in disguise, as it was felt that it would actually attract attention. This appeared to work, as the car was never subject to a press scoop. Registering the car in Cheshire, and obliterating the manufacturer's name from the tax disc avoided all reference to TVR and Lancashire.

Another system, which consumed much time, was the exhaust. The prototype was built with a 'one off' system to get it running. While it worked well, it also tended to heat the middle of the car up. The Chiswick Exhaust Company in Blackpool agreed to help. It built up systems around its existing tooled parts, and developed it to meet

The prototype on durability testing.

the legal noise requirements. One afternoon, Martin was at Bamber Bridge, when Chiswick telephoned to say that its latest development system was ready for assessment. Martin drove me over in his Ferrari Boxer. When we pulled into Chiswick's car park, the project engineer was astounded, and questioned where we had driven from. He had called Bamber Bridge, 25 miles away, on the far side of Preston, and here we were, in less than 12 minutes.

Later, after production had started, we changed the supplier to Grundy, which developed a fine stainless steel system at its factory in South Wales. The 400-plus-mile drive down there on motorways, and back through mid-Wales, was the kind of journey for which the Tasmin was built. Adrian and I got to know this quite well, as Grundy needed the car a number of times. Naturally, the system had to meet back pressure, installation clearances, cost and noise level requirements.

Suspension tuning was done with Armstrong, in York, some 80 miles across country. I drove over with a TVR fitter each morning for a day's work, some five or six times. We were working to get a good ride without losing handling, by following the Chapman principles of soft springing with very well controlled damping. Great attention was paid to ensuring that the wheels could rebound onto droop very quickly – the moorland roads around the north of England showed that it was important to be able to maintain control over the crest of major humps. Using a rough railway level crossing near its facility, Armstrong raised the speed at which the car could cross in full control by a large margin, much to the chagrin of the crossing keeper. Unfortunately, over the later life of the TVR, the ride became much firmer, making bumpy cornering more of a challenge.

When I joined TVR, I was led to believe it had never used a full part number system. TVR parts were identified by 'word of mouth,' and the date and type of vehicle on which they were used. I therefore introduced a similar system to that at Lotus. In fact, there was a comprehensive part number system that had been developed by Mike Bigland, but we were not made aware of it – quite why, I don't know.

Another feature that gave an amusing break was the headlamp lift system. At one o'clock, very early one morning, my door bell rang, and I descended to find the local policeman at the door. Apologising for the late call, and accepting a cup of tea, he explained that the car was raising and lowering each headlamp alternately, with a flourishing flash at top dead centre. As there was no one near the car, he thought he had better make me aware. Removing the battery leads solved the problem short term, but the cause was water seeping into the electrical

relays which controlled them. This was not the first time sodden relays gave specialist producers nightmares, but, despite many requests to the well-known supplier, sealed units were never made. The relays were subsequently moved to a dryer part of the engine compartment.

The provision for a radio aerial was a challenge. Electrically retractable masts were bulky, heavy and expensive. A supplier came up with a way of using the tailgate heater element, and this worked well – almost something for nothing. I believe this was an industry 'first.'

The upper reaches of the M6 motorway provided space for high speed running. Outside peak holiday season, traffic was sparse between Lancaster and Shap summit. (I often drove that way on the way to work.) The need for this was to stress the cooling system, as the engine would be at high load for a significant distance. These runs also showed that the tyres were giving vibrations. As the wheels were carefully balanced, it could only come from the tyre construction. We changed to Goodyear NCTs, which cured the problem.

Members of the M6 Motorway police often dropped into Bamber Bridge for a chat and a cup of tea, and were made most welcome. I explained the nature of the project, and showed them round the workshops, and they were sympathetic to our challenges. One of their biggest concerns, they said, was the danger caused by cars travelling too slowly on the motorway, as it caused difficulties for everyone else, especially the trucks. They prosecuted as many for this, as for speeding. However, their message to me was: "Make sure you see us before we see you!"

Bamber Bridge had a section for bodywork, with two specialists from the Blackpool factory. They produced models and patterns from which moulds would be taken for the glass fibre parts. In the summer of 1979, a representative from the local employment services visited me to see if I could take any trainees. Remembering the benefits of my own training, I agreed to have a body shop apprentice. As well as learning on the job, they would be enrolled at Blackburn Technical College. The first tranche of potential applicants had application profiles best described as unemployable. No examination results at all, and no hobbies or pastimes. One had filled in as their only pastime, "Hanging around on street corners" – yes, really!

The second attempt brought an application form with some modest academic results, and a hobby making model aircraft and cars. I liked the sound of this, and the young man was subsequently successfully trained in the skills of woodwork and glass fibre bodymaking. However, one untrained addition to the body experimental staff was not enough to make the unit capable of handling the production of the main body moulds. As Mike Rawlings had left Topelec, the work was put to IDAT down in Essex, which made a fine job of a master body with a superb finish. The resulting moulds produced bodies with a very high standard of surface finish, and accurate rebates for the opening panels and glass. This left Bamber Bridge free to make the tooling for all the other glass fibre parts. This work consumed a number of months.

Although Nick Fulcher had produced the prototype interior trim, he was unable to handle production quantities. The Coventry firm of Callow and Maddox produced the trim, using glass fibre mouldings sent from Blackpool. Initially, all the cars were built with a dark brown leathercloth and creamy beige knitted nylon, contrasted with walnut veneered panels. The veneered panels were sourced from a furniture factory in Nottingham, which made a fine job of them.

The interior of the TVR Tasmin.

In the autumn of 1979, my relationship with TVR hit a problem: I felt TVR had not been totally fair with me. All the other employees had received a summer pay rise, which I had not. Lotus had been in touch, and a contract was agreed between us. I presented a resignation letter to Martin Lilley, who was most upset. A fruitful discussion between us saw matters put right, and I had the embarrassing job of withdrawing my signature from the Lotus contract. Fortunately, Mike Kimberley understood the dilemma, and all was settled amicably.

One sunny morning, I was returning to Bamber Bridge with Roy Wood, the buyer from the Blackpool factory, fairly fast, in the prototype. As we approached an interchange on the M55, there was a lurch from the rear, and I became aware of a wheel overtaking me down the slip road. Coming safely to a halt on the hard

shoulder, we retrieved the wheel, complete with hub, and telephoned for help. The entire hub had come off, as both rear attachment threads were right-handed. Often, they are opposite-handed to ensure the securing nut tightens on acceleration. No serious damage was done, but a good helping of Loctite on the proprietary hub was specified henceforth.

Another suspension-related development issue was rear wheel tramp under 'racing' start acceleration. A large hole was cut in the prototype floor to study the radius arm bush, and visual markers aligned to the wheel hub. The car would only do it occasionally, and we never found a solution, despite many suspension bush changes.

Martin was unhappy with the steering feel, and asked for the rack to be lowered. This allowed some kickback, which he preferred (his Ferrari did that rather well), but, later, *Motor* magazine would have preferred a bit less!

Bit-by-bit, the suppliers were producing production specification parts. Long-serving TVR employee Terry Lendrim, with the help of sub-contractors, was putting together the production assembly fixtures for the chassis, door beams and other brackets; and Formula Fabrications was producing the final drive mounting. TVR was to build the chassis frames at Bristol Avenue, and send them out for corrosion treatment. Much time was spent on the vexing question of how to treat the steel, with plastic dipping given strong consideration. The final decision was oxide submersion and paint.

So, how did Tasmin become the name for the new car? One evening in the summer of 1979, Martin Lilley, Jerry Sagerman (the United States TVR importer) and I were having dinner at a the Haighton Manor near Longridge. The conversation moved to names, and many ideas were aired – some sensible and some less so. We decided we needed to maintain the letter T at the start of the name, so worked round that. Two names kept recurring, Tasman, after the antipodean race series, and Tamsin, a girl's name. No one could fix a connection with the former, although Martin may have had some with the latter. It was he that put the two together to make Tasmin, which immediately felt very comfortable.

Throughout the development period, a great TVR enthusiast and friend, John Bailie, had followed the project with interest. As a graphic designer, he produced all the company literature from his Blackpool business, Image Publicity. He created a new TVR logo, featuring horizontal bars, that fitted well with the grooves on the bumpers, and which has lasted many years. He also came up with the TASMIN script, which adorned the rear flanks of the car. He planned all the launch literature, and carried out the photography.

The prototype at the Last Drop Village, with the name logos covered for John Baillie's brochure research.

TVR received full support from the Ford Motor Company, and, to give Ford confidence that the installation of its powertrain was satisfactory, it arranged for tests at MIRA. An engineer from Ford checked out the installation, and then wanted to measure the fluid temperatures in high load conditions. A chassis dynamometer (a trailer with an engine which applied a drag load to its wheels) was towed behind the prototype, simulating the effects of a never-ending steep hill. It was necessary to run the car at the fastest steady speed possible for long periods, towing the dynamometer. Two hours on the banked high speed circuit, at 120mph, had still not stabilised the oil temperatures, but the test was cut short by a horrific accident to another vehicle. The facility was closed, while the unfortunate driver was removed to hospital, where he subsequently recovered, but, when it reopened, neither the Ford engineer, nor I were keen to continue. After a full examination of the results over that long period, Ford concluded all was fine, and gave its approval.

The clutch release became the subject of study shortly before production started, as the Triumph TR7-sourced pedal box used a hydraulic system, which was not compatible with the mechanical linkage on the Ford clutch. I had devised a method of holding the clutch inner cable to allow the outer cable cover to release the clutch arm. It worked very well on the prototype, but, to operate properly, needed a large clearance hole in the firewall. Although a substantial rubber gaiter was used to seal it, there was the potential for major noise and water leakage. Martin Lilley thought there might be a better way.

Enter Broadspeed: Broadspeed was well known to the company, as it built the turbocharged engine for the 3-litre TVRs. These had a hydraulic release system concentric with the clutch output shaft, which allowed the whole system to become hydraulic. This worked well – until the seals, which had to endure much heat and output shaft rotation, gave up their fight to contain the fluid. Eventually, the manual system returned.

Bamber Bridge was busy building the (only) pre production car which emerged, in bright red, in November 1979. The factory at Bristol Avenue was completing the last of the Taimar range, and preparing to build the Tasmin. I redesigned the factory layout to have a chassis assembly section, with a number of stages, and a sub-assembly area alongside.

The first production TVR Tasmin, in the winter sunshine, at Hoghton Tower.

The body mount stage was aligned with the area set aside for electrical harness construction. TVR was unusual in making all its own wiring, as major industry suppliers were uninterested in low volume producers. A cut cable store was built in the form of a wheel, from which the loom build operators could select parts easily. Unfortunately, it was not feasible to stock many different-coloured cables, so they were all black, with marker flags at the ends.

Once the fuel tanks and wiring were installed in the body, it was lowered onto the completed rolling chassis. The car was then completed with the connection of all systems, glazing and interior trim. The first car down the line was in Champagne Gold, and was built to European, left-hand drive specification.

With no Production Engineering Department, we sent staff from Bamber Bridge to 'educate' the Bristol Avenue staff on how to assemble the car. The Body Moulding Shop had already built about 40 bodies ahead of assembly operations, so that was settling down smoothly. My recollection of this period differs somewhat from the section of a recent book, which quotes Stuart Halstead as saying that "the cause of the production troubles was rooted in the inefficiency of operations at the Bamber Bridge research and development unit. He explained: 'Oliver Winterbottom's responsibility there had been to develop the Tasmin right up to the stage where it could be built to a high standard by the guys at Bristol Avenue. But Oliver's efforts left much to be desired. There weren't even enough engineering drawings to substantiate the design.'" My recollection is that we spent many hours at Bristol Avenue assisting the build operations.

Like all new designs going into production, the workforce had a lot to learn. Richer manufacturers spend many months honing their pre-production processes, but TVR did not have the luxury of either time or money to do that. The Blackpool workforce soon had the processes working to a very high standard. Roy Wood had filled the stores with all the new parts necessary – he would have found this difficult, if drawings and specifications had not been released.

The red pre-production car was now ready for brochure work. I joined John Bailie at the first location, the Last Drop Village, outside Bolton. Here, a stone village of shops, cafés and a hotel had been created from a derelict old farm, and we had a couple of hours exclusive use, early one Sunday morning, before the public arrived. The Sunday afternoon was spent shivering in thick fog on Rivington Pike, which produced the dramatic cover for the brochure.

Hoghton Tower, where King James knighted his dinner beef to create sirloin, was next. John hired a gigantic plate camera, and spent hours hiding under a black cloth with it, to produce some outstanding shots. It always seems that, whenever good car pictures are needed, it's at a drab time of the year!

I also had to put together the basis of the owner's handbook for John Baillie to complete, and worked out the service schedules. The TVR Service Department took over this, and administered it for production. To show that the car was ready for production, the handbook and service book were part of the press pack. As the announcement date drew near, the motoring press was invited to come to Bamber Bridge and gather data for its articles, to coincide with the launch.

Steve Cropley and Mel Nichols arrived from *Car* magazine. Martin came over from Blackpool, and, after I had given them a full description of the car, and showed them round the engineering facility, I recommended a test route. It took them over the Pennines to Hawes, back to Settle, and down the M6. They had to use the prototype, as the pre-production car was not completed. The weather was awful, with a full-blown gale, and rain, but, in due course, they returned, impressed. They agreed to feature the Tasmin on the front cover, and a photo shoot was arranged at a redundant brickworks outside Blackburn. The resulting article was more than we could have wished for.

Autocar and the *Motor* also had to contend with the prototype for their driving impressions. *Motor* was also impressed with the stability in gale-force cross winds, and the ride and handling. "Traction" it wrote, "was outstanding." It summed up: "With lots of showroom appeal, including much of what marketing men call 'perceived quality,' and plenty of go to match the show, the Tasmin is an impressive car for such a small manufacturer. TVR couldn't wish for a better springboard to the '80s."

John Bolster made an enjoyable visit, on behalf of *Motorsport,* and enjoyed the car nearly as much as I enjoyed our lunch together; and was impressed by its professionalism. The generally positive attitude of the motoring press was a big boost to the company.

Stewart Halstead, Sales Director, organised the dealer launch in mid-December 1979, featuring the red car and a show chassis. This was held at Blackpool, so we were not involved.

The pre-production car was taken to Chorley Corporation weighbridge, and revealed that, as the payload was increased, the weight distribution settled at around 50% on each axle. Although driver-only, with four gallons of fuel, was 53% front; adding a further ten gallons, Adrian as passenger and 50kg of luggage, reduced the front to 49.2%. The kerb weight of 1065kg compared well with competitors.

At Christmas, there was a panic. Triplex produced the glass for the car, and had neglected to drill the holes on the tailgate for the hinges and latches. The Champagne car was due at the Brussels Motor Show for the public launch, in early January, and there was no hope of getting new glass in time. I had some hinges made, to be bonded to the glass, but, with my previous shattering Lotus Elite experience (see page 46), I had little confidence they would be durable. The car left for Belgium, with instructions that the tailgate must not be opened on any account. A photograph of the show stand shows this instruction was successfully ignored.

Martin Lilley, Stewart Halstead and I drove to Brussels in Martin's Rolls-Royce. The simple show stand I had designed had the car on a raised platform, and, at right angles, down at ground level, a show chassis. The stand space was modest, but the reception on the press day, January 15 1980, certainly was not.

"TVR Comes of Age," wrote *Motor* magazine; "the Tasmin marks TVR's promotion to the ranks of 'establishment' motor manufacturers."

As TVR made a splash on behalf of the British motor industry, various dignitaries visited the stand. An enthusiastic Bob Lutz, from Ford, offered lavish praise, and any help we might need in the future. One of the dignitaries from the British Society of Motor Manufacturers and Traders congratulated the company, and asked if there was anything it needed help with. I mentioned that we had been let down on the glass back window, and dare not open it in public. The dignitary then let on that he was a director of Triplex Safety Glass. The problem was resolved as soon as we were back in England, and, following the replacement of its engineering representative, our account was handled by a new and more efficient man. New glass was in Blackpool very shortly afterwards.

The Tasmin coupé was put on the British market at £12,800. This compared well with other similarly powered sports cars, such as the AC 3000 £13,238; Porsche 924 Turbo £13,629, and Lotus Esprit £14,175. It was, however, a rise in average selling price for a TVR, as the M series cars cost from £8000, to £13,000 for the Turbo model. Unfortunately, potential customers tended to compare the price with the previous model, rather than some of the more expensive opposition.

Brochure picture of Tasmin, taken at Hoghton Tower.

	Quoted performance
Acceleration 0 – 50mph	5,6sec
Standing ¼ mile	16sec
Maximum speed	133mph
Fuel consumption	24/30mpg

With production under way, the government type approval inspector arrived to check on 'Conformity of

The joys of brochure work in winter: sunset at Hoghton Tower.

Production.' This entailed his inspecting the vehicle and components at random. The parts had to conform to the designs and specifications submitted at the time of testing. All went well, until he found some Ford engine parts without the matching identity markings to the originals. He was very displeased, although it turned out that, unbeknown to us, the reason was that Ford had two suppliers for the identical parts. The explanation was grudgingly accepted, but it was a lesson in how legislation can be overwhelming to small business. The cost and time it took to check Ford's own sub-suppliers – when TVR was buying a standard part from Ford – was an overhead of no added value.

Shortly after the Tasmin began delivery to customers, two cars suffered fractures of the rear suspension hub carrier. Fortunately, there were no harmful consequences, but the issue was serious. I clamped an aluminium casting in a vice and gave it a light blow with a hammer – it shattered like brittle cast iron. Immediately, I visited the foundry that made them, where the quality control was, to say the least, poor: floor sweepings being disposed of in the melt crucible, and no analysis taken of the final alloy melt. Laboratory checks showed major deviations from the finely balanced constituents of the LM25 alloy. The quality of the supplier had been taken for granted, as its literature was literally covered in Kitemarks, BS symbols and Ministry of Defence certification. Only later, we found that the parts made for the defence customers were – basically shrapnel! I assume they stayed in one piece until they reached the enemy.

A new supplier in the Midlands was brought in to take over the casting, and Ian Jones came up to Lancashire to ensure the design was not overstressed. Despite his finding that it was more than adequate, the TVR directors, somewhat unnerved by the incident, insisted

on a significant increase in material thickness, just to make sure. A sound lesson was learned never to take quality on trust. The prototype had proved capable, but had components from a different supplier.

This episode created our one major recall, as some 30 cars were at dealers, all with the same potential problem. These were returned to Blackpool, where the parts were changed.

Shortly after the launch, Stewart Halstead and I took the prototype, and the red production car, to Europe. We revisited Brussels for the Belgian type approval people to inspect the car, and to allow J P Yseboot to start selling them. We then continued to Germany, where the TVR importer, Ron Christopher, was our host. Ron, a Geordie, was doing good business selling cars to the American forces personnel from his small headquarters, at Hannau, outside Frankfurt. Here, the government inspectors were more demanding.

It was necessary to prove the maximum speed quoted in all literature, for consumer rights legislation. The autobahn between Frankfurt and Darmstadt was the chosen venue, and the inspector sat alongside me, to time the car between the kilometre posts. It was vital that the car could exceed 200kph for marketing reasons, and the run, in both directions took a lot of time as the junctions where we could turn round, were far apart. We achieved a mean maximum of some 131mph (211kph), with the southward run spiced up by a small car pulling out in front, close to the end of the run. Although I kept my foot down, it was close.

The brakes also needed proving, and the Alfred Teves Company allowed us to use its test track. This had a real 'wall of death' banking at one end, as the site was constrained by the nearby autobahn. It was a strange sensation as we cornered virtually at some 80 degrees to datum. The inspector was most impressed with the handbrake, as the car (perfectly adjusted) had huge Jaguar rear brakes.

Another daunting test was for noise. The Tasmin was not a particularly loud car, and had satisfied the British authorities' 'drive by' test. The Germans, however, measured the noise statically, by revving the engine, with microphones located all round the car. We managed to fail this, but after some diplomatic discussion, they decided to approve the system. This was, of course, long before the arrival of European Whole Vehicle approvals – we were going for local, low volume acceptance.

On the way home, with the German approval as good as done, we visited a company outside Beilefeld, in Germany, which took the prototype, to install a turbocharged engine similar to its 2.8 Capri conversions.

It engineered a very tidy system, with the turbo mounted at the front of the engine. The prototype was soon back at Bamber Bridge, and went extremely well. Sadly, it blew up after two exhilarating months, possibly due to the compression ratio remaining at 9.2:1 compared with the Lotus Turbo at 8:1.

Back in England, after an overnight crossing to Hull, Stewart was driving up the A1 early on a Sunday morning. The speedometer had failed in Europe, and he was maintaining a good pace. Out of a slip road, came a police car. Stewart explained that he did not kno he was speeding (by a considerable amount), as the speedometer had failed. The constabulary said that anyone should be able to judge their speed reasonably closely, so Stewart offered them the TVR keys and said – "OK, you drive it at 70mph without a clock." I remained as passenger, and the policeman was impressed with the refinement and ease with which the car drove. Stopping in the next lay-by, it emerged the police driver had maintained a steady 90mph in the test. That was probably somewhat less than the original speed they had seen that morning, so they prosecuted Halstead anyway.

One piece of information which the German authorities required was an engine power curve with the TVR exhaust system, as it was completely different to the standard Ford offering. Back in the UK, I arranged for Ford Power Products in Coventry to do the work, and a Tasmin exhaust was duly supplied. A couple of days later, I received a call from Ford Power Products saying that it could not achieve the Ford power figures. Surprised, it then fitted a standard Ford system and failed again. For over a fortnight, every possible engine specification was measured and checked. The camshaft lifts and overlaps, the bore and stroke of the engine, the compression ratio, the timing and fuelling, but in the end it admitted defeat. Ford took over the job, and I had a perfect power curve plot on my desk within three days, from another of its approved test houses. This anomaly has never been explained, but the Tasmin would not have achieved 130mph with much less than its specified 160bhp.

With a successful launch complete, the Tasmin coupé settled down to production at Blackpool. Meanwhile, Bamber Bridge had much still to do. A convertible prototype was under construction; the body pattern for the revised rear had already been made by Topelec, in Norwich. The car was running by the late spring, and, initially, had no soft top.

I was working on ideas to make a foldable 'rigid' roof. Inspiration came from the concept of battens in boat sails. I attempted to create a 'sail,' which was a series of rigid sections as close together as would allow folding,

covered with a flexible fabric. The difficulty lay in how to link them together as a rigid structure when erected, and still get it to fold into a small space. It soon became apparent that it was beyond our time and resource limits. I subsequently developed the rigid centre section/folding fabric rear, which long outlived the Tasmin. The use of the rigid panels and a stout glass fibre rear hoop meant that good water and wind sealing could be achieved. I was amused to read that, after I left TVR, Adrian Morrell spent a damp time in the local car wash perfecting the sealing!

In order to make a tidy seatbelt arrangement based on the coupé components, I came up with the concentric shoulder belt mount with the soft top pivot. This allowed the belt to run unaffected by the folding of the hood, but required that the hood pivot was located within the legally allowed seatbelt geometry.

Concerns were raised about the stiffness required for the windscreen structure, which was the same cross section as the coupé. Lancaster University conducted research to establish the worst loading and the acceptable amount of deflection, and found that the worst case would be from large adults levering themselves out of the car, using the top of the screen post. A load of 250lb (115kg) applied at the top corner should not allow more than 3mm deflection. We achieved this by filling the inside of the pillar with continuous filament glass fibre, and running the lower ends into the hinge post and front wing line, to spread the load over the widest area possible.

All this took time, and the convertible needed general development. A chassis stiffness rig was built, and tests showed that the frame had very even distribution of torque. A single extra diagonal was added in the centre backbone, in preparation for the convertible.

Adrian Morrell and I made a visit to the Department of Transport in Bristol, in the convertible prototype without its soft top (which had yet to be fitted). The day started with a pleasant, sunny drive down from Lancashire. Adrian noted that there was little wind noise or draught, as we cruised down the M6. However, as we were leaving Bristol in the evening rush hour, the heavens opened, and, while the cockpit stayed dry when moving, it didn't when static! The hearts of the Bristolians must have been in right place, as everyone gave the car and its soggy occupants priority at junctions, so that we could keep moving – a very effective jam beater.

Bamber Bridge was kept busy investigating cost savings for the Tasmin. One exercise involved making some body parts moulded in Kevlar instead of glass. If one layer of the aramid fibre could do the work of two layers of glass, the production time and cost would be reduced. Weight saving was also a potential (but not the primary)

The TVR Tasmin Convertible on Southport sands.

objective. However, parts made in this way were deemed too flexible, and the idea abandoned.

Adding fillers to the resin was a success, though. It not only reduced the resin cost (oil products were rocketing in price at that time), but increased the panel stiffness – with no weight penalty. Unfortunately, just as the material was being introduced to production, the supplier liquidated, and, with no direct replacement, this idea also foundered. Another job was to redevelop the heater with one fan instead of two.

Martin wanted to try a Rover V8 in the Tasmin, but when I laid out the installation, the top main frame tube passed exactly over the centre of the rear cylinder exhaust port. There was no obvious solution, although Martin suggested bending the frame tube – brought up on Colin Chapman's structural principles, I was against it. History has shown how wrong I was, as the Rover engine in the Tasmin was developed into cars which built TVR's reputation for ultimate performance, with bent top tubes which had no ill effects. Had we managed to shoehorn the V8, with its five-speed gearbox, into the car, and experienced the transformation in performance, I would, perhaps, have tried harder to find a solution.

The Engineering Department was busy not only getting the convertible to market, but also a 2+2. Martin Lilley felt that a 2+2 would expand the company into a market that was very large, and, as yet, untouched by TVR. He came up with the idea in May 1980 – it had not been pre-planned, as some books suggest. It was also a way of altering the visual balance of the coupé.

The coupé body was extensively modified, with a more aggressive front air dam, sill extensions which flared into the wheelarches, and a softer break in the lines over the front wheels. The upper body was unchanged, except for a longer tail (by 67mm), with the vertical rear glass running at an angle. The front overhang was unchanged (despite some authors suggesting otherwise). The bumpers were modified, with softer corners, and the rear wrapped round. This was all intended to make the car appear longer – which it was! The fuel was housed in a single tank over the rear axle, similar to the prototype installation, and the space behind the seat vacated by the twin tanks was remodelled into two small 'child' seats.

In the summer of 1980, Lilley started thinking about a small economy car to swell the TVR range. He asked me to draw up some ideas based on the Ford Fiesta running gear, but it was low priority, and never progressed beyond the concept stage.

To increase the customer base, Bamber Bridge installed power steering, and squeezed in an automatic gearbox, both made available as options. Customers could order any paint colour they desired, for extra cost; the paint being mixed and delivered daily to the Blackpool paintshop.

The Bamber Bridge Engineering Department was located in the Central Lancashire Development Corporation New Town, and TVR was seen as a prestigious company to have on board; so, when asked to participate in an advertising campaign, TVR jumped at the opportunity. Photographs were to be taken on Southport sands, which,

The TVR Tasmin 2+2 coupé by the River Wyre.

at low tide, stretch for miles. The rendezvous was very early in the morning, and I drove out to the photo shoot. Quite some time passed while all the sand was brushed from the tyres and their tracks disguised. When the pictures were 'in the can,' the photographers asked if they could do some speed shots. Agreeing, I set off, driving at over 60mph, with the cameras clicking.

There was a little white van, looking innocuous enough – but it contained the beach police. The speed limit on the sands was 5mph … The combined arguments, in my defence, from the advertising agency and the Development Corporation, resulted in my receiving just a verbal warning. It was probably the biggest margin I have ever had for speeding. The advertisements ran in the national press, and featured alongside some of the other local employers.

Mid-summer saw Martin bring in potential marketing support for TVR. The insurance broker, Sanderson and Law, was based in Lancaster, and was run by keen sports car enthusiasts. We held a meeting at the Imperial Hotel, Blackpool, also attended by Peter Purves, the TV presenter, who added his media expertise, and plans were made for a grand presentation extravaganza. It centred on a guest list of the Worthy and the Wealthy, each of whom would receive a golden car key with their invitation. The holder of the key that unlocked the prize Tasmin would take it home. The guest list included members of the press, motorsport, civic dignitaries, film stars, etc, and a superb display and banquet was planned. Ultimately, it never happened, although I believe a similar extravaganza took place after I left the company.

In mid-September 1980, I was clearing my desk at Bamber Bridge prior to leaving for a week's holiday, when Bill Bickerstaff, the company finance man, arrived with the news that my job was to cease. The company was not enjoying a prosperous time, and needed to make savings.

The timing was unfortunate for me, but I negotiated a stay of execution until after the holiday. I hoped that, with time to reconsider, there would be a change of mind.

The convertible and the 2+2 were poised for launch at the British Motor Show, in October, and the USA variants were planned as the next job. I had a miserable holiday, having decided that, as the decision was not final, I would spare the family the potential news. Upon my return, there was no reconsideration, so I packed my things, had my faithful old drawing board delivered to my home, and rang Mike Kimberley at Lotus.

The TVR period had been, in general, a most happy one. The company worked as a true team, with everyone accepting requests, or demands, by word-of-mouth. In the two years up north, I only issued one formal memo: the service schedules to the Service Department. Martin, Stewart and I would discuss ideas and issues, informally, in the evenings, and I always felt part of the action.

Unfortunately, Martin Lilley was having a very a tough time financially, as events conspired to make life at TVR difficult. It had built over 30 3-litre cars, which were still in stock when I left. Quite why they were built and remained unsold is a mystery. At the same time, in the United States, 25 3000S models were impounded by the authorities over a paperwork error. Combined, these tied up a considerable amount of cash, and the bank was not being helpful.

Sales of the Tasmin were seen as disappointing. The planned annual production was 432 cars, which was very optimistic. In 1979, they had made 308 3-litre cars, but, of those, 140 were for export. With no USA market open until Tasmin was 'Federalised,' and with the effects of the serious recession in 1980, the 144 built was probably as much as could be expected. With low volumes by car industry standard, parts were being delivered way above production needs, as many had to be committed for 12 months in advance.

The recession hit the whole specialist car business, and TVR actually out-performed many in 1980-81. While, in 1980, TVR saw a reduction in production of 53% from 1979, Lotus dropped 61%, and the Triumph TR7 by 82%.

Martin had a target selling price (in the UK) of under £10,000. However, the bank insisted on £12,800. This was a major increase from previous models – excepting the top Turbo – and a lower price could have seen higher sales volumes. Unlike the 2010 recession, the 1980 version did not enjoy an exceptionally low bank rate. In fact, the Bank of England interest rate went up, in November 1979, to 17% at a very sensitive time for the company.

Despite criticism in certain books, the teams at Topelec, in Norwich, and at Bamber Bridge succeeded in creating a product for far less cost over far less time than its rivals. The Tasmin took 23 months from concept approval to production, while the 1974 Lotus Elite took 37 months, and the Lotus Elan M100 36 months. Lotus had far greater resources of manpower and equipment to support its projects.

The TVR wedge stayed in production in various forms for 12 years, a timespan only exceeded by the TVR Chimera. It also had the second highest production volume. Although the Rover V8 gave it the extra performance we had always wanted, interestingly the number of V6 cars produced was nearly the same as the V8: 1228 and 1390 respectively.

The Tasmin range, was, I felt, a significant move for the company. I believed, just as the contemporary press had noted, that it moved them forward, so, when I have read more recent criticism of it, I feel some of it is unjustified. Its angular shape was an extreme example of a style which lasted another ten years. As a specialist car, it needed to push boundaries. Sharp-edged cars continued to emerge from manufacturers, such as the Mitsubishi Starion (1982), Audi Quattro (1983) and the Maserati Biturbo (1984). Today, I am greatly impressed with the enthusiasm of the current owners of this TVR.

However, for me, the TVR story was over; I was heading back to Lotus after a three-year absence.

www.velocebooks.com / www.veloce.co.uk
Details of all current books • New book news • Special offers • Gift vouchers • Forum

95

Chapter 8

The car that never was – part 1

Arriving back at Lotus, on 8 October 1980, I saw that much had changed. Engineering, under Colin Spooner, was hard at work with the DeLorean project. I was given an office in the complex of buildings opposite the main factory: a rambling collection of low buildings, built when Hethel was a wartime base.

Colin Chapman, Mike Kimberley, Tony Rudd and Colin Spooner had decided that Lotus needed an 'affordable' sports car to replace the late lamented Elan. It was obvious that the high-investment components must be sourced from a major manufacturer. The supplier needed to have superlative quality products, and be enthusiastic about participating. A shortlist was drawn up, and Chapman wrote to the, mainly Japanese, companies. The one that most relished the opportunity was the Toyota Motor Corporation, so the new car was to be designed around its components, although they did not all have to come from one model.

Although some preparatory work had been done, and a fifth-scale model constructed, before I arrived, I was instructed to start with a clean sheet of paper. The project was to be completed in total secrecy, and a team was installed in the room next to mine. Chris Dunster, who had worked on the Elite, supported body and chassis, and Ken Heap, an ex-Jaguar man, was the suspension expert. Alan Bradley, also from Elite days, looked after the engine and transmission. Shortly afterwards, he was joined by Malcolm Leeds, now departed from the boat company. The chosen donor vehicle was the 2-litre twin-cam Celica, and one was duly acquired, along with service books, to get as much data as possible. At the beginning, the Japanese kept a low profile, as a formal deal had not been signed. To enable us to draw components, we stripped the Celica. The engine lived under a dust-sheet in the locked project office, but somehow news of its likely future was leaked to the press. Luckily, it was only published in a small circulation newsletter, but it meant that the security clamp was applied even harder.

The M90 fifth-scale model – made prior to my return to Lotus – which launched the project.

The project was assigned the name 'M90.' Our first task was to decide on the layout and outline specification, which had to be front-engine, rear-drive, as Toyota only had one model without that configuration, the Tercel. The Tercel was front-wheel drive, with a longitudinal engine over its transmission. We felt that this low output powertrain was underpowered, with a too-high centre of gravity, to be a donor for a mid-engined design.

The 2-litre Celica, with five-speed gearbox, and a final drive suited to an independent suspension, was chosen. Although the car had a live axle in Europe, independently sprung variants existed in Japan. The Lotus Sales Department suggested that a 2+2 would attract up to five times as many customers than a pure two-seater, so that was included in the requirements. Colin Chapman agreed that a steel-backbone frame would be the best option for the structure, clothed with a glass fibre body. Open and closed body variants were specified.

Colin Spooner had already taken up the challenge of exploring alternative methods of making injection-moulded bodies, with no undercut shapes that necessitated split moulds. He came up with a mould split which used two sides, a top, and a bottom, moulding. Although the body would be made from four, instead of two, major

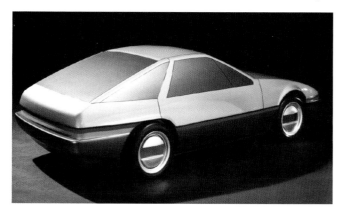

My first design ideas for the Lotus M90.

mouldings, it dispensed with add-on gutters and sills, and removed the need for an obvious styling feature to conceal the mid-height joint line. However, there were difficulties concealing the seams of the mouldings down the edge of the front wings, windscreen and rear wings. In the end, the decision was to continue manufacturing Lotus bodies as two pieces, top and bottom mouldings, joined at the widest point.

After much discussion with Colin Chapman, to get a feeling for his direction, along with the assistance of his old friend and co-director, Peter Kirwan Taylor, I laid out a smooth, fastback coupé. Chapman was impressed with Italdesign's Medusa, and suggested that it was used for design direction. The design was drawn on paper by 25 November, and a wooden model made by Christmas.

It met the objective of keeping the lines simple, although it failed to meet the 'no side windows behind the door' criterion – Colin's yardstick for a 'sports car.' Chapman liked it, and more detail design work started. Under the impression that Chapman wanted to push ahead as fast as possible, the team began to build a seating buck. One Saturday morning, he came in and found us at work on it. He was not best pleased, and stopped the work immediately. Instead, he insisted on a complete parts list for the proposed design, with all costs shown. He *did* sit in the buck, however and concluded that the rear seats were too big for a sports car, so it partly vindicated itself, and formed a useful decision indicator.

To meet Chapman's edict, Chris Dunster and I obtained a copy of the Lotus Eclat cost list, and amended it wherever appropriate. As Chapman had pointed out, all cars had the same basic parts, and, even if they were not all designed yet, the parts list made you think harder. Every deviation had to be justified and explained, and the job took a couple of weeks of full-time work to complete. When it was finished, Chapman opened a couple of pages at random, and queried the entries. One of these was the exhaust system. He could not believe that the reduction suggested – from £130 for the Eclat to the £50 proposed – was attainable, until I explained that the allowed cost was £5 more than the production TVR stainless steel system, and that was for a Vee-engine. Happy that the exercise had been done properly, Colin used his copy of the bulky roll of paper as a doorstop in his Ketteringham Hall office. Chris never got over the ignominy of it. It had, however, made us all think much harder about how we could reduce costs to a bare minimum.

With the failure of the first model to bring enough sporting feel to the project, I cut off the fast back, and created the notchback design. Work on the details continued through March 1981. It was more suitable

Fifth-scale model of the notchback variant of my first M90 design.

for conversion to a convertible, but still did not get anyone's 'juices' flowing. Then I drew up a simple wedge design.

The car company was facing financial difficulties as a result of the recession, and Chapman decided that Lotus Engineering should set up as consultants. He reasoned that it could maintain a much larger engineering skill-base for Lotus' own use, with other clients funding this resource. As well as DeLorean, Talbot was a client, and we did work on a Turbo Horizon, as a sister car to the Lotus Sunbeam: the interior was rebuilt in magnolia hide, the bright red exterior was bespoilered and louvred, and the Powertrain Department produced the engine. Art Blakeslee, the Talbot chief stylist, came to Hethel and liked what he saw, as did his engineering colleagues who drove it. However, times were difficult for them, too, financially, and it proceeded no further.

John Greaves, a colleague of mine in JCL Marine, came over to Lotus, as the first stage in the expansion of Styling Design, and was charged with finding new clients. This he did admirably, designing two prize-winning pieces of avant garde furniture for a Nottingham company. The glass fibre structure of his chaise longue was made at Lotus, to supplement the work in the Car Body Shop.

I was not involved in the DeLorean project, beyond advising on the centre console. This had to house a specified number of music tapes under the armrest. The resulting design prevented the driver from using the gear selector properly, so I had a look, but could not come up with anything that improved it. I did suggest that next time. they should "put a house brick on the tunnel, and try it before committing to tooling!" When Chapman found out I had spent a couple of hours on it, he expressly forbade further involvement.

As DeLorean wound down, the M90 project moved across to the main Lotus factory. A secure room behind the main office was refurbished to house Chris Dunster, John Greaves and me. Although the budget was low, we managed to create an efficient and pleasant environment. The room was kept locked at all times, and we had no windows, so were often surprised by weather changes when we set off home!

Ken Heap and Alan Bradley moved into the vehicle engineering area of the main office, as the basic running gear for the car was complete. That was now being developed for project M55, the Excel. This utilised the new chassis and suspension, with the Toyota gearbox and final drive mated to the Lotus 2.2-litre engine. It immediately overcame many of the reliability problems of the original M50. The Lotus engine was retained, as it had 160hp to the Toyota's 115hp. The frame carried new suspensions designed by Ken Heap.

Colin Spooner took charge of the external changes to the Eclat body shape, the most notable difference being the adoption of glass fibre for the 'bright trim' components for the screen post and gutters, originally made in polished aluminium. This saved a considerable sum of money, and made it possible for the design to include flexible shapes, as it did not require constant production of sections by rolling or extruding the metal. The work on the body was extensive, as the transmission dictated a new tunnel in the undertray. At the same time, we took the opportunity to introduce a new interior, and it eventually absorbed a lot of resource. One aspect that I was sad about was that the seats were redesigned much thicker than the originals. This lost a significant amount of rear passenger space. The Excel was put into production in 1982, lasting until 1992, extending the life of the front-engined luxury cars to 18 years from the Elite's announcement.

The M90 wedges were created in May 1981, designed in both coupé and convertible configurations. We built fifth-scale models, including an accurate backbone chassis frame (in card, which allowed deflection areas to be studied), made by Chris Dunster; and a body structure model, with its foam-filled sections for sills and other box

M90 Convertible wedge design model.

members. Comprehensive presentation brochures were produced to communicate the ideas to Japan. The models were rejected by the Japanese, due to their width: this could not exceed 1700mm (66.9in) without attracting severe tax penalties in that market at the time. Toyota explained that even its Crown luxury car conformed, that being why it was so long – it couldn't pack everything in, in anything shorter!

The specification included a Toyota four-speed automatic gearbox, set to do a sprightly 73mph (118kph) in second gear. The car sat on 195 60VR 14 tyres on 6in rims. It carried 12 gallons (55 litres) of fuel, under the luggage compartment floor. It compared with rivals, thus:

Model	UK price	0-60mph (97kph)	Maximum speed
Lancia Montecarlo	£8100	9.0sec	115.8mph (187kph)
Datsun 280ZX	£8742	10.4sec	117.8mph
Mazda RX 7	£8699	9.0sec	119.0mph
Porsche 924	£9103	9.3sec	121.3mph
Triumph TR7	£6880	10.0sec	108.5mph.

We thought we were on the right lines with our predictions of 0-60mph in 7.8 seconds, and a maximum speed of 134mph (217kph). While projects were at the paper stage, we used to set a lot of store by the use of comparisons with selected rivals.

Chapman felt that he would prefer the wedges toned down a bit, and we spent hours applying tape to the side of the models to flatten the wing line. This was done in two distinct steps, but when the models had been built and presented to Chapman, the flair had died, and they just looked very ordinary. Included in this work was an extension of the wheelbase. This was to lead to the adoption of the same wheelbase as the forthcoming Lotus Excel.

A fifth-scale model with tape applied to study a flatter wing line.

The coupé version of the wedge.

The flattened-wedge wing line took away the design's flair, and was scrapped.

Concurrent with the M90, Chris Dunster, John Greaves and I were supporting potential clients of Lotus Engineering, one of whom was Norton. During March and April 1981, we worked on a proposed car, which would utilise a development of the rotary engine used in its motorcycles. This water-cooled unit had an inter-cooled turbo, and drove through a proprietary car transmission.

The engine was very compact, so we designed a front-wheel drive 2+2 coupé and convertible to suit world markets. Designated Project Nora, dry weight was estimated at 590kg, propelled by 90hp. This was projected to give a 0-60mph (97kph) acceleration of 8.75 seconds – the same as a Golf GTI – and a maximum of 124mph (200kph), some 13mph (21kph) faster than the

Project Nora, the Norton rotary-engined coupé.

comparators. To achieve good overall road performance, the car would have had to be driven with full use of the gears, as the lack of torque made fourth and fifth very lazy.

The body was to be a glass fibre monocoque with foam-filled box sections. The engine and suspension were carried on steel subframes mounted to the body on rubber isolators. The front suspension was by double wishbones, with longitudinal torsion bars, and a damper on the upper link. The rear had transverse torsion bars acting on semi-trailing arms. The 10-gallon (45-litre) plastic fuel tank had its underside faired into the upswept vehicle floor profile, designed to be a ground effect diffuser. Estimates for parts and tooling, and assembly costs were made, and it was presented to Norton, at its plant in Coventry.

Colin Chapman, Tony Rudd, Chris Dunster and I attended the presentation to Dennis Poore, Norton's Chairman, who seemed a bit bowled over by the amount of detail already done. Chris and I had drawn the vehicle out in fifth-scale, and raised a parts list, in order to cost it. We went back to Hethel with high hopes that the project would proceed, as we all found the car an exciting challenge. Messages came and went, for some time, between Norton's powertrain engineers and Lotus, but it gradually became apparent that its rotary powerplant was not ready for automobile use.

Colin Chapman was very aware, as was I, that many styling designs did not adequately package all the vital components. The result was that the initial shapes presented were often changed so much in proportion that the original flair was lost. Worse, sometimes very complex and expensive solutions had to be found later in the programme, when systems just would not fit into the vehicle. The very wide, low radiator on the Esprit was a case in point: it needed three expensive (and heavy) electric fans, due to the package height restriction. Therefore, before the drawings for a scale model were released from the drawing board, Chapman would inspect and critique the layout, to ensure all the main elements were packaged.

The layouts would show the engine, gearbox and final drive, obviously, but I also had to show how the engine and gearbox could be removed from an assembled car – very embarrassing to find it could not be removed without tearing apart the whole car! I drew in the proposed structural frame, with its suspension, and laid out the wheels for full bump and rebound, and steering angulation. The driver was shown, with foot pedals and the necessary stroke that he would need for full depression. As brakes usually need over 100mm of stroke, there is a major 'dead' space below the feet in normal driving. The

Project Nora, compared with the Mini Metro, was very low it was, due to the compact powertrain.

radiator, steering column and heater units would be laid in, and the driver's basic visibility checked. The battery had to have a home: they are only available in a range of sizes, which cannot be 'compressed' to suit circumstances. The fuel tank was laid out, with the necessary volume specified, and an intended route for the filler considered. The material from which the fuel tank was made was important, as small companies like Lotus could not afford complex metal pressings. It had tanks made by wrapping sheet metal round end plates and welding up the seams, as in an oil drum – later, these became plastic.

I estimated luggage capacity (my famous 'Elite' suitcases again!), housed the spare wheel – another big and incompressible chunk – and checked the lights for basic legal position. Colin had suffered problems with confined pedal spacing and foot-wells in the past, and, while he would never allow excess in his designs, he needed to be shown the space allocated was adequate. The doors were always shown in cross-section, as the glass had to drop and clear the lock mechanism, and the structural beam, needed for side impact protection.

While this package of components and systems was physically laid out on plastic drawing film, the other considerations that control the success of a product were also in consideration. Chapman would not allow the models to proceed until their manufacturing process was clear. Mainly, that meant how the body was moulded, bonded together and painted. We drew diagrams to show typical moulding conditions, which could not have shapes which locked into two-piece (male and female) moulds. Chris Dunster spent much time on this work, and he and I

were always attempting to come up with radical solutions to the basic body engineering conditions. We devoted many hundreds of hours for the M90 on this subject, and the conclusions are described later.

Another major issue was weight. Not only the total weight –that enemy of performance – but also its disposition in the vehicle. When I proposed locating the spare wheel at the front of the vehicle, Colin had me do a basic weight distribution check, before he would accept the idea.

My thoughts were influenced by contemporary industrial design, and, in this case, I drew up a shape inspired by an electric razor. Luckily, no one else guessed the source, as it didn't look like one! Chapman was keen to exploit this direction, and I suggested that a basic model could be made to half the usual size, at tenth-scale. This was done by 28 June, on the M55 (Excel) chassis, fitted with the Toyota 2-litre engine, with the spare wheel housed in the nose, over the radiator. This allowed the tail to be very compact. The tenth-scale model was given the immediate 'go ahead' to be developed in more detail at fifth-scale, and I created the drawings to support this.

The design moved to a fifth scheme and model. The models were built of wood – usually jelutong – in the Lotus Pattern Shop. At Jaguar, all the hardwood used was mahogany, but its long-term availability was in question, so Lotus substituted jelutong. Later, artificial resin-based materials would oust the use of natural wood altogether. These new materials were much more consistent and dimensionally stable than trees, which were sometimes found to contain old spearheads or barbed wire! As the

Tenth-scale concept model had a removable roof section, to show the convertible.

The basic concept model, with the coupé roof.

and the selection of these components played a major part in this. For instance, a door release was used from the Renault 5 as it had no handle, just a small lever attached directly to the lock. I needed to find the minimum usable dimensions for the access cut-out in the door panel, so a model was made of the area, and various people inserted their gloved fingers to test it out. When a consensus was agreed, the detail could go down on the drawings.

Presentation drawing of the tenth-scale concept, produced by our technical artist, Geoff Devlin.

Presentation drawing of the tenth-scale convertible concept.

The drawings of the tenth-scale model showed a new solution to body panel jointing.

shapes progressed, I would advise on design detail. When the shape was to my liking, the surface was sealed with body primer paint, and flatted down with 'wet and dry' paper. Typically, the model in fifth-scale would take two weeks to build. It was then spray-painted in colour paint, and the windows masked up and painted in a darkish grey gloss. Mick McIssacs had returned to Lotus, and built many of these.

Chris Dunster was a past master at applying lighting units made up on paper, along with the number plates. The panel shut lines were applied with very thin body decal tape, and the whole set off with model exhaust pipes and wheels. The tyres were made from turned wood, with a flat on the bottom to represent the normal standing height of the tyre. Aluminium alloy wheel models were fabricated in the Lotus Machine Shop, and inserted in the centre of the wheels.

Often, after the model had been approved in principle, a mould was taken, to allow fibreglass replicas to be made. These had a number of uses. First, the convertible variant was developed on a cut-down coupé. A wind tunnel model was also built, with as much underbody detail as was feasible, and with a simulated radiator.

The work now concentrated on the coupé; now that the design was 'real,' we needed suppliers for all the components. Weight was always a serious consideration,

The first of many fifth-scale models, which led eventually to a running prototype.

The dark grey lower panels were impact-resistant RIM plastic.

Wraparound bumpers were becoming common, so we figured that we could use them for the total front and rear lower visual body. The door sills were separate, to allow the seal-mounting flange to be inset, so we saw little penalty in sweeping the ends of the sills up to the same height as the top of the bumpers. The space behind provided an accessible cavity for the substantial door hinges and latches. Most of the length between the wheels was taken up by the door, anyway. The bonnet was made as a front-hinged clamshell, and extended down to the top of the sill and bumper mouldings. Calculations showed that the clamshell bonnet saved a total of £12.50 (in 1982) over the conventional front fender and bonnet design.

The upper body consisted of the engine bulkhead, screen pillars (A-posts), roof, rear quarter panels, and rear deck. The undercut needed, to place the door seals inset from the glass line, was achieved by incorporating a foam-filled section inside the edge of the roof, which also provided a stiff structure.

With the whole of the lower part of the car clad in RIM impact-proof plastic, the floor, wheel housings and

lower sides could be designed as functional-, rather than visual-, styled parts in a one-piece undertray moulding. This allowed the rear lower edge of the door, shut, to have a curved line, which was impossible with the original two-piece bodied cars, which were vertical to avoid mould lock up. The bumpers incorporated the side and tail lamps, number plate recess, and lower front and rear valences.

The doors, made from an inner and outer moulding bonded together, were normally moulded at right-angles to their surfaces. The use of RIM for the visual lower body presented an opportunity to approach the construction differently. Usually, all the door mechanisms are fed into the door through large holes in the inner panel. I thought that led to ultimate stiffness issues for the door pull/armrest and the window motor system. I therefore made the inner panel very stiff, with only the body-painted outer upper part bonded to it. Access to the internal systems was achieved by removing the lower panel. All this led to the development of the mid-body joint.

The previous cars (and boats) were joined with an out-turned flange, parallel to the ground, bonded together and covered with an extruded plastic finisher. This ran round the whole vehicle, including the wheel arches, and was hand-finished flush in the door openings. The M90 was subject to strict width limits in Japan, so the width of the joint finisher was of no packaging value. The undertray had a flange turned out and down, to make the joint face down instead of out. The edge was precision cut and radiused, prior to painting. Chapman thought the painting might lead to sags and drips on the cut edges, so a trial section was made full-size, and put through the production paint process. There were no problems, so he allowed this to proceed. A by-product of this joint was that the area to be bonded could almost be of unlimited size. This joint only applied around the rear half of the car, behind the doors, as they and the bonnet covered the rest of the joint.

A single windscreen wiper was employed, as it wiped all the legally required glass area. The Elite had this feature, but suffered from poor serviceability. If the mechanism failed, the instrument panel and air-conditioning had to be removed first, making repair a two-day job. I designed a one-piece bracket that held the motor, linkage and the wiper spindle. It attached to studs on the engine side of the bulkhead for instant removal, and allowed all the reaction forces to be absorbed in one unit.

Single 7in round headlamps were chosen as the best compromise for light output, weight, space utilisation and cost. The front and rear lighting was a challenge, however. No suitable donor was apparent, until I visited the supplier of the Aston Martin Lagonda tail lamps.

These were expensive, but their modular opportunities were obvious for keeping the tooling costs to a minimum. There was just one illuminated lamp in either red, amber or clear plastic.

Concurrent with the design detailing, scale models were honed in the wind tunnel. A number of visits were made to MIRA over the autumn and early winter. A lot of work was concentrated on the airflow under the vehicle, with refinement of the front intake and lower lip and the tuning of the rear lower valence to permit the exit of underbody air. The design had low lift and drag, despite disposing of the cooling air under the car, rather than up to the top of the bonnet.

John Greaves, Chris and I were still kept busy with Lotus Engineering client work. We put together a series of ideas to face-lift a truck cab, but failed to win the contract. John was working on a milk float. Internally named Project Ernie, his role was to assist Hunting Plastics, which had taken out a licence on the Lotus injection-moulding process. It, in turn, was working with its customer, who made milk floats and wanted to push the design barriers forward. John worked hard on this and prototypes were made, but I don't remember that it ever came into production.

In the summer of 1981, Chris Dunster inherited a drawer full of old drawings from somewhere in the organisation. Among assorted drawings of little interest was an original early scheme for the Type 14 Lotus Elite. Drawn and signed by Colin Chapman, it compared various dimensions, weights and performance predictions with the Alfa Romeo GT. We were fascinated to see he had been working in much the same way, for a long time. The next time Colin visited the office, we showed it to him, and he was very emotional at seeing it. He asked Chris never to lose it.

The under-tray 'mould' under construction (viewed from the front).

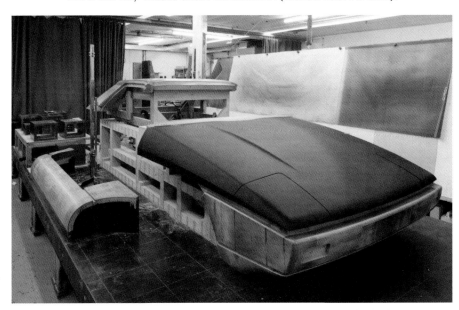

Each section being built up on the heavyweight central 'cube.'

Lotus was traditionally bad at preserving its 'archive,' but it was not for the want of trying: it was more that there was no space to house and document it all – it was a prolific organisation! In recent years, some people have suggested that Chapman had no time for the past, a view I do not share from my experience of him.

Colin was, as always, very busy. He was taken with the possibilities for free movement potentially offered by

The cube allowed each area to be made simultaneously on the bench.

A view of the rear of the coupé in the Lotus Pattern Shop.

laid out on the huge tables in the Engineering Department in the Lotus main office. Once the body lines were smoothed, by eye, to my satisfaction, and the detail engineering issues resolved, the drawings went to the Pattern Shop for translation into wooden oversize models. A small increase was made to the dimensions, to allow for resin shrinkage during the tooling and moulding cycle.

The under-tray or lower body, with floor and wheel arches, was built as a wooden mould; unlike the visual outer skins, built as a model, from which moulds would be taken. It was much easier to make this way round, as the wheel housings were solid domes rather than hollow shapes. The surface finish, while very good, did not have to be to Class A visual standard. It also meant that a whole step could be saved in the programme. Heavily shaped areas, such as the wheel housings and the sides, which had to conform to the visual body, were made in gelutung, but the flatter areas were fabricated in high quality birch plywood.

When the wooden under-tray mould was finished, the body process manager took a dislike to the swages and interruptions that broke up the flat shapes of the floor and tunnel. From his point of view, they would make the mouldings more complex, but it was the cheapest and lightest solutions for the finished vehicle that mattered. Flat glass fibre, just as flat metal, would transmit noise. Sound deadening was heavy and expensive. Better to stabilise the panels in the first place. More complexity for body manufacture would be more than offset by the savings.

The vehicle was split into sections, and a heavy wooden cube frame constructed. Each area was shaped, on the bench, usually by teams of two, with the work referenced to datums that were on the central cube. Apart from speeding up the work, it meant that the dimensions

microlight aircraft, and had a design under development in the United States. One day, he asked me to do a colour scheme. "You can do anything you like, as long as the top of the wings are white," he explained. The reason was that the foam-filled wing sections could not be allowed to absorb heat, or they were likely to explode!

On 8 August 1981, we began work on the full-size drawings of the M90. Led by Ron Warke, they were

The full-size model on display for the directors' viewing in the Vehicle Workshop.

The model was badged 'Lotus Elan.'

could be held with great accuracy, usually to within half a millimetre. The timber used for the patterns was first machine-planed into blocks about 200mm thick. These were then glued together, and clamped to make bigger blocks. The main shape was marked out and the block put through a band saw, close to the desired line. After sawing, the pattern makers would clean up the sawn line accurately using block planes, chisels, gouges and spoke-shaves. They would then manufacture templates from the sectioned body line drawings, and carve down at each section point. They would remove the remaining wood in between each section, and smooth the surface with fine glass paper. I, and the body lines team, would supervise closely, to ensure the surface details were as desired.

As the various pieces of the visual body were attached to the cube, final finishing took place. The surface was sprayed with filler paint, and rubbed down the same way as the scale models; the final paint was polyurethane-based. Lotus had been finishing body patterns with this very hard-surface material for some time, as it created very good surfaces. There was a limited colour range available, so yellow was chosen. Colin Chapman was suspicious of silver as a presentation colour, as he felt that it tended to flatter most designs, leading to disappointment, when they were seen in other colours, later.

As the M90 full-size model presentation neared, windows were fabricated in thin plywood, and lights made from textured plastic. The windscreen wiper, radio aerial, and door handles, were fitted, along with an exhaust tailpipe, mirrors, and number plates. Support for the weight of the cube, to give the desired ground clearance, was hidden behind the wheels, and painted matt black. Decals were cut out by hand by Chris Dunster, and rubber tube inserted round the side windows to simulate the seals.

As had happened with the Elite presentation in 1971, comparative vehicles were brought in. They were a Mazda RX7, Triumph TR7, and a Porsche 924. Workshop space was cleared, the comparator cars arranged, with the M90 in the centre. At 11:00am, on 14 February 1982, Colin Chapman came to view the model. Mike Kimberley,

From the left: Spooner, Putnam, Kimberley, Chapman and myself at the full-size model viewing.

A fifth-scale model with the revised body mid joint.

the Managing Director, Colin Spooner, Head of Vehicle Engineering, and Roger Putnam, Sales and Marketing Director, also attended, while I explained the features. The event, as I remember, was not as dynamic as previous first viewings, and little use was made of the comparator cars. In the past, Colin Chapman had become totally immersed at such an event, making it hard to keep up with him.

This model was much fresher to Chapman, who, unusually, had not spent much time in the workshops while it was built. He asked for very little to be changed – the rear spoiler was to be faired, to extend the body surface, and that was about it. He was not sure about the body mid-height joint design, and a revised fifth-scale model was built, photographed, and copies sent to Chapman, at the Brazilian Grand Prix on 1 March, from where no comment was forthcoming. There was an apocryphal story that he left the pictures there, on the pit counter, but that was unlikely.

In January 1982, I joined Martin Long and Chris Wynder from Purchasing, Colin Spooner and Mike Kimberley, at Heathrow to visit Japan. We spent a week with Toyota, clarifying the parts we required for the M90 and the M55 Excel. The Japanese were fine hosts, and sitting down to a traditional Japanese boxed lunch on the first day, the British all picked up chop sticks, whilst all the Toyota staff picked up the carefully arranged knives and forks and were highly amused.

One evening, our hosts arranged a banquet at the Toyota museum. This was a private collection, housed in a magnificent modern building. The lobby was decorated with priceless European paintings and oriental porcelain. I was talking to one of the senior managers present, explaining that my grandfather had once lived in Japan.

I knew he lived at Saitazaki, but had never located it on a map. The manager said, "Oh, I know where that is. I was born in the next village." Small world. After dinner, we were shown down to the basement, where Toyota had a collection of its historic vehicles. These included racing sports cars, and the famous James Bond 2000 convertible. We were very flattered to be guests at this rather special evening.

The technical discussions were very drawn out, as the Japanese operated at an incredible level of thoroughness. Lotus noted that the gearbox proposed for the M55 had a torque rating below that of the Lotus engine. They just smiled, and said that, although that was the official figure, it had been over-engineered by more than enough for the Lotus.

We had a tour of the Export Packing Department, where components for foreign-assembled Toyotas were prepared for shipment. It was a massive operation, utilising a moving assembly line, and they explained that all the Lotus components must conform to their system. No special modifications could be contemplated – use standard parts, or go elsewhere.

After the exacting week at the company-owned Toyota Castle Hotel, we left for a night in Tokyo. Martin Long, Chris Wynder and I met to decide how to spend the evening. We were all very tired, and, when I pointed out that there were 13 restaurants in the building, we elected to stay in and choose one. The French restaurant won the vote, and we were shown to a table by the Japanese maitre'd, in traditional white tie and tails. A string quartet played gently in the corner, as we enjoyed a pleasant three courses and a bottle of wine. This break from Japanese food was much appreciated, as was Martin's offer to

A sketch of the 'cathedral' design.

pick up the bill. Back at Hethel, a few days later, I received a call from him to say he had now done his expenses and worked out the value of the dinner bill. I expected it to be fairly expensive, but was surprised when he said it was £125. "As much as that," I said. "Each," said Martin! This would equate to £428 in 2015.

Returning from an early season Grand Prix, Colin decided to alter the construction of the body. He was convinced that the contemporary Opel/Vauxhall Astra had its widest point at the top of the doorsill. Dunster and I contested that, but it was an order, so we schemed out a theoretical design, with the joint at

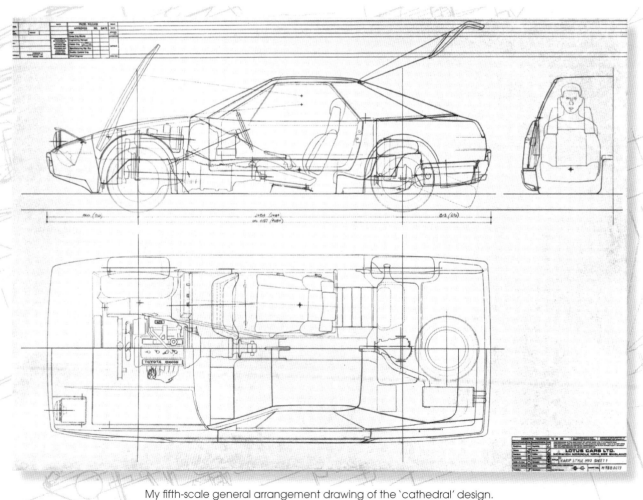

My fifth-scale general arrangement drawing of the 'cathedral' design.

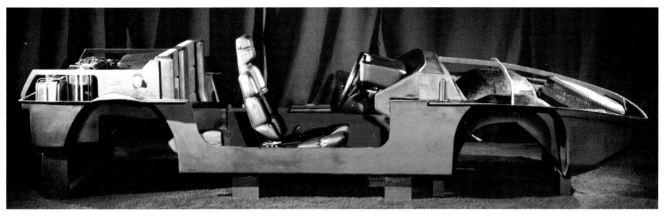

The M90 package buck, built on an undertray moulding. Spare wheel in the nose.

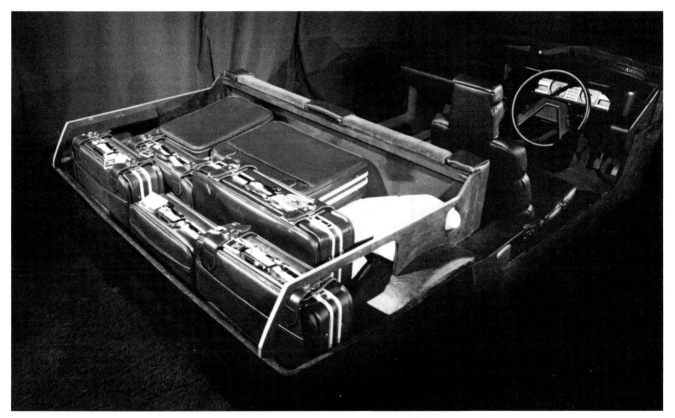

The packaging buck, with luggage, and model fuel tank in yellow.

sill level, and running around the wheel arches. Known in the office as the 'cathedral' designs, two models were built, but we could not make them look acceptable. Chris Dunster found an Astra, and had a template made from the door section. It immediately proved that the widest point was conventionally halfway up the door.

Colin was not best pleased to be proved wrong, but the project went back to the mid-height break, and the original presentation design. Chris and I were wondering if this was a stalling tactic. As soon as the full-size body model could be approved, the next step would have been mould making and prototype build. That was expensive, and I doubt the company had enough money to proceed at the time. An additional reason for slowing down the project was that Toyota had still not signed the formal supply agreement, although that was not far away.

In the spring of 1982, Sam Shimada, Toyota's product specialist and primary contact in Japan, visited Lotus,

The M90 full-size model repainted in silver for the Toyota presentation.

and let it be known quietly, that it had a new engine. It would be smaller, lighter and more powerful than the 2-litre already packaged. No details were available at first, but Sam was paving the way for a change. Soon, we had the overall dimension details of the forthcoming 1.6-litre 4AGE engine. We leapt at the opportunity to benefit from its advantages, but that was going to take time.

In the July 1982, Toyota made it known that it would be visiting Hethel in September. Mr Toyoda and a number of his directors would expect to see the M90. Chapman asked for the full-size model to be repainted a flattering silver!

A moulding was taken of the undertray, and a basic cockpit built up, with seating. The fuel tank was modelled in polystyrene and painted yellow, luggage fitted in the boot, and the spare wheel in its intended position in the nose. Wooden sections were cut to show the shape and position of the bonnet, and it was mounted at the correct height from the ground.

A mock up 1.6-litre engine arrived in early August, and was put into an Excel chassis intended for the car. It didn't fit very well, but served its purpose for the September presentation.

The high profile visit by the Japanese was a very important event for Lotus, as it was to make the joint participation of the M90 'official,' although some agreements already existed. It also marked an acceleration in engineering projects that Lotus would be getting from

Toyota, the most prominent being the design and development of a V6 engine.

To show the M90 in a suitable setting, the Lotus Directors' Garage was cleared, the walls draped with surplus brown trimming cloth, and part of the floor carpeted in leftovers from a Motor Show. The Directors' Garage, a 'drive in' covered space for some ten cars, was both private, and, conveniently, alongside the executive suite.

I located some theatrical stage lighting, and the full-size model, seating buck, and chassis were arranged on the carpet. The remaining concrete floor was repainted, and a production Turbo Esprit in matching silver, brought in. We also installed a coffee table and some casual seating, with presentation booklets containing the specification, performance expectations, and cost information. The table featured Norfolk's best attempt at an oriental flower arrangement.

Mr Toyoda and his entourage were delighted with what they saw, and pledged full support. Mr Chapman was cheered up a bit, as well, and three sets of M90 components were ordered for January 1983 delivery.

Chapman had been uneasy about M90, since the full-size presentation the previous February. Beside the 'cathedral' exercise, I had also done a clay and a plaster fifth model of alternatives. Chapman had called in his old friend John Frayling, the Type 14 Elite designer, in the summer, and set up a room for him on the first floor of Ketteringham Hall, where I gave him as much assistance as I could. John worked on some clay ideas for two or three weeks, but his heart did not appear to be in it. Nothing emerged, and he left as quietly as he came.

I believe that Chapman was having confidence problems. He had many years of groundbreaking success in the automobile world, and may have been worried about how to follow that. He was busy with active suspension, twin chassis racing cars, microlight aircraft, and the gathering storm created by the DeLorean project. He spent much less time at Hethel, leaving the running of Lotus Cars to Mike Kimberley, and Engineering to Tony Rudd. I found this most unusual, having been used to his thrice daily visits to my drawing board, in the past.

He was a lot 'easier,' almost as if his infrequent visits

to our project office were a way to escape. Road cars had frustrated him ever since the Elite, ten years before, as so much was governed by legislation. When he was not away racing, he spent most of his time at Ketteringham Hall. The other factor, which may have had even more influence on his actions, was that Lotus did not have the money to proceed any further with the M90. The next stage, building running prototypes, was going to be expensive. He was unlikely to say "yes" to a design, and then suffer the frustration of being unable to proceed with it.

The project had gone quiet for a while, but was re-invigorated by the enthusiasm of the Toyota representatives. In mid-November, Chapman looked at drawings with the lower cladding panels integrated into the top body, and with a Lotus 2.2 engine fitted in the M55 standard chassis. Sitting on 205 60 14 tyres, it would have been a rapid car – but also much more expensive. However, the 'Lotus-engined' variant always remained a possibility.

With the project now back on the rails, I took the opportunity of reviewing the vehicle layout, as the 1.6-litre engine needed packaging properly. Better still, was the Toyota offer of a smaller five-speed gearbox, and a more compact final drive unit. The final drive was unique to Japan, and would save space and weight over the units in the Excel. These remained unchanged, as, due to the power and torque of the Lotus 2.2-litre engine, it had to continue to use a larger and heavier final drive.

I was at the 1982 Motor Show in Birmingham, when Colin Chapman came back to the Lotus stand, and went into the private office. He was completely bewildered and very upset that American Express, who had significantly helped with Lotus funding, had turned down his request for finance for the M90. At first, he could not believe it, and then he became angry that it would not support the company's growth. I realised that it was a very worrying time for him, and that the M90 was still facing an uphill struggle.

That Motor Show was difficult, as I had to keep morale up among potential suppliers. Many had agreed to supply specific items for the M90, and were concerned at the lack of progress. Many were enthusiastic and helpful, but we were all getting very frustrated at the lack of forward progress. I had started talking to selected component firms, for the non-Japanese-sourced parts, many months before, with the promise of a rapid development programme. Phil Moss, of Wardle Storeys, was one of these. It was a supplier of trimming materials, and he was its designer. He spent a lot of time with me, helping to refine colours and textures, and providing fresh solutions to reduce the weight and cost of items, such as the lightweight sound

absorbers. He also provided a useful sounding board on industry design trends, hosting a lunch with David Basche, the ex-Rover Chief Designer, which I found most stimulating, as I was somewhat isolated in my locked room at Hethel.

By the beginning of December 1982, I showed Chapman the result of my reassessment of the package. By sweeping the front suspension crossmember forward of the engine sump, I could locate the lighter engine further forward. The steering rack moved back to a position behind the wheel hubs. The manual, and the relevant automatic, gearboxes were packaged, and gave a small increase in cockpit space, while the final drive was compact enough to allow the exhaust to run under it. The spare wheel moved to a vertical position in the luggage compartment – where Chapman felt it always should have been. The reduction in luggage space was acceptable as the deep-floored design had more than enough capacity.

Colin Chapman was much happier with these changes, which reduced the wheelbase by 176mm (6.93in) to 2308mm (90.86in). He obviously felt the car was much more on the lines he had always envisaged, without surplus bulk and weight. The cockpit toe board was now just forward of the back face of the front wheel housing, which allowed space for the pedals to stroke without cramping the width over their pads. A significant reduction in size meant the same for weight and cost. The project was truly back on track.

A week later, I came into the office about half-an-hour before the official starting time of 8:15am, as I usually did, to find Colin Spooner at his desk, ashen-faced. Assuming the worst, I asked him if the company had gone bankrupt. "No, worse," was his reply, as he asked for all his staff to assemble in the workshop. Colin Chapman had died earlier that morning, 16 December 1982, at his home, at East Carleton. Not a word was spoken. Slowly, we went back to our workplaces, speechless and dazed.

For all the staff at Lotus, the news was devastating. The local vicar held a short religious service in the main assembly hall, standing on wooden pallets. Everyone attended, and it was pretty emotional.

The funeral was at his local church, in East Carleton. The building was very small, so attendance was by invitation only. With his wide-ranging contacts in motorsport and industry, and his significance to the County of Norfolk, there were numerous high-ranking persons in attendance; there had to be limits to the number of Lotus staff attending. Wendy and I were privileged to be invited. The factory was closed for the day, as a mark of respect. The Bishop of Norwich conducted the service.

I had worked closely with Colin for the majority of

Part of the Toyota presentation – inside the Lotus Directors' Garage.

With Mike Kimberley (right), and an opportunity to view the M90 outside.

The Lotus Esprit (right) shows the compact size of the M90.

the previous eleven years. He was a very dynamic man, with wide-ranging interests. In the time I worked for him, he was involved with racing and road cars, luxury high-performance boats, racing hydroplanes (with his son Clive), and microlight aircraft. He possessed the art of understanding the foundations of what he was doing, and never forgot the basic rules of physics. He was an avid reader, and could absorb books in depth, rapidly, using them as a valuable source of information. Colin could be very patient, when new challenges were being developed, and would take time to explain the logic behind an idea. Some of these ideas were failures, and he knew the value of that: readily advising us from his long experience. Unlike Henry

With the M90 model outside the offices at Hethel.

Ford (reputedly), he had time for history, and used it to supplement his own experience.

He was very skilled at getting what he wanted from people. Colin could charm anybody when it suited, and he could be very tough when that suited, too. I had experience of both, but, if you were doing a good job, you somehow knew he realised that, regardless of his prevailing mood. I remember that when I first joined Lotus, it was having a bad racing season. I expected Colin to be in a frightful mood, the Monday after a race disaster. In fact, he was usually very contrite, but God help you when he was winning!

Blessed with a tremendous memory for detail, and a very broad knowledge of world affairs, his opinions were always worth listening to. He had impatience with the status quo, authority, and rules for the sake of them – and for products of engineers who 'always did it that way.' Colin was a stickler for tidiness – the factory, the back yard, the office desk, workshop, everywhere. The grounds of the factory and Ketteringham Hall were maintained to immaculate levels, as he did not believe you could do a quality job in a second rate environment.

Despite the pace that Colin demanded, I knew that his process steps had to be observed. They were derived from previous project errors, and were there to ensure that money was spent wisely. Like many successful entrepreneurs, he treated investors' money as his own, and would not take kindly to it being wasted. We could

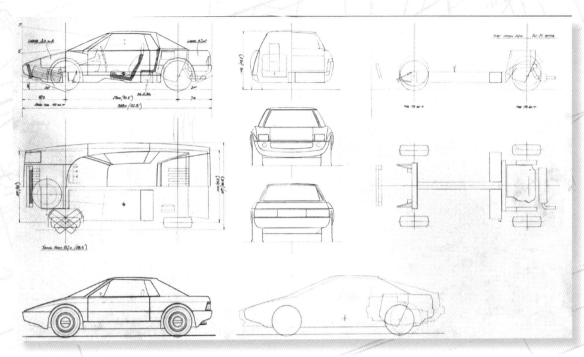

A mid-engined 2+2 concept, with either a Talbot Horizon or VW Golf engine, early in the project's history. The bottom right shows an outline comparison with the Lotus Esprit

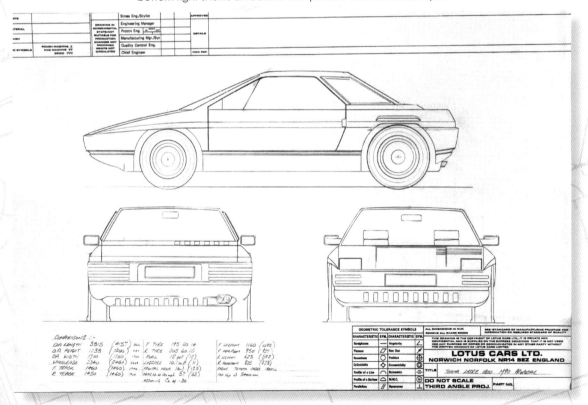

Another mid-engined 2+2 with a Toyota Lasre 1.8 powertrain, dated 25 May 1982.

The short-wheelbase 1.6-litre, 1:5-scale model coupé.

The short-wheelbase convertible 1:5-scale model.

sounds so logical today, and large companies have rigid processes, but it is surprising how many people want to charge on into the unknown, without all these 'ducks in a row.' He was a man who exuded enthusiasm, and relied on it to keep his staff. I never got rich financially working for him, but have no regrets. Never one to overpay for anything, his parsimony was part of his efficiency. It had been an enjoyable privilege to work for him.

As far as the M90 project was concerned, I am certain he would have preferred a mid-engined design, had Toyota had suitable components. Over the course of the project, I drew out a number of concepts, but they never got off the drawing board. We were not aware of Toyota developing its own mid-engined sports car, the MR2, but, if we had managed to move to that configuration, in my opinion, I fear Toyota would probably have advised us against it.

Despite the difficulty of packaging 2+2 seats in a mid-engined design, the wheelbase of 2340mm was only 32mm longer than the front-engined short wheelbase M90. The length of 3815mm was 87mm shorter overall, while the height was 42mm lower. This would have given a useful reduction in frontal area, and, probably, aerodynamic drag.

not proceed from scale models and layouts, without the parts cost, manufacturing process, schemes for market variants, and the dynamic performance predictions. It

Colin Chapman was much happier with the short-wheelbase models.

www.velocebooks.com / www.veloce.co.uk
Details of all current books • New book news • Special offers • Gift vouchers • Forum

115

Chapter 9

The car that never was – part 2

Lotus was now in serious difficulties. American Express wanted its money back, Chapman had gone, and the car business was in a serious recession. The staff were under no illusions that the company was fighting for survival. Lights were extinguished upon leaving a room, the telephone was used briefly, and only in the afternoon, when the rates were cheaper, even the stationary was used as sparingly as possible. Merchant bankers Guinness Mahan had to sign off the company accounts each month, to keep American Express on board – a lifesaving deal done by Fred Bushell, the long serving Finance Director – while the directors searched for new finance.

There was certainly no money for new projects, so Mike Kimberley put the M90 on hold. Chris Dunster returned to the Engineering Department, and I was left on my own in the project office. I sat down, and started to draw out the complete short-wheelbase car, in full-size. I completed

the general arrangement drawings, by 14 January 1983. The undertray was completed by 2 March, and the chassis assembly drawings by 1 April. I continued throughout the

The M90 project office at Hethel.

whole vehicle, body, fuel system, suspension, headlamp system and trim. I got a lot of useful help from Ken Sears on suspension and steering geometry, and trawled the company specialists for direction on many aspects. It was a slightly strange life, in a windowless room, alone. I was once so absorbed, that I stopped for lunch only to discover it was 3:30 in the afternoon!

I did a complete weight and centre of gravity analysis, and refined the parts list. New presentation books were created, and, during the summer of 1983, various potential investors were brought in to view the M90 display in the Directors' Garage. Among these was Sir Clive Sinclair. He did not become an investor, but he brought to the company his concept to develop an electrically-powered tricycle.

I worked on the concept for a week, before handing the papers to Colin Spooner, and asking to be excused that one. Colin Spooner put the work into his Engineering Department, and the Sinclair C5 trike eventually went into production. The rest is history, as the world failed to take to it.

Toyota was helping Lotus in it financial plight, giving it a V6 engine project, taking an equity holding in Lotus, and keeping the cash flowing, by paying its invoices instantly. By the summer, David Wickens of British Car Auctions brought along other investors, to create a majority holding in Lotus. This prevented Toyota from gaining control, and I have often wondered what would have happened if the Japanese had created a European Research Centre at Lotus. They were interested in Formula One and Le Mans, and had a genuine respect for the company's abilities.

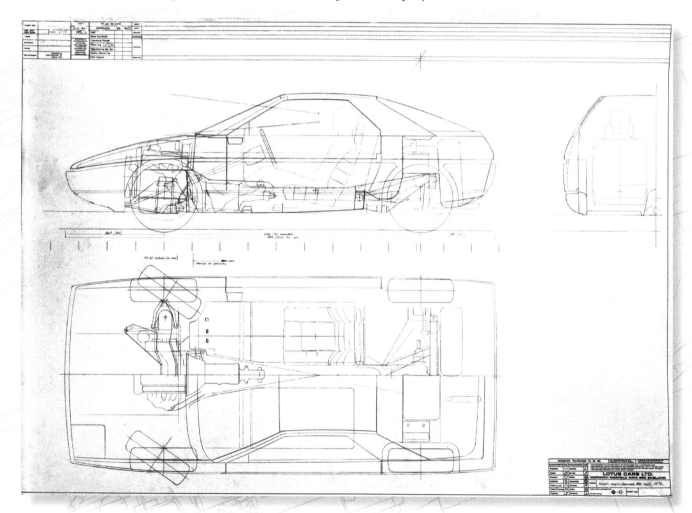

Throughout the project, we examined alternative ideas. This was a unitary construction glass fibre body, with steel sub-frames, using the general arrangement of the short-wheelbase M90.

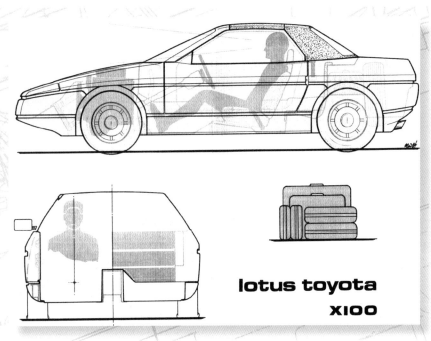

lotus toyota
X100

The Lotus M90 becomes the Lotus X100 (from the centre spread of the prototypes handbook).

Things were picking up at Lotus, when the 1983 Motor Show opened in London. Reading a report in the *Eastern Daily Press*, my local paper, I was astounded to see that David Wickens quoted as saying that the M90 was dead. I decided there was little point in going to the Hethel office, so I drove to London instead.

I found Mike Kimberley, who was shocked to hear the newspaper's story, and set off to find out if it was true. It transpired that Wickens had given an impromptu press conference at his hotel, and that, to stamp his authority on the project, it was now project X100. Mike said the car must be recognisably different to the M90, so I returned to Hethel, and remodelled the front bumper to be a positive slope, instead of an undercut. It did the trick politically. I was not so sure I liked it so much scenically! It made the front appear too long, as the eye followed it forward to its peak.

Don MacLauchlan worked hard on the company's public relations. He arranged for *Car* magazine to offer a newly-announced Excel as a competition prize. To make it more special, I was asked to customise its colour scheme. I followed the X100 route, and specified red on the upper half, and metallic grey below the body joint. The interior was in shades of grey leather, with red carpet. I also used Toyota alloy wheels.

As part of the long-term build up to the launch of the X100, Steve Cropley, the editor of *Car* was allowed to follow the project, under strict confidentiality. From his ongoing involvement, it was hoped that a true 'insider' piece of journalism would tell the full story, when the car was announced. Although this never happened, due to changing circumstances, he got started by spending a day with me. In combination with a feature on the special Excel being built for his magazine, we had an enjoyable time discussing the aims and aspirations for the new car. He also covered my chequered history, and the resulting interview was published in the December 1983 issue.

"Now an amusing, wry and somewhat well-used man of 39, Winterbottom is Lotus' 'head of design.' He's also become Britain's most prolific specialist designer of sports cars, though, because he's worked on plenty of vastly different projects, he probably wouldn't be content with the title. For the past several years, he's been at work on what is probably the greatest challenge of his life – breathing life into the Lotus M90, the 'second Elan' of 1985."

Cropley went on to record my past exploits, and finished on the M90 again. "One gets the impression that there have been hiccups in M90's progression, though Winterbottom, staunchly loyal, lets nothing significant slip. It's clear, though, that the M90 is his most carefully crafted car yet. They're building a mock-up now, to show investors – of money and old-fashioned faith – how the new Lotus will look …"

At the end of October 1983, David Wickens gave permission for a one-off prototype to be built. It would help raise money for the project. Lotus still needed about £7 million to complete the engineering, testing, development, durability, legal compliance, and for the tooling and factory expansion. Investors were more likely to get involved, if the car was drivable, instead of being a lump of wood and a book of good numbers.

I calculated that it would take £94,000, and five months to complete the prototype. The plan was approved, and work resumed in the Pattern Shop, which had to modify the undertray and the body patterns for the short wheelbase. The original model was of a coupé, and it was felt that the convertible would excite investors more, so I also had to detail that variant.

The Pattern Shop team had a formidable workload, as the only pattern which could go for mould-making,

The wooden patterns being modified for the short-wheelbase convertible.

unchanged, was the rear bumper. The undertray had to be shortened, and the revised transmission tunnel and boot floor incorporated. The front bumper needed to be modified, and the sills needed to be altered for the reduced wheelbase.

The bonnet also needed a total rework to be shortened, and a completely new convertible rear upper body had to be made. The door outer upper was new, as it was swept up to meet the rear deck, and the inner panel needed making from scratch. A boot lid was required with an inner panel. They took the windshield surround from the existing coupé model, with new detailing to accept the soft top, but had to build the firewall bulkhead to a new drawing. Finally, they had to build the rear cockpit bulkhead.

Meanwhile, in the Metal Fabrication Shop, Ted Fleet started to construct the steel backbone chassis. I had detailed each piece from the assembly drawings, and produced a blank shape drawing for them. Ted, an ex-Team Lotus fabricator, built up the structure on the surface table, carefully welding to reduce heat distortion effects to a minimum. He completed the frame in about three weeks, and it was given a quick paint in red oxide primer and gloss black, to contain basic corrosion. If it had been to production specification, it would have had a more thorough finish.

Keith Hare took on the job of vehicle assembly. Keith was a long-serving fitter in the Development Workshop. He was also made responsible for ensuring that the weight of every component was recorded before assembly. This involved the use of everything from the vehicle weighbridge for heavy items, to the mail room scales for the lightest. This, he did comprehensively, and a log was recorded.

The stores contained the three sets of Japanese components delivered the previous January. Ted Fleet went on to make suspension links, engine, gearbox and final drive mountings, to feed Keith with the parts, as needed. I attempted to release the components in the order required to make the build process as efficient as possible, and kept an eye on the overall timing and coordination of the work. Special steering arms were made for the 'behind the hub' rack position, and they were shaped to provide Ackermann effect on the wheels. Colin Chapman disliked using much Ackermann – the inside wheel turning more than the outer to maintain them on true radii. Lotuses had ploughed many a loose driveway on full lock in the past!

By 2 December 1983, the undertray was on the chassis, with the front and rear bulkheads in place. A substantial aluminium rectangular section was bonded and riveted to the sills, not only for beam stiffness of the car, but to also take the seatbelt lower loads.

X100 under construction 2 December 1983 with the chassis mounted to the undertray and bulkheads.

Andy Harrison started work in the experimental trim pen. He had to reduce and re-shape Eclat seat foams, and work up the vinyl and woven polyester textile covers. From time to time, he would cut and fit sound deadening and carpet to suit the build process. The sound deadening was by lightweight closed cell skinned polyethylene foam on the floor and in the luggage area. The firewall had a double layer of foam, and barrier mat, to prevent engine noise. Great care was taken to ensure there were no gaps or openings, as these would destroy most of its effect. The gearbox and the final drive had thick, spongy absorbers to soak up their noise emissions.

By the beginning of January 1984, the rear body was moulded and bonded to the undertray and bulkhead. This process of building up the body, as parts became available, was not the planned production sequence, but helped minimise the programme timing. Thanks to the accuracy of the work, there were no dramas fitting it all

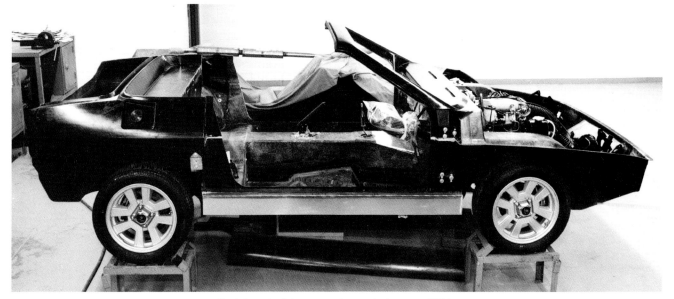

Prototype build progress by early January 1984.

together. John Page had joined Keith on the vehicle build, to look after all the fibreglass work. The fuel tank was under construction, in stainless steel, to replicate the weight of the proposed plastic one, and the same supplier, Langford, fabricated the exhaust system.

John Mountain had to design and build the vehicle wiring systems. I saw that as a black art, and John had, first, to fathom out the electrical principles of the Toyota components, before integrating them into a complete system. The wiring harnesses had to be built and installed in stages, to suit the build process, as most are hidden away under trim components.

The interior dashboard, console, door trim and instrument housing were all put on paper, and the patterns and moulds built at The Dove Company, in East Dereham, as the Lotus capacity for this work was already filled. I kept the design very simple, as, not only did the parts have to fit 'right first time,' but also Andy Harrison had to trim them in foam and vinyl, with little time for development.

The Pattern Shop continued to provide models to the Body Toolroom for moulds to be made for the glass fibre parts. Following the main body, details such as the headlamp pod inners, the heater intake plenum, ventilation ducts, fan shrouds, and the patterns for ABS vacuum-formed sheet mouldings, were all created. The fuel tank and battery had moulded covers, as did many small components such as the boot lock.

The little team had a couple of prestigious visits during the build period. Prince Michael of Kent, a great motoring enthusiast, came to Lotus informally a number

Discussing the X100 during the build with HRH Prince Michael of Kent (right) and Mike Kimberley (left).

of times. He was obviously very interested to see the little car grow, and spent some time discussing it. I remember that he could clearly recall the progress between visits.

On one of these informal tours of the workshop, he came across a prototype Sinclair C5. Climbing aboard, he accelerated down the workshop with his personal detective in hot pursuit, on foot, while everyone shouted instructions on to how to stop it! Neither he nor the machine came to any harm in the ensuing collision with the firmly shut workshop door.

X100 build progress on 2 February 1984.

By mid-February, the car looked nearly complete. The door inner panel mouldings were hinged and hung, and the window lift and guide system built and fitted. The Pattern Shop had made fixtures of the periphery of the glass parts, and St Gobain made six sets of windscreens and side windows. The number of pieces made reflected an insurance against breakage, and the development of the side glass system consumed a couple of sets. All the glass was laminated, including the side windows, to reduce tooling cost.

Andy Harrison was now developing the folding hood. I based it on the targa folding system I had developed on the TVR Tasmin. A rigid glass fibre centre roof panel was trimmed in vinyl hood material, had a soft lining, and carried rubber glass seals. The rear section consisted of a glass fibre hoop, pivoted behind the doors, and I added a refinement by having a supplementary steel support hoop running above the rear window, which folded automatically. The rear window was flexible PVC and the interior was lined with knitted nylon. When removed, the rigid roof panel fitted over the fuel tank, and consumed virtually no luggage space.

I wanted to be sure that every planned production part was on this prototype. I felt that anything less could send the wrong messages to Toyota and potential investors. Type approval and warning labels from other Lotuses were affixed in the relevant locations, the jack and wheel brace fitted, all external decal badging was designed, and, in the glove box, a handbook. All contributed to weight, packaging, and cost of the car, so they were all there. The only non-operational components were the exterior mirrors, which were rigid wooden models with real mirror glass. The investment in fully working ones was considered unjustified.

Some ingenuity was needed for some parts of the specification through low investment. Ford Fiesta reversing lights with a yellow bulb for the front direction indicators, and a clear one for the side lamps were used. The instruments came from the Opel Monza, modified with red lighting, and were adapted to the new input information. We used Toyota road and steering wheels, although the wheel was a bit cumbersome for the car, and the road wheels heavier than the bespoke items intended.

The handbook was written with real information. Although brief, it explained the operation of all controls, instructions on general maintenance of the mechanical and electrical systems, and the operation of the soft top. It carried a full technical specification, and comprised of 16 pages, in a bespoke silver and red cover. I had visions of VIPs taking the car away for trial and, being an untested 'one off,' getting marooned with a fault. Luckily, this never happened.

By the end of February 1984, the car was in the Service Department Paint Shop. They worked the whole weekend applying the silver two pack acrylic paint to the body, stripped of all locks, detail parts, and on slave wheels. It returned to the workshops for final build on the Monday morning.

First attempts to start the engine on the Wednesday were thwarted by a reluctance of the petrol pump to operate. Traced to a wiring misunderstanding, the car was ready to run the following evening. Accompanied by Colin Spooner, Ken Sears and, in case of trouble, Keith Hare, I covered 35 miles of the Hethel track with no problems.

We had done it! It was on time, and I believe it was about £1500 under budget. It was a fine example of a small team working together with no communications problems, in the traditional Lotus way. To say the team and myself were euphoric would be an understatement. It was a great landmark, after the frustrations since I had first put pencil to paper some 40 months earlier.

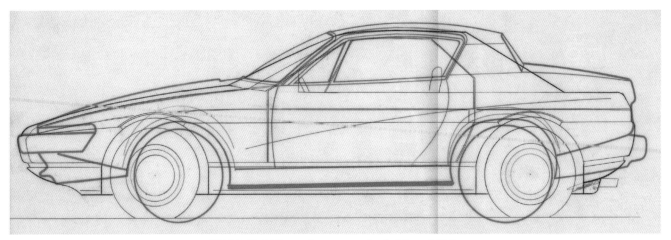

X100 (with M90 nose) compared with Triumph TR7.

Now we had done it, what had we got? The vehicle was 257mm (10.1in) shorter and 226kg (497lb) lighter than the Triumph TR7, but carried four people.

Overall length	3921mm	153.4in
Wheelbase	2308mm	90.9in
Overall width	1698mm	66.8in
Overall height, roof up	1187mm	46.7in
Ground clearance, exhaust	130mm	5.1in
Turning circle, kerbs	8.68m	28.5ft
Kerb weight	895kg	1973lb

The finished weight was influenced by at least 20kg of non-standard equipment. This included the solid wooden mirrors, the stainless steel fuel tank, the Toyota steering wheel, and alloy road wheels. The production intention was to design alloy wheels to the minimum structural requirement, with no concessions to style. They would be covered with very light plastic discs, modelled on the type seen in endurance racing at the time. With further work on the interior mouldings, chassis crossmember, roof panels and details, the design could easily have got down to the 850kg (1870lb) target.

The directors' brochure was photographed in a dismal March.

X100 overhead view.

The interior featured red and grey.

The X100 with its panels open, showing
the good engine access.

The brochure attempted to portray all the X100's features.

The semi-rigid convertible roof worked well.

X100 at Heydon Hall with my children in the rear seats.

Ron Middleton, of Focalpoint Norwich, returned to photograph the car – this time for real. The results were bound as a book. Directors got the large size, and lesser bodies the reduced edition. As seems often the case with new projects, they mature in the gloomy part of the year. A damp March is not the best month for flattering photography!

The car was presented to the directors. Perhaps due to the sudden relaxation of activity, I remember nothing of that event. The directors had a static viewing, and then drove on the test track, leaving with the facts and figures and their brochures. The company generously voted me a cash bonus (tax deducted!) for my efforts.

Shortly after the presentation, Ron Middleton hired a video camera. These were comparatively new at the time, and he rented a 'professional' one. Ron was the first to admit that he was a still photographer rather than a movie man, but a damp, dreary weekend was spent on the track at Hethel, recording small pieces of action. The results convinced senior management to invest in a professionally-made film of the car. The prime purpose was to try and avoid sending the X100 to Japan for Toyota's assessment, on cost grounds.

A small company in Norwich spent about a month making the film. Lasting 20 minutes, it thoroughly showed off the X100, and also included some historic company background. I, with Don MacLauchlan's help, arranged for a variety of historic road cars to be brought to Hethel for filming. These included a Type 14 Elite, which gave me the chance to drive one – 25 years after my visit to the Team Elite showrooms (see Chapter 1). Although only a very short experience, I loved it.

The finale of the film was a 'weekend away' in the X100. With Hazel Chapman's kind permission, arrangements were made to start a fictitious journey at her home, East Carleton Manor. To get the car there, early one Saturday morning, I drove it the two-and-a-half miles on the road – the only time it was ever out in public. After 'leaving' the imposing front door of the Manor, I drove down the long drive on a sunny but cool morning. The car was then loaded onto a trailer to reach the 'arrival' venue.

Haydon Hall in Norfolk co-operated, and the car was filmed on the estate roads, before turning up at the front of this magnificent building, and sweeping to a halt. The Hall's owner, Captain Bulwer Long, and his family 'met' the car, helped with the luggage, and we all went inside. Filming finished with a zoom-in on the car, bathed in cool spring sunshine. In the midst of enjoying a cup of warming coffee in the drawing room, we had to rush out and erect the soft top when the snow arrived!

The video was completed with professional voice-overs and music. Two copies were made in PAL, and two in SECAM, for use with Toyota and potential investors. The success of this film led to the company making a video of its current products and facilities, for general publicity.

With the car built and running, analysis of whether it met targets was made, and showed it was very close to predictions. On 2 April 1984, I wrote my first impressions of the car, entitled 'Initial Report X100 Prototype 01.'

X100 outside Heydon Hall, with my wife, Wendy, and children on board.

"The stainless steel exhaust system produces a pleasant sporting sound which unfortunately is some 4dBA over the legal requirement. The two main silencer boxes are only 30% packed with absorbent material, so development of a legal system should not prove difficult. The system does not transmit any vibration to the vehicle but a foul between the down pipes and the steering rack has been noted. Realignment to overcome this problem can easily be carried out. Exhaust fumes do not enter the cockpit with the hood down or erected.

"The light weight and good aerodynamics combine to produce an outstanding fuel consumption of 48 miles (78km) per gallon at 56mph (90kph). The 13-gallon (58-litre) tank fills to maximum with no blow back or frothing.

"The suspension settings have not been tuned, making the ride 'over damped' as a result of using damper settings from the much heavier Excel model. The car exhibits initial understeer on entering a bend but this can easily be neutralised by the application of power. The cornering performance is already similar to the Excel. Small ridges are absorbed very well on the tyre pressure setting of 22psi.

"The manual steering is light at all speeds and does not suffer kickback. A slightly quicker ratio may be desirable and requires investigation as the wheel rim load could easily be raised without disadvantage.

"The brakes have proved powerful and very light in operation suggesting that a smaller servo may be desirable. The front brakes lock first although no balance valve is used, and pull up straight every time. The handbrake holds the car easily on steep loading ramps.

"The driving position is comfortable with all the controls falling conveniently to hand. Visibility of the instruments is 100%. The large doors permit easy access to front and rear although a wider opening angle should be investigated. The hidden exterior door release handle works well but an improvement is required to assist gripping the door to pull it open.

"The front seats are very comfortable. The lever to release the tilting seatback is easy to use, located near the recline knob but can painfully intrude occasionally when entering the car and must be altered – it can also snag the seatbelt at times. Tilting the seatback forwards can operate the centre horn push on the steering wheel when the spokes are set centrally. Entry to thc rear seats is very good assisted by the sliding lower mounts of the seat belts. The seats can carry two children adequately while two adults may be carried for short journeys.

"The heater produces plenty of heat and airflow while the controls are easy to use and reach. The location of the window switches and cigar lighter on the tunnel top is convenient but relocating them in the centre of the dashboard would tidy up their appearance and reduce costs. The lockable glove compartment is very large, easily holding handbags and cameras, etc, but the lid is difficult to use and hold open.

"While the extreme corners of the car cannot be seen from the driving seat, the visibility is good with the car being easy to place on the road and easy to park. The single windscreen wiper provides a very good view while the side windows and soft top rear window stay free from running water. The side glass does not vibrate or get sucked free from the seal, up to 110mph. The interior stays free from draughts with the hood down, up to 110mph – the fastest speed yet tested.

"The beam strength of the structure is adequate with no problems of rattling door locks but the torsional stiffness of the bulkhead and the stiffness of the windscreen post/hinge post require improvement. The screen structure can take a load of 100kg (220lb) on the top corners with the hood down.

"OC Winterbottom 2nd April 1984."

	Lotus X100	Porsche 924	Mazda RX7	Triumph TR7
Engine capacity	1600cc	1984cc	2292cc	1998cc
Maximum mph (kph)	132 (214)	121 (196)	119 (193)	110 (178)
0-60mph (97kph)	7.5secs	9.3secs	9.0secs	11.2secs
Length mm (ins)	3921 (154.4)	4216 (166.0)	4318 (170.0)	4178 (164.5)
Width	1698 (66.8)	1684 (66.3)	1676(66.0)	1681 (66.2)
Height	1187 (46.7)	1270 (50.0)	1270 950.0)	1267 (49.9)
Weight kg (lb)	895 (1967)	1026 (2257)	1001 (2202)	1121 (2466)
Luggage capacity cu ft	8.2	4.8	4.7	9.3
Turning circle ft (m)	28.5 (8.68)	33.1 (10.08)	29.4 (8.96)	29.0 (8.84)

The prototype X100 in the MIRA wind tunnel, with a temporary coupé rear window. Drag figures are now lost.

I felt this was a pretty good first attempt with no serious issues, if the torsional stiffness of the structure could be improved. Later that year, I tackled that. So how did the car compare with its selected rivals?

Keith Hare and I recorded performance figures, using light beam recorder equipment on the test track at Hethel, but unfortunately the results are lost. I remember that all the acceleration times were better than predicted, and that interior noise recordings were comparable to a fixed-head motorcar.

All basic aspects of the performance were measured, and, on one occasion, brought near disaster. Keith and I were circulating the Hethel track, at speed, for cooling system checks. Approaching a sweeping bend at around 100mph (161kph), a large game bird rose from the trackside and hit the windscreen directly in front of my face. I flinched, and immediately saw the concrete fence posts on the inside of the bend rapidly approaching. Applying opposite lock, the car responded by leaving the outside of the bend, taking to the ploughed field – on its side. Keith and I hunched down, looking at each other, as the car came to rest on its wheels. Selecting reverse, we regained the tarmac, spreading tons of soil to mark the event.

Relieved that the vehicle had not turned over completely, we were amazed to find that the bird had escaped, although probably mortally injured. While Keith attended to the only damage, a deflated tyre, I hightailed it to Mike Kimberley's office to get my story in first. With the car back in the workshop, we found the only damage was a very small scratch on the corner of the front bumper, which was to remain untouched, as evidence, throughout the car's future at Lotus.

As far as performance and effectiveness went, the car looked pretty good. For the costing and pricing work,

Toyota sent one of its planning accountants over to assist us. Mr Nishiyama checked and double-checked all the calculations on tooling, factory facilitisation, material, labour and overhead costs. The formulae were looked at from every direction, paybacks extended and contracted. Every time we thought we had completed a solid financial model, he looked at them a different way.

Finally, the UK selling price was set at £9990 for the coupé and £10,490 for the convertible, and we were all confident that the car would make a useful profit. The profit percentage was slightly increased on the open car, which was now thought to be the higher volume variant, although its costs were very similar to the coupé.

The pricing exercise covered world markets, with France, Japan, Australia, and the USA all included. More powerful variants were also planned. Toyota had a tubocharged version of its 1.6 with a possible 75hp increase on the drawing board, and we looked at installing the Lotus 2.2 engine. Extras were planned, and included power steering, automatic transmission and air-conditioning.

The comparisons with the competition had changed, as the Triumph TR7 was out of production. In its place, we chose the new Mitsubishi Starion with a competitive 0-60mph of 7.5 seconds and a maximum of 130mph (211kph).

Mazda RX7	£9599
Lotus X100 Coupé	£9990
Lotus X100 Convertible	£10,490
Porsche 924	£11,495
Mitsubishi Starion	£12,499

Checking the car on the Hethel track, before shipping to Japan.

Carefully packed for the flight to Japan.

If all proceeded to plan, we thought we'd cracked it: value, performance and practicality, with low cost of ownership. I was most keen that the car was not expensive to run and maintain, to maintain customer loyalty and satisfaction.

Despite our best hopes, the video idea didn't stop Toyota wanting the car in Japan. So, at the end of June 1984, it was loaded onto a pallet, fuel system purged with nitrogen, and covered with a black fabric shroud for secrecy. In the glovebox was the handbook, and, in the boot, the luggage.

I flew out to Toyota Technical Centre near Nagoya on 11 July 1984. Our contact, Sam Shimada, took me to the Toyota Castle Hotel, where I was resident for the following three weeks. Various meetings with Toyota engineers, to explain the specification and try to find more components, culminated in a unique event.

Toyota had eight styling studios, each dedicated to a particular vehicle line, which had never come together for a single presentation, until the Lotus was put on show on the roof of the studios. Sam was having lunch with me just prior to this event, when he casually mentioned that I would have to present the car to all the senior heads of the Toyota design studios. Not having been forewarned, or done any preparation, I felt somewhat apprehensive, and Sam emphasising the gravity of the event did not help. Direct entry to the studio buildings was forbidden, and I was taken through miles of corridors to reach the roof, without seeing any of the design studios' work.

In the event, the show went well. There were many positive comments from the studio heads, and I managed to get them to write a report on their views. They suggested softening the corners, reducing the slope on the rear of the side glass and shortening the nose. Although these changes would reduce the extremeness of the design, I welcomed them as being a positive stamp of approval. Once the styling viewing was complete, the prototype went to Toyota's proving grounds.

I made a number of visits to Toyota's suppliers and learned a lot. Toyota asked some interesting questions on the issue of whether Lotus engineers would be comfortable working in Japan. I thought that could be difficult, unless some sort of ex-patriot community was set up, as it would be impossible to drive, or even do basic shopping, unless one knew the language. Toyota City was remote; far from the more cosmopolitan larger cities.

I also visited Toyota Motor Sales offices in Tokyo. I stepped from the air-conditioned bullet train and took the more basic suburban railway to its office. The summer weather was very hot, and I had on a suit, tie and jacket on. By the time I reached the office, I was bathed in sweat from head to toe – in fact, it looked as if I had been in a shower with all my clothes on. I was politely shown a rest room and given a fine towel. After washing and drying myself as best I could, I offered back the towel. "Please accept it as a gift," they said!

The following day, I was offered a drive in the new Toyota MR2, with a young salesman. He drove me down to Yokohama Chinatown, where we had a fine lunch. After lunch, we went to see the Great Buddha, at Kamakura. This was a second visit for me, but I suspected they wanted me to realise the similarity of girth between us! While we were there, we drove up a narrow side street, until the mirrors of the MR2 touched both sides. Reversing carefully, I realised why Japan had a width limit on vehicles.

Giving me the keys to drive back to Tokyo, the salesman fell asleep in the passenger seat. Unable to read the road signs, I navigated by the direction of the sun. I got us well into the evening rush hour traffic jams, before my guide awoke, surprised to find that I was only

The multi-studio styling viewing at Toyota City.

two blocks from the hotel. The car was great, especially the gearshift, but the traffic was so bad, it was a limited experience, with no opportunity of really getting to explore its performance.

Toyota returned the car to England, flying it to Heathrow from Tokyo. When it arrived, Customs demanded an astoundingly-high duty payment of over £12,000. As it had cost under £4000 to send it out to Japan, I contested this, only to discover that international airfreight does not work on the basis of a journey one way being the same in reverse – it all depends on take off and landing charges. Customs then demanded to know why I was smuggling suitcases. Not realising the contents of the boot should have gone on the shipping manifest, it was a case of pay up or lose them. We elected to kindly donate them to HM Customs, who gained one case with a large hole in it, where Lotus development foreman, John Freeman, had drilled through it to release the boot lid when the lock failed.

Upon my return to the office, work progressed to move the project forward. A chap was brought in to plan it in detail, and covered acres of graph paper, with the timing for every event needed to bring the car to production.

I spent a lot of time discussing the opportunities offered by computer-controlled modelling and drawing, with Chris Dunster and Ron Warke. I had little experience of these techniques, but they had seen tremendous improvements in both speed and accuracy, when working on the DeLorean project. Our challenge was to prove there would be a net cost saving. We all believed there would be, but the investment was high compared to the slower, old hand-crafting methods.

Ken Bell, an old Lotus hand, returned to the company to plan the production process details. Thyssen, in Germany, was contacted as potential chassis suppliers. I was all set to visit Thyssen, but this was cancelled at the last minute by my senior management, with no explanation – which alerted me to some potential funny business.

Jerry Booen also joined us in the project office. Jerry was ex-Team Lotus, and was to be a significant player at Lotus for some years to come. He and I sat down to improve the torsional stiffness. The car was not that bad, better than the convertible Tasmin, but it was not up to Lotus, or our, expectations. Of course it had been over ten years since the company had made an open-topped vehicle, and the automobile structural yardsticks had been extended in that time. We came up with a perimeter frame, in steel, cantilevered from the backbone, to replace the bonded aluminium boxes in the prototype sills. We had sawn the roof off an old development Excel – it took about 20 minutes – and studied the effects of various alternative body mounts. We made the most progress linking the foot and toe boards to the frame, which gave us the evidence for the perimeter structure.

Mike Kimberley and Colin Spooner were trying to get us to engineer a glass fibre structure. I suggested that the physical properties of steel were multiples better than glass fibre, and significantly better than aluminium. The steel perimeter frame had a net weight penalty of 2.5kg. I felt that was a small price to pay for a significant improvement. Much of the pressure to use materials other than steel was driven by the desire to make the specification more exotic. With the paucity of major structural space on the convertible, this could have led to a long development exercise.

As well as the frame stiffness, the car needed an improved rear door post structure. I had originally designed a simple rear bulkhead to run straight across, behind the rear seats. A new design, acting, in plan view, as an arched horseshoe, would link the door jambs much better. I modified the front hinge post in detail, and proposed a de-mountable cross-tubular structure to run over the engine.

A modified Excel chassis was built up with the perimeter frame, and tested. It met the targets suggested, but had little charisma. It was not ever put into the car, which

A Lotus Excel frame with perimeter extensions under torsional test.

Toyotaka Ikeda in the X100, at Hethel on his world trip.

design. They made visits to Norwich to observe clothing, furniture and general design trends in the shops. It was this attention to international tastes that helped the Japanese to move their products in export markets so successfully. Toyotaka and I got on very well, and we had a stimulating few days together. I was most flattered to receive a letter from him after the event, in which he wrote "The meeting in your office I shall long remember for its excellence and it was one of the most impressive times I have spent in Europe." Toyotaka maintained Christmas contact for a number of years, and I would have enjoyed working with him more, if circumstances had permitted.

had undergone some suspension development upon its return from Japan. This development had highlighted the torsional problem under extreme conditions, and possibly influenced some people's views. It might have been better to have fixed the structure first.

Early in October, Colin Spooner invited me to join him on a visit to Italdesign in Turin. It had built a show car based on an extended-wheelbase Esprit chassis, with the intention that it would become a Lotus V8-powered successor. We went to Ital's new headquarters in Moncaleri, and Guigiaro greeted me as a long lost friend. I was delighted to meet him again, and most flattered by his reception. The Etna was on display in the factory yard. Guigiaro seemed less than 100% happy with the car, and spoke to his staff in Italian about a number of aspects of it. I felt the glazing solution to the rear window was a bit contrived, but some of the ideas eventually re-emerged in the revised Esprit, some years later. The interior was fabulous, but sadly the car never got beyond the exhibition stage.

October, and the 1984 Motor Show was held in Birmingham: Toyota had asked if I would host a visit by three of its designers. I was delighted to do so, and escorted them round the show, discussing the finer points of the displays. Upon leaving, they picked up their stored luggage and I was horrified to see the amount. They had plenty, as they were on a world trip lasting some time. I had my company Lotus Sunbeam in the car park and eventually got everything in, but the uncomplaining rear passengers were under a lot of bags.

Led by Toyotaka Ikeda, Chief Styling Designer, they were on a world trip to research all aspects of taste and

A couple of times that autumn, Colin Spooner had asked me to supply him with copies of various Toyota drawings. This was difficult, as they were all strictly rationed to one copy, for security. A replacement would only be forthcoming if the original went back to Japan. I began to wonder what the purpose of these bits of information was, as no explanation for their supply was offered.

In October, I was asked to build another full-size model, a bit more up-to-date, as everyone was getting bored with the shape. I had already got some direction from the Japanese designers, so I had some ideas as to what to do. I was, however, very unhappy at being told it was to be in polystyrene foam. I had no experience of this as a medium, but knew it could not be painted. Colin Spooner found a modeller experienced in this, John Chittenden, who turned out to be a first class chap.

We worked together building this shape in matt white foam, which incorporated the trends suggested. One side was finished as a convertible, the other, the coupé. We were both aware of an 'atmosphere' as we proceeded, being left alone to get on with it, without any interest from anyone else.

While visiting Llanelli Radiators, in South Wales, to discuss the cooling system, I was asked to call on Peter Stevens at the Royal College of Art, in London, on the way home. This I did, and found Peter very interested in the X100. I put my philosophies across with some unease, but left hoping all was under control. Peter had done work for Colin Spooner on the Excel, but had remained off site, so we had not met before. What I learned, years later, was

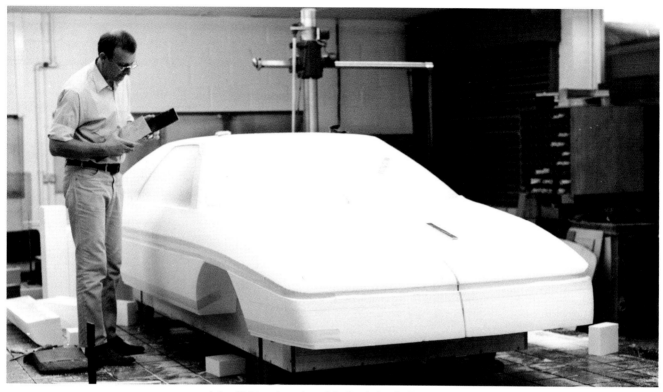

John Chittenden at work in the Lotus Pattern Shop.

that Peter had made a model for the X100 some months before – without my knowledge. That he assumed I knew of this, did not make the meeting any easier. Peter's model was a two-seater – it seemed his information was different to mine. The 2+2 layout had been a project 'given' requirement.

After Christmas 1984, John Miles, the ex-Team Lotus Grand Prix driver, became involved in the project. His opinion was that rear-wheel drive was not usual in cars anymore, and that there were many motorists who had never driven anything but front-wheel drive. He felt that as an affordable sports car, the X100 should

The rival X100, after delivery to Hethel from Italy, 11 February 1985.

have familiar and safe handling –and, to him, this meant front-wheel drive.

He arranged a trip to the Goodyear test track in Luxemburg, so that Jerry Booen and I could form our own opinion. A rear-wheel drive Toyota Corolla GT and a front-wheel drive Peugeot 205 were at our disposal. After John used his skill to demonstrate both cars' abilities, we had the track to ourselves. I found the front driver much easier to take to the limit, which Jerry and I thoroughly enjoyed for most of a morning. However, I wondered if it was all quite fair. The Toyota was not a bad car, but the Peugeot was one of the best of its type. This heavily influenced subsequent events.

At the end of January 1985, I was informed there would be a presentation of the polystyrene model, and that there would be another competitor. I got the white foam slab into the Directors' Garage and was putting the finishing touches to it, when a truck arrived. A full-size model of a front-wheel drive two-seater coupé was unloaded. It had been made by Colin Spooner and Peter Stevens, at CECOMP in Italy – that was why they wanted the Toyota drawings in the autumn.

I felt devastated; here I was, in competition against a fully-painted car with a new driveline configuration and seating layout of which I had been kept unaware. Apart from the biased aspect of the visual presentation, I was upset at the total change of mechanical configuration. I was, after all, the Project Manager of the 'affordable sports car' programme. I was also rather sad, given the long relationship that I'd had with my senior management, that I was the last to know of this development among my Hethel colleagues. I suspect the secret was a strain on some of them.

My polystyrene model was shown with matt black windows and black tape for shut lines. Of course the matt white finish had no reflections or highlights on its surfaces, and no contrast or deep shadows. Its shape was the culmination of the idea. The rival was loosely based on Guigiaro's Lotus Etna show car. Not in the least surprised, given the clues over the preceding weeks that something was afoot, I left for home knowing that I had lost the vote at the presentation, before it had even begun.

I sat down and wrote a Private and Confidential letter to Mike Kimberley. In it, I asked for an explanation of why there had been so much going on behind my back. The response was rapid. He passed the issue to Colin Spooner,

The finished polystyrene foam model, in February 1985.

The polystyrene foam did not show highlights or reflections.

who discussed the letter with me; the outcome was that I decided to resign.

Naturally, I was not very happy and my conclusions, many years later, are this: I believed I had done a good job under less than easy circumstances. The company grew tired of the car, because it had been around in one form or another for some time. The outside world hadn't seen it, though. I worked hard to get the company a marketable and profitable product. I have seen criticism since, that it was not technically advanced enough. So what? I believe most of the car-buying public don't care what their car is made of, or how it delivers, but just want what it delivers. Later experience suggests that by moving into unconventional technology, a project could be made more expensive and riskier for both manufacturer and customer.

I knew the M90/X100 was competitive on price, had excellent performance, and was a very usable package for passengers and their baggage. A lot of thought had been put into low cost of ownership. Others thought that Lotus Cars should be a showcase for Lotus Engineering.

I was subsequently fascinated to see that rear-wheel drive sports cars had not disappeared. Mazda's MX5 Miata has been a huge success, and is not unconventional or technologically advanced.

The Lotus M90 finally happened, when the new front-wheel drive Elan (M100) was announced, in the autumn of 1989, nearly five years, and many millions of pounds, later. It was notable that it had a steel backbone chassis with prominent steel reinforced sills, outrigged from the central structure. If we had taken the computer-aided development route, the market could have enjoyed the X100 at least three years earlier.

Factoring the selling price of my X100 to 1989, the year the M100 Elan was announced, the convertible would have sold for £14,400. The Elan M100 naturally aspirated was priced at £17,850, and Turbo model £19,850. The X100 actually undercut the Mazda MX5 by £550. It also was quicker, to 60mph, than all but the M100 Elan Turbo.

X100 at Heydon Hall, Norfolk, before the snow in March 1984.

Chapter 10

Cadillac, Oldsmobile and the USA

So I had left Lotus again. My colleagues were sympathetic; one of them suggested that I contact a company called Hawtall Whiting. I did so, and went to discuss the possibility of working in the United States, as it already had contractors there. Hawtall Whiting explained that the remuneration was reasonable, there was no tax to pay, and also detailed the living costs that one might reasonably expect. I signed on to work with General Motors, in Detroit, as a body engineer.

I flew to Detroit, via Toronto, on 24 March 1985. I already had a visa to allow me to visit the United States on business. However, the family couldn't join me until they had the relevant visas.

There were few people are on the flight to Toronto; there, customs and emigration procedures were carried out on behalf of the American government. Detroit had become increasingly inaccessible for English engineers, and the immigration authorities could sometimes be very obstructive.

Hawtall Whiting had promised to have someone meet me. Not for the last time, promises did not seem to go quite as planned. Failing to find the welcoming committee, I got a taxi to the Coventry Inn, opposite the General Motors Technical Centre, and checked in.

Early the following morning, I crossed the road to the Technical Centre, where I was asked to wait in reception. This I did – for about two hours. Eventually, I was introduced to a young man who informed me that I would not be working at the Technical Centre, but would be working 'off site,' a few miles away. Because of this, I would need transport; this had already been arranged – a Ford Escort. I was a bit unhappy about this, as I had hoped

to be able to build up some cash reserves in the first few weeks by dispensing with road transport, in order to be able to set up home for my family.

The young man, Brian Backman, explained that the Ford was the cheapest rental car they could find; cheaper than anything from General Motors! I followed him across the city to a smart new office building located in Stirling Heights, where Brian introduced me to my new boss, John Peck. John worked in the Buick Oldsmobile Cadillac (BOC) Specialty Vehicle Activity: a new group set up to deal with low-volume and niche vehicles. John needed an assistant, and it was felt that my experience in the low-volume business in Europe would be ideal. I was to assist John as a programme manager, a role in which I had much more experience.

Most of the low-volume projects were carried out in liaison with subcontractors, to prevent them affecting GM's technical resource or manufacturing efficiency. John had a number of projects under his control, including the Cadillac Deville Touring Car with the ASC Corporation, and the Buick Grand Sport project. The department covered many low-volume vehicles, such as the Buick Reatta and the Cadillac Allante, plus the stretch-wheelbase Cadillacs converted at Hess and Eisenhardt, just around the corner

To relieve John of some of his workload, I was to concentrate on the Deville Touring Car. This Cadillac was an attempt to Europeanise the company's high-volume model, with assertion that it was for "… the people who find it fun to drive, so they want a little more out of driving than comfort alone. They want a car that lets them hug the road a little more closely."

The Cadillac Deville was built in huge numbers, at the Lake Orion plant, north of Detroit. The covered area of the factory exceeded 80 acres (32 hectares) and had a railway line through the centre of it for parts deliveries. Apart from the difficulties of finding my way around, the presence of robotic Tallus trucks prowling the walkways was unnerving. Although they had sensors to prevent them from mowing down a pedestrian, I never trusted them.

The Cadillac was a spacious, unitary-bodied, front-wheel-drive V8 four-door sedan or two-door coupé. Most of the Touring Car changes to the Deville were cosmetic; grey plastic cladding on the lower parts of the body, fog lamps in a front air dam, and a small rear spoiler. The interior, trimmed in grey leather had the steering wheel and major controls finished to match.

The suspension was slightly stiffened, with revised damper settings and a bigger rear anti-roll bar. The contemporary literature claimed that the firm ride and responsive steering "… do not bully the road. Instead, they conquer it more with subtle finesse and quiet confidence in their abilities." Unfortunately, it was not in the least 'European.' The 4.1-litre engine was left untouched, with a lazy 130bhp, so it still drove much the same as the standard product. Somewhere, the product planners had missed the point of what the best from BMW, Mercedes et al, offered.

An administrative chore that needed to be done was to open a bank account. It had to be at the National Bank of Detroit, due to my immigration status. One amazing aspect was that they gave me an immense box, with at least a dozen chequebooks in it. They must have had a very optimistic view of the level of financial activity I was likely to achieve.

A couple of days after my arrival, everyone was called into the conference room. The buildings were new, so it was to hear about the precautions needed in case of a tornado. I was not familiar with these powerful events, and was quite horrified when the emergency authorities described the full force that they could produce. They reinforced their message with films and pictures, one of which showed a huge railway locomotive that had been lifted from its tracks.

The Specialty Vehicle Activity had not been in these offices for very long, so the authorities searched the buildings to find the best place to shelter. Their conclusion was that we should all go to the toilets, because the pipes were the strongest things in the building. It would have been a strange place to become familiar with new friends, in times of dire emergency.

The Cadillac Deville Touring Car.

The Cadillac Deville Touring Car did not seem very 'European' to me.

This meeting was a great opportunity for me to meet some of my other colleagues. Gerry Mahoney was head of the department; supported by Dave Clark as his right-hand man; and Vic Fontana in the purchasing role. They all had long histories with the Fisher Body Division of GM, and I think many resented the absorption of that old company into the corporation.

Not long afterwards, I had to join John Peck on a visit to the ASC plant at Lancing, Michigan. At this plant, ASC converted fixed-roof vehicles, supplied by the nearby GM plant, into Buick Riviera convertibles. The removal of the fixed-head roof was spectacular to watch.

I also had to go to the ASC headquarters, south of Detroit. This provided me with my first view of the skyscrapers in a large American city. I found the buildings very exciting, and, later, when I visited Chicago, got through rolls and rolls of photographic film on the same subject.

The late Heinz Prechter had started the ASC business in California, developing sunroofs and, later, vinyl roof toppings. The major manufacturers liked the idea of being able to easily customise their products, and soon he had a major business going. As an expansion of this, ASC had moved into more sophisticated niche models for all the Big Three American manufacturers. It had become well known for its convertibles, and was able to count Toyota among its foreign clients.

Tom Hughes, working for Art MacNee, ran the Cadillac programme, and I spent many hours in meetings with them. General Motors seemed able to hold bigger and longer meetings than I had ever known before. One serious problem emerged during the low-volume discussions. The role of Specialty Vehicle Activity was to ensure that the subcontractors designed and built the vehicles to conform to General Motors quality standards. GM marketed the finished products alongside the regular production offerings.

The problem was that the quality staff at General Motors had never worked on such a low-volume project before. They therefore demanded extensive long-term tests, using literally hundreds of prototypes. This was unrealistic, as the project was only due to last two years, with a production of around 3000 vehicles per year. I took up the task of explaining and negotiating this with the General Motors, and, in due course, managed to get the acceptance qualifications to be within more reasonable levels.

I also found that there was something of a confrontational relationship between GM and its subcontractors. It was terrified the contractor might be making a fast buck out of it. This was the opposite of the trust I had seen between Japanese companies and their subcontractors. Later in my stay in America, I was able to move the relationships into a much better position.

As liaison managers, the Specialty Vehicle Activity brought all the needs of the Corporation together. I had to work with the sales and product staff, the plant management, planners and quality personnel, and the engineering release staff at the GM Technical Centre. I then had to ensure that ASC could satisfy these demands, and negotiate any differences which arose. It meant a lot of travel, which was generally very easy, with the exception of during downtown rush hour.

The Cadillac project was not going particularly well, as ASC's own subcontractor, making the RRIM plastic add-on panels to fit on the lower body, was struggling to achieve the dimensional requirements. The attitude of the man who ran this small operation was very aggressive. At one point, he even refused to allow either General Motors or ASC personnel into his plant, despite extensive offers of help from both companies.

The shortage of panels to supply the pre-production build of the Cadillac led to its delay, and the same issue delayed production start-up. An amusing aside to this was the name that GM gave to the RIM deformable plastic bumper covers – flubber!

A job for the weekends was searching for somewhere to live. Hawtall Whiting had told me that a monthly rental of around 700 dollars would secure a pleasant apartment. Visiting a number of real estate offices, I soon found that 700 dollars didn't secure anything.

I was becoming quite desperate, when somebody suggested that I take a look over to the west of the city, where the landscape was dotted with many lakes. Although this was a much more expensive area, it was also a much more suitable area to bring a family with children, although the monthly rental cost $500 more than my guide budget. Eventually, I found a three-bedroom rental house in West Bloomfield.

My working visa and the family's linked ones were taking a long time to process in London, and I was becoming increasingly frustrated over this. In early May, Tony Rudd visited Detroit, and invited me to dinner. I enjoyed the opportunity to catch up on old times, and was quite emotional, when he brought gifts from my family, whom I had not seen for quite a long time. I had to drive back to the Coventry Inn in pouring rain, in the dark, with no cats eyes – a most unpleasant experience. Telegraph Road is about six lanes wide, each way, and, under those circumstances, it appeared as a wide reflective sheet of water. Trying to maintain good lane discipline on something that looks like Lake Windermere proved both dangerous and difficult.

Notice that the visas would be ready for collection finally came through. It meant a flight home to collect my family, and the visas from the American Embassy in London. Sadly, while there, we had our luggage stolen from the parked rental car. The next day we had a good flight to Detroit – a first for the children. In due course, we were allowed to enter the United States. It was 18 May 1985.

Work proceeded at Lancing to get ready for the production of the Cadillac, and I made quite a number of visits to the plant. However, the saga of the ill-fitting plastic panels continued, with extensive laboratory testing carried out day and night.

I had to make a number of visits to the General

Motors Technical Centre. This was a huge complex, the site measuring one mile by one mile. It included its styling complex, research laboratories and the massive engineering block. Finding my way around was not easy, and there were whole rooms filled with experts on such exciting parts as armrests, glovebox doors – in fact, every detail part of an automobile.

Working in the Specialty Vehicle Department, I had to learn to write my reports in American English. One particular issue was my use of the word 'fixing.' At Lotus, it was used to cover general nuts, screws, washers, bolts, etc, but, for the Americans, it had something to do with 'arranging things,' not a subject they wanted me to suggest in a report. Great care had to be taken with all written documents, as courts investigating liability cases had the power to subpoena them.

Another aspect of the Corporation I found interesting was the total belief that everything it did was perfect. On one occasion, I saw a senior executive park a new Jaguar. He joined me in an elevator. I asked what he thought of it, and got the reply "a bunch of junk." Upset, I explained my past connection with the famous concern, and that I doubted it was junk. He couldn't offer anything more specific to expand his opinion. I believe he was really just 'being corporate.'

From time to time, the department was loaned competitors' vehicles for comparison. I had the use of a number of them, and remember being very impressed with the Honda CRX coupé. Despite its size and sporty characteristics, it was a delight to use after the softer home grown products I was becoming used to.

The Mercedes 280SL was, however, a disappointment. It was rather soft and had lazy performance, but it was the plethora of rattles, and general instability of its structure, which really surprised me. (Perhaps the Lotus X100 hadn't needed any structural improvement at all!) I had been looking forward to driving it, as it was a car I aspired to. I did not enjoy driving the big Cadillacs, as I found the overall softness detracted from all driving pleasure because you were totally divorced from what it was doing – although the comfort levels were superb.

Less pleasant was the announcement by Hawtall Whiting that all British contractors would have to pay income tax. The US authorities had finally woken up to the fact that there were hundreds of foreign contractors in the city, not the handful originally anticipated, and some of them had been there quite a few years. The long-termers had to get out. The Inland Revenue Service froze their bank accounts, and put demands for tens of thousands of dollars back tax upon them. They left. For me, it meant 30% of my pay was immediately withheld, and that I

owed back tax on everything I had earned to date – quite a serious cut. As I also had to pay State property taxes, and medical insurance, a lot of money was going out.

It certainly seemed draconian, and a little unfair to render back tax, as it was the Internal Revenue Service that had waived it in the first place. As time went by, many of the contract activities moved over the Detroit River to Windsor, Ontario, the Canadians being more supportive of the industry.

9 September 1985, one month late, the GM Lake Orion Plant started building the base vehicles for ASC to convert to Touring Cars. John Grettenburger, Head of Cadillac, came to see the sparsely filled line at ASC Lancing three days later, and was not very happy with the delays – all caused by one weak subcontractor.

At the beginning of October 1985, the Specialty Vehicle Activity took delivery of a concept car from Oldsmobile. To be called the 98 Touring Car, it was to include more comprehensive changes than had the Cadillac. Besides the plastic lower cladding panels, the body had a chrome spear moulding along each flank, and the interior had very advanced seating, developed by Lear Siegler, which allowed for every conceivable adjustment. The door trim was new, as was a centre console. The steering wheel and instrumentation was upgraded, and a floor-mounted transmission selector specified. A rear spoiler, front fog lamps and revised rear lighting was set off with new cloisonné (enamel) emblems. Stiffer suspensions made this four-door sedan, on a similar platform to the Cadillac, perform in quite an acceptable manner.

Five companies responded to the invitation to bid for the engineering and production conversion work. John Peck was busy with a number of other projects, and I was asked if I would take the job on, as manager. I was delighted, but a little apprehensive of falling foul of the American anti-trust laws, in place to ensure I was scrupulously fair to each contender.

The concept car was presented to all the bidders, simultaneously, on the afternoon of 22 October 1985, so everyone had identical information. Any subsequent questions during the bid preparation time had to be relayed, with the answers, to all the bidders. I had to present the car to the plant management at Lake Orion to get its production planning started. It would be building the base car on its production line, with the uprated suspension, but with many of the Touring unique parts missing, ready for the converter to assemble subsequently. The cars would have to drive off the production line, so a slave seat and steering wheel were arranged. The production lines could not build the complete specification of this limited edition, as their assembly stations were tuned to the standard

A brochure shot of the Oldsmobile 98 Touring Car.

specification vehicles. For instance, the seats were far more time-consuming to mount and fit, so would have gone far past the assigned line stage, if done in the plant.

The afternoon of Friday 8 November 1985 was exciting, as the bids came in. Two companies withdrew, leaving three to choose from. Strangely, one of these refused to break down its submission in the manner we requested, so that left two. The following morning, I discussed the quotes with Gerry Mahony, Dave Clark and Vic Fontana, and was asked for my final choice. I chose not the cheapest, but the one I trusted to deliver a good project. That was ASC.

After the many delays the Cadillac Touring Car had suffered coming into production, ASC held a full post mortem, with the participation of the Special Vehicle Department. Many detail issues were reviewed, and new procedures adopted. One issue that I was keen to resolve was the relationship between the contractor, ASC, and the client, General Motors. I preached the dogma I had learned from my Japanese experiences: that the project should be to the benefit of both parties. If successful, they would both make money; if not, their competitors would be the beneficiaries. I therefore became a part-time member of the ASC team, as well as being the General Motors representative. This worked well in practice, as I participated in the 'private' ASC weekly project review: then, a few days later, in the GM project review. If there

were any issues that I could help resolve with corporation assistance, then I obtained it. I worked hard to ensure there were no conflicts of interest to give one party the business advantage.

Art MacNee put a young man, Don Wallace, in the position of ASC programme manager. All the design work was done on Catia CAD terminals at ASC's Southgate, Michigan headquarters. Dale Paes put Jim Sherrill in as the manufacturing engineer on day one, to ensure that the build process would be achieved within the planned financial targets.

I was in the ASC design office one day, when people started to ask why the building was shaking. I managed to miss this phenomenon, but soon learned 'I had survived the Detroit earthquake.' Centred a few miles away, in northern Ohio, it had enough power to empty supermarket shelves, although not enough for me to notice it!

The plastic body cladding panels were given much thought, in view of previous project difficulties. Contour Plastics took on the moulding of these, with Lear Seigler responsible for the seats, Norriss Industries the console, and Irvin Industries the door trim, so there was plenty for me to co-ordinate. All these parts had to meet the approval of the engineers in the Oldsmobile Division, while the C/H Vehicle Platform team at Flint, Michigan, oversaw the details.

Dave Fletcher was the special vehicle manager in Flint,

and had a team of 18 specialists to support him. They ranged from vehicle build co-ordinators to specialists for each detail part. I had regular meetings with them, which filled a very large room with a lot of people, although most said little or nothing. My biggest challenge was understanding what one engineer from the Deep South, USA, was saying, as his accent was so thick. After the meeting, I used to call Fletcher to get a translation.

The winter weather in Michigan could be very severe. I had to rise very early in the mornings. My alarm clock went off at 20 past five in the morning, and I would be in the office just after six. One day, I set off with the temperature at minus 28° Fahrenheit (minus 33.3°C). I had left my gloves in the car overnight, and, putting them on as I drove, I nearly screamed with the pain, they were so cold.

General Motors were good at keeping staff trained, and the department had a two day training seminar at the Service School at the Tech Centre. As a finale, I presented the Lotus X100 soft top system as an example of problem solving. I found, as I subsequently did in England, that these sessions were better for staff bonding than intellectual enrichment.

My H2 work visa was due for renewal by the end of February 1986, but the authorities in Detroit were proving awkward and US immigration had stopped issuing visas. They dragged their heels to such an extent that the English engineering companies took their case to law. Despite the judgement going their way (on discriminatory grounds), the visas were still frozen. This meant that neither the family nor I could regain access to the USA, if we left the country.

Although we stayed for another six months, it was never renewed, despite a subsequent enforcement order from the presiding court. Someone must have wanted us out real bad. It had begun to feel as though authority was against the British engineers, despite the proven need, and satisfaction with their work, from the Big Three motor companies.

The spring of 1986 saw the announcement of the new Toyota Supra. A 2+2 hatchback coupé, its shape had, in my opinion, some resemblance to my Lotus X100, although less extreme. Although a much larger vehicle, with a 3-litre straight six engine to accommodate, it shared a similar treatment to the door glass and the back window, although that was divided into three parts, and it had a prominent black accent where the Lotus had its body joint. I was most flattered that my ideas had perhaps been of some stimulation (I modestly assumed), and the car remained in production until 1993, by which time over 1.3 million had been produced.

I heard some shocking news from home that spring, when a colleague in the office announced that GM had bought Lotus. I found this hard to believe, and only accepted it when I saw it in print on the GM news service. In due course, both companies paths would cross for me, and my experience of Detroit and GM would prove very useful.

At around the same time General Motors imposed an overtime ban. I had been working 10 to 15 hours over the standard 40 per week, and needed the money. With the imposition of the unexpected income tax, there was rather less surplus cash than the original deal had suggested. General Motors rules were simple, get the job done, but you won't get any overtime pay.

Gerry Mahoney and Dave Clark did their best to try and work out a solution to my overtime issue. They even got senior management permission to offer me permanent GM employment, and the chance to qualify for a Green Card. Flattered though I was, I did not want to commit the family to permanent residence in the USA. To solve the problem financially, they arranged a move to one of the few departments in the corporation permitted overtime. This was due to the lateness of its project in hand.

I was sad to leave the Special Vehicle Activity and the project at ASC. The Oldsmobile 98 Touring Car was running on time, with good relationships between all parties. In January 1987, when back in England, I was delighted to get a letter from Don Wallace telling me that the Oldsmobile had gone into production on time. This was particularly significant, as it had been some years since a General Motors project had met its timing target.

In mid-May 1886, I joined the Buick, Oldsmobile, Cadillac C/H Platform team, on the fourth floor of the Ameritech building in Troy, Michigan, where I was liaison engineer between Hawtall Whiting and the General Motors platform engineers. They were working on a new Cadillac Deville, which was seriously behind schedule.

The styling studios at the GM Tech Centre would send the basic bodylines to the office, where the technical feasibility was checked. Most of the work involved ensuring the door glass would drop and seal correctly, which was a challenge, as the designers wanted the glass completely flush with the body skins. Ingenious mechanisms were used to get the glass to move inwards as well as dropping into the door.

With the project stalled at this early stage, I had little liaising to do with Hawtall Whiting, back in the UK, where the prototypes were to be built. Time and again, designs would shuttle between Styling and Engineering, as the styling was far from settled. As the project ran later and later, so the overtime allowance increased.

General Motors was now using design computers extensively on new projects. However, it did not use them on this type of work between Styling and our feasibility group. At that time, software programs to operate compatibly with the body surface designers had not been developed, so we used good old hand drawing methods.

With little liaison to do, I worked on the body engineering. On the drawing tables, many sections were cut through the door and A pillar, the most challenging being radial sections at the transition of the windscreen post and the roof. The office opened at 6am and there were long days, with often nothing to do at all, if the work had been referred back to Styling. There were three other English contractors in the office, and we were all told that we must 'appear' to be working at all times.

1986 Toyota Supra.

1982 Lotus M90.

The building was fitted with security systems on every main door, which recorded the passage of each individual's security pass. The Ameritech building had a number of shops and a café on the ground floor, so each contractor, in turn, would 'lead' the rest of us down there. At least this gave us the opportunity to escape four times, morning and afternoon.

Three weeks later, even this relief was lost, when the project moved to a new office building. There were no cafés or other distractions there, and life became even more tedious. One of the most difficult times was Saturday morning, when we would check in at 6am and stay until lunchtime. There were few American staff present at the weekends, and, if there was no work to be done, we had a hard time getting through it. I found it a strange way to manage a project, but, if the department ceased doing overtime, it would lose the right to it for good, so we had to keep our useless attendance up.

One project we undertook during that time was to build ourselves a rocket. Made of cardboard and propelled by a solid fuel motor, it was designed to deploy a parachute at its peak altitude of over 1000ft, for a return soft landing. We carefully constructed a very light, high tech card fabrication on the drawing tables. When finished, I took it home for testing. Meticulously set up on a launching stand, ignition cables attached, it rapidly gained altitude on launch. Unfortunately, the carefully constructed monocoque body was not completely straight, so it described a complete half circle and disappeared deep into Moon Lake, still on full power, long before the homemade parachute could deploy. It was lucky that it was bent that way, or it could have hit something useful.

June was Detroit Grand Prix time again, and Senna, in a Lotus, dominated both qualifying and the race. The same week, I wrote to Tony Rudd, in England, to ask him if he knew of any opportunities for work among his worldwide contacts. Although I also contacted some other potential employers, it was Tony who came back to me, with an invitation to meet for dinner on his next visit to Detroit.

He said that Lotus would like me to return. The directors had discussed the idea, and now that Lotus Cars had its own Engineering Department, under Graham Atkin, there would be a place there for me. Lotus made me an offer, which I accepted, and I made plans to start there on 1 September 1986.

My time at General Motors had been interesting as a contrast to the decisive processes at Lotus and TVR. I had enjoyed it, although my family had mixed views. My wife suffered in particular, as she could not take any paid work. With both daughters at school, she had a pretty dull time.

Chapter 11

Back to – guess where?

The Lotus to which I returned, in September 1986, had changed completely over the 18 months I had been in North America. General Motors purchased the Group on 22 January 1986. With GM came ambitious plans for product and plant expansion, and an undertaking to control the company with a 'hand's off' approach. This allowed the Engineering division to continue working with other manufacturer clients, as their projects remained confidential. It was also hoped that the policy would allow the spirit and flair for which the company was famous to be maintained.

I returned to the position of Project General Manager in the current Engineering Department of Lotus Cars. It was a relatively new group, overseeing all the work on past, present and future Lotus Cars products; design and construction work was carried out by Lotus Engineering. Upon my arrival, the department was working on a heavily revised Esprit: Project X180. Besides a new body, penned by Peter Stevens, it had revisions to the interior, and utilised a Renault five-speed transmission in place of the Citroën unit. Lotus Engineering was hard at work, at a relatively early stage of the project. Initially I had little to do with it, spending most of my time on product planning.

By mid-October, the first requirements for a new supercar, the X200, were being discussed with Sales and other parties. As well as the new model programmes, the department had to look after customer complaints, warranty claims, and assist the service representatives.

A project that was kept away from the department was the M100. While I had been in the USA, work had proceeded on the Etna-style coupé (X100), with front-wheel drive Toyota running gear. Prototypes had been built and run. Much time and effort had been expended on trying to develop a composite (glass fibre) structure, but it all went back to being – believe it or not – a backbone-based frame made of steel, with a metal reinforced perimeter frame.

By December 1985, the board was growing tired of the styling. The convertible design was not entirely loved, and

A Toyota-engined front-wheel drive X100 prototype.

The convertible version.

there was concern over its structural integrity. The plot had consumed some money, but not really moved on the project much. With the arrival of General Motors, sadly, Toyota left the scene, and the running gear needed re-sourcing. Toyota, however, with typical Japanese etiquette, stood by its agreements to supply parts for existing models for the remainder of its ten-year agreement.

The new small sports car then became the M100, and utilised a powertrain from Izuzu, in which GM had a significant shareholding. Behind closed doors, the project progressed, reaching its first major landmark, when the board would select the style. Intensive security was laid on for the presentation on 14 November 1986.

I was invited to view the contenders after the official board presentation, and was furnished with a special high security pass. Upon entering the large presentation area, there were three models on display. General Motors had created one of them in its studios in the USA. It had very pure and pleasant lines, but a major flaw: it was a very large car; far too big for the proposed market: not the compact, light, responsive product that Lotus was aiming for. Opposite this was a model from Guigiaro's Italdesign. I was most disappointed with this effort, which, perhaps, was 'the exception which proves the rule.'

In the far corner, stealing the limelight, was the model of what was to become the Elan. It was compact, sporting, and boasted a fully detailed interior – unlike its rivals. I was not surprised to hear that the board had unanimously chosen the 'in house' model, but I was disappointed to see some of its proportions change on the path to production, as a result of packaging issues. Following the presentation, the project was maintained with absolute security, in its own locked premises.

Mike Kimberley, Lotus Chief Executive, had promised the new owner that the X180 Esprit would be in production 18 months from kick-off. However, GM was sceptical, and kept the project under scrutiny to ensure it was completed within the promised time. The work was beginning to fall behind, and I was asked to assume overall management, taking over from Chris Dunster. Chris was doing a good job, but it was felt that the authority of a General Manager would ensure absolute support throughout the factory and with suppliers. I felt somewhat embarrassed to be brought in over him, as I had known Chris for more than 15 years, and knew he was perfectly capable. To his credit, he took it well, and we just got on with it.

By April 1987, I had officially moved from the car company back to Lotus Engineering. The Lotus Cars Engineering group was secreted away in a temporary Portacabin to get on with the supercar, and little was seen of it.

A prototype Lotus X180 Esprit on test at Millbrook Proving Ground.

Chris and I drove the Esprit development on: pre-production car number 1 went onto the assembly line on 23 June 1987. With everything going to plan, we fought vociferously against some last-minute trim changes, as they could have been the one-step-too-far in getting to the start of production. Sales and Marketing, however, won the day – despite this, we did achieve the start date, but I wonder if everyone realised how close it was. Chris and I went down to the Royal Garden Hotel, in London, for the dealer launch, just before the press day at the 1987 Earls Court Motor Show. The car was an immediate success, and developments of it were still in production in the new millennium.

Lotus USA was in the process of changing ownership, and the new operation was looking for investors. As a bonus, they would get 'an investor special' Esprit SE, as the new X180 model was named. Mike Kimberley asked me for colour and trim ideas, at very short notice, and I came up with two: metallic white paintwork with shades of blue and cream Alcantara suede and leather; and a pale Champagne gold metallic with rich brown and biscuit interior. They were adopted, and the fifty investor's specials duly left for the States.

With the Esprit SE settling down in the factory, I was offered the position of leading the work on the installation of airbags in the Esprit and the forthcoming

Lotus Esprit X180.

Lotus X180 styling model with the neat engine vent under the rear window similar to Italdesign's Etna.

The production Lotus Esprit X180 was unable to replicate the neatness of the vent.

Elan. Twice I turned it down, thinking it was a rather dull and isolated sector in which to become involved. The third time, Lotus Engineering's Managing Director Cedric Ashley mentioned that the project started in two days with attendance at a conference in New Orleans. That was an opportunity too good to miss, so on Monday 9 November 1987, Clive Roberts and I stepped aboard the Delta Airlines Tristar en route to the home of jazz, via Cincinnati.

Clive was an ex-Triumph Motor Company apprentice, who had been part of Graham Atkins' Engineering Department, when I came back from the States. He raced a Caterham Seven with enthusiasm; Caterham being his previous employer.

We landed at New Orleans, and set out to explore the old French Quarter. The next morning, we were up early to attend the Stapp Safety Conference. The conference was founded and chaired by Colonel Stapp, who pioneered work on assessing the physical limits of force and acceleration that the human body could withstand. He simply strapped himself to a rocket-powered sled mounted on rails, launched himself at speeds up to about 600 miles per hour, and stopped suddenly in a water trough. If he lived, then the threshold was greater than the figures recorded; if not, then they were lower. He survived, and his research formed the backbone of the acceptability levels required from dummies used in safety testing. A brave man, whose contribution to the progress of human safety cannot be overstated. He lived to a ripe old age.

At the conference, we met representatives of the General Motor's companies that were to support the Lotus occupant safety projects. Now that Lotus was in the GM family, it's help was at our disposal. Byron Singer, of Delco Electronics, was our host, and we dined at a traditional restaurant, where the appetising starter was the quaintly named Gumbo Ya Ya. Then Clive and I hit the town again, Clive nearly decapitating himself trying to affix Lotus business cards to a bar ceiling adorned with a powerful ceiling fan. I began to find that vehicle occupant safety was actually quite fun.

The following day, the conference continued, and the complex nature of the safety world began to sink in. We met Phil Hopf and Bob Jones, from the GM Inland Division, who had been working on airbag protection for years. We also met Mike Fitzpatrick, an independent safety consultant, who had developed pioneering computer simulation programs for occupants in a crash.

We enjoyed our final night in jazz town, and wondered why we had bothered to get a hotel; we had seen little of it. The following morning, the conference finished. We flew to Detroit to start a tour of all the supporting cast for the Lotus airbag projects. We went to the GM Milford Crash Laboratories, and drove to Saginaw to discuss steering columns suitable for airbag installations.

We then had a six-hour drive to Chicago, where we were to meet Gerry Doe, the Lotus Legislation Manager. Gerry was in charge of safety issues at Lotus, back in the UK, and had many years' experience. At that stage, the installation of airbag systems was expected to be his ultimate responsibility. However, once we grasped the magnitude of the task, I took it on as a stand-alone discipline, while Gerry continued to look after all other safety and legislation issues.

He was due to arrive on the Sunday lunchtime, so I took Clive on a site-seeing trip to Chicago in the morning. We were a few minutes late back at O'Hare airport, and rushed to the arrivals area. It was very crowded, but Gerry was nowhere to be found. Worried, we set off on the long drive to Kokomo, Indiana, discussing what could have happened to the hapless Gerry. We arrived at 10:30 that night, and found Gerry sitting in the hotel lobby waiting for us. Upon arriving in Chicago, and unable to find us, he had immediately rented a car and set off on his own – the atmosphere was a mixture of relief and anger.

Kokomo, Indiana, became the destination for many a visit. The town sign, dominated by the biggest gas holder (probably) in the world, proclaimed it was a 'City of Firsts.' It cited the first American automobile (make unknown), something to do with a huge cow, and some other historic firsts, but, for us, it was the home of Delco Electronics. Delco was to take the lead in ensuring that Lotus did an adequate job of providing a safe system. As suppliers, Delco Electronics would provide the crash sensors and the electronic control unit, which would have to match the Esprit and new Elan crash characteristics.

Of the two issues we discussed, the first was the content. We were told that a typical major GM platform needed up to 70 crash tests and around 80 simulated sled tests. A 'brief' programme, such as that done by a subcontractor on the Chevrolet Corvette, ran to 24 barrier impacts and 50 sled runs.

The sled is a giant gas gun. It propels the cockpit of the vehicle with an acceleration pattern that matches the deceleration in a crash. This mirrors what happens in a crash, and subjects the dummies aboard the cockpit to the equivalent forces of a vehicle impact. The beauty of the sled test was that it only needed cockpit parts replacing between tests, saving on the consumption of whole cars.

The suggested quantity of cars needed to develop the system was far beyond that which Lotus would expect to finance, and, after much work looking at the reasons for

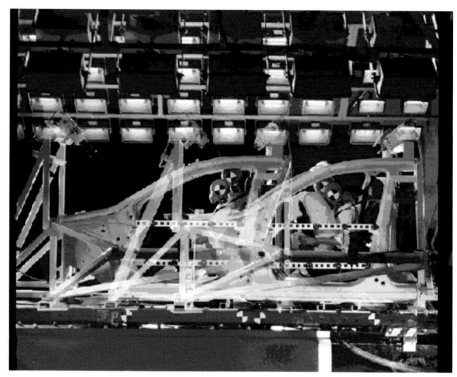

A double exposure picture showing a Hy Ge sled moving to the right with the dummy being accelerated into an airbag.

set off for Cincinnati and the flight home, without. The problem was that we didn't have enough money to pay for the rental car, which had clocked up many miles, and was far from its Detroit home.

So we hatched a plan: upon arrival at the airport, we made for the Radisson Inn, and timed our departure for the flight check-in to the last moment. Then, we parked on the yellow lines outside the terminal doors, and rushed to the Delta airline counter, presenting the car keys and papers to the Delta staff, and explaining we had no time to return it. Fortunately, the airline accepted this extra burden, and we ran for the flight. Gerry was very worried about this tactic, but could not come up with a better one. In due course, the American rental car company sent the bill to England, where it was settled satisfactorily.

Back at Hethel, we constructed the timing and resource plans from the copious information we had obtained in America. By 10 December 1988, the plans were in place, and I presented them to the Lotus Cars management. I put together a basic guide to passive restraint: what it was, how it worked and why it was needed.

The United States government wanted airbags introduced as quickly as possible, and offered temporary exemption on the passenger side, as encouragement. The airbag industry had to be created from nothing, and everyone realised the magnitude of the industry's task.

Mid-December, Gerry Doe and I returned to Inland, and quickly reached the conclusion that the only steering wheel with anything like acceptable European styling was that of the forthcoming Pontiac Firebird. There was no way that Lotus could afford a uniquely styled one.

We moved on to Kokomo, where there was to be a crucial meeting. A local American candidate was due for interview that afternoon, for the role of Lotus' representative with Delco. At the appointed hour, he was shown into a large conference room to face a sea of Delco Electronics staff and a couple of foreigners – from Lotus. The man, Don Orem, did a fine job. When he had completed his presentation, Gerry and I left the room to discuss it. Despite suggesting it, I felt a little uneasy,

the numbers, we were able to reduce it to a total of 12 crash tests, to develop and validate the Esprit system.

The second subject for debate was a requirement that Lotus supply a project representative to Kokomo for the 18-month programme. I knew how difficult it would be to find someone who both knew Lotus, and would be prepared to settle in Indiana for a year-and-a-half. Anyway, I could not imagine what the person would find to do with all their time, so I came up with an alternative. I suggested that Delco find a local person for the position, and that Lotus would pay their salary, with any surplus time available for other projects. Delco agreed, and we left for our next port of call.

We all set off together for Dayton, Ohio. The Inland Fisher Guide Division was responsible for steering wheels and airbag modules, and also had a sled for the system development work. Here we were received by the 'Three Wise Men,' Phil Hopf, Bill Shaw and Bob Jones. Phil was to be the Lotus programme manager, while his two colleagues gave much support on technical issues.

A couple of days earlier, we had asked Lotus to send us some extra American money: we had been in the USA much longer than planned, so had run short! While we were at Inland, we made frantic attempts to find out if the extra funds were coming. Apparently they were not, so we 'taking on' a person on behalf of Lotus, but we agreed we had no better ideas, and Don became the Lotus man at Delco.

Early in 1988, the first set of Esprit crash cars were leaving for TNO, Delft, in Holland, under Ken Evans tender care. Don Orem arrived from the States, and joined us in Delft for the testing.

The first suite of six Esprit tests was to establish the crash characteristics of the vehicle, and the acceleration inputs to all the potential locations for the crash sensors. The final test was to collide with a simulated animal at 50mph (81kph). In the northern United States, deer strikes are surprisingly common. In order to preserve the airbag system for use in a secondary crash, after the animal strike, the sensor calibrations should achieve a 'no fire' input. Detecting this type of impact was essential, as the system had to discriminate between a 'full' crash and a deer impact. Severe secondary crashes in such situations were very common.

The Esprit was set up to run from the crash laboratory to collide, outside, with an 'animal' built from rubber tyres standing on wooden legs. The car's braking system was activated by remote control to halt it after the impact. The Esprit emerged from the TNO building at a steady 50mph (81kph) and collided with the hapless animal as planned. The tyres and wooden legs were thrown into the air, and the Esprit just kept going unabated. The remote brake system had failed, and the car continued down the test yard, across an internal road and into a pile of builder's sand left fortuitously beyond. Had the sand not been there, it was 'next stop Rotterdam!' The car was half buried in it, but suffered only light damage.

Preventing the airbag from firing, when it was not needed, was as difficult as sensing when it was. Tests were run on proving grounds over many severe conditions. All the sensor input data was recorded and sent to Delco Electronics for assimilation.

Ten sled tests were run at the end of April, and, during this time, we took delivery of a road-going Esprit. This was used to increase our partner's knowledge of the product involved, and many senior Inland and Delco people took it

for a drive. Most were quite overawed by it, and couldn't believe the performance "from a four-cylinder engine."

The Inland engineers, who had been working on these systems in the GM cars for a long time, treated the test results with some amazement. The head injuries were less than 20% of the permitted level, and the chest was similar. The Lotus knee bolster worked well to return less than 30% of the permitted loads.

The knee bolster was an innovative Lotus approach. Most manufacturers used the deformation of metal sheet to absorb the impact energy of the occupant's legs. I winced at the thought of this, and, working with Lotus material expert, Andy Clough, we came up with a structural foam contoured to accept the upper shins in the most medically friendly way.

With the specification and design proven on the Hy Ge sled, the Esprit project team could release drawings for the prototype cars to be built.

The first live pre-production airbags were being prepared for shipment to Lotus. To meet the laws of the land, Lotus needed an explosives licence. Alan Charles, an ex-UK Government Explosives Directorate employee, had set up as an adviser for this, and he explained the storage needed, and arranged the licence. In the longer term, this became an irritating issue, as each specific pyrotechnic device had to have its own licence. For instance, if we wanted to try out another design, we had to clear the

The airbag-equipped Lotus Esprit with the knee impact absorber below the dash.

government paperwork for that particular device, before import could take place.

The first week of July 1988, Esprit crash testing with the production airbag system commenced. The low speed impacts verified that the fire/no fire thresholds worked as planned, and injury levels were as expected. Once all the slow motion films and the audited test results and measurements were available, I took them across the Atlantic to present them to our partners. Delco and Inland were impressed with the results, and no one could see any hidden problems from the tests.

In between the Esprit activity, we had to provide a system for the forthcoming M100 Elan. During spring of 1989, initial crash testing was carried out, in Holland, using up five prototypes.

The Elan crash tests showed it had a rather more severe situation to handle. We had to do a lot of preparatory work to get the front-wheel drive package to crash with a satisfactory performance. Although we were not very experienced at the time, the results should have given us a warning. In early November 1988, I was offered, and accepted, the role of leading the Opel/Lotus project to build a high-performance saloon. Originally based on the Senator model, it was to be shown at the Geneva Motor Show the following March. The project meeting, in Germany, a week later, had it change to the Omega/Carlton. By 24 November 1989, an Omega 3000 arrived at Hethel for the team to start examining.

Also in November, with the temperature well below freezing and snow on the ground, we started sled work on the Elan in Dayton. It did not go well. Where the Esprit had exceeded predictions on injuries, the Elan did the opposite, and after various trials and tribulations, we left for Christmas with a lot yet to do.

With the path ahead for the Elan looking increasingly difficult, I suggested, sadly, that I should resign from the leadership of the Opel Lotus Omega project, so that I could focus on the Elan. This was accepted as the best thing to do, under the circumstances.

The next round of Elan development ran from mid-March to April 1989. Working seven days a week, we got the driver system to work, with a greatly revised airbag specification, but still had some issues with passenger protection. In the course of testing back in the USA, we broke a major unique Elan component. While the Inland workshops did a superb repair job, they were very impressed when a replacement part arrived from the factory in England within 24 hours, via Concorde.

August 1989, and the airbag-equipped Esprit went into production. Initially only for the North American market, we soon found that the Germans were insisting on having it as well.

Arnie Johnson, at Lotus USA, kept me informed of customer concerns, the only ones being that the steering wheel design was bulky, and that the driving position less favoured than the previous model. Nothing could be done about either issue. It would be some years before new technology would shrink the size of an airbag module.

Shortly after the Esprit reached the USA public, the first airbag deployment crash occurred. The driver, who hit an oncoming vehicle head on, was unhurt, despite the collision being at over 45mph (72kph). Over the years, the system has proved to be all that was hoped. No reports of unwanted deployments, a few crashes, but with one extreme exception, no serious injuries or fatalities. The extreme exception occurred at an impact speed over 100mph (160kph), where the car was completely destroyed.

In Mid-February 1990, the Esprit was back on the Hy Ge sled to run tests on a passenger airbag. We ran a number of these, and the very first produced the lowest head injury levels seen at that time anywhere in the GM Corporation.

Inland was keen to move into the safety arena in Europe, and a number of opportunities were followed up, with Lotus cast as the 'Whole Vehicle Engineers.' I coined the phrase, because my growing experience in the area had showed me that, to make a

Lotus Elan, with driver airbag.

safety system work properly, there were many interacting influences which had to be balanced. While each supplier of equipment and components was an undoubted expert in their field, balancing the whole could be done most effectively by a vehicle design house. I made this the platform for future work of the newly-formed Lotus Occupant Safety Department.

Over the summer and autumn of 1989, the Elan was the subject of considerable further development, and, by the time it was ready for validation tests, in early July 1990, I had been in the USA for a total of 73 days.

However, not all my time was spent on the Elan project, as Lotus Engineering had a number of potential engineering client projects on that continent to visit.

The United States specification Elan went into production in late 1991, and I moved back to Lotus vehicle work. As General Manager, Lotus Product Engineering, one of my first tasks was to improve the Esprit. I had driven one over a weekend that summer, and wrote 18 pages of my thoughts over a weekend in Dayton.

We got permission to 'improve' an old development car to show off our ideas. These were many: as well as power steering, and an effort assister for the clutch pedal, a new stiffer chassis was built with a revised frame, that incorporated a new torque box structure at the front of the engine bay. The backbone centre section was reduced in height, giving the cockpit a major increase in space.

The seats were modified, and incorporated a removable under-cushion, which allowed for very tall occupants to sit lower. Details were changed, such as the size of the internal rear window which was increased, the door and windscreen trim altered, and a fully integrated central locking system, with colour-matched door handles, incorporated.

Not all these changes were to be adopted; the chassis change was seen as too radical, given the funds available. This was a shame, as the increased stiffness would have helped both the quality feel of the car, and the roadholding and cockpit space. The other ideas were approved, and the car announced in 1992 became the Esprit S4.

Another Esprit project was the limited edition X180R. Dave Minter was the engineer responsible for specifying this road-going race car replica. Built only for the USA, to commemorate the huge success of the car in SCCA racing there,

it featured a full race roll cage, AP racing brakes, and numerous weight savings, such as the deletion of the air conditioner.

The prototype was finished in late October 1990, and all the cars needed to be landed in the USA before the end of the year, to avoid the forthcoming luxury tax. We just managed it. The X180R led to the development of the Esprit Sport 300, possibly the best Esprit ever.

The department was also responsible for ongoing engineering issues on the Elan. Andrew Walmsley had become Engineering Director of Lotus Cars. I had been offered this post when I was in America, in the summer of 1991, but I turned it down, due to some of the personalities involved at the time. History was to show that my decision spared me subsequently being marched off site under escort!

The Elan was running at some 3000 units per year, but some suppliers were struggling to keep pace. One of these was the chassis supplier, which had to make the welded sheet frame to very high tolerances. The design had become much more complex since it had quoted in the early days of the project, and relations were not happy. Andrew and I realised we had to bring the two sides together, and would set off for Coventry every Wednesday to try and achieve this. Where there were production problems, I would try and find a way to ease the supplier's constraints.

The Excel was still in production, and a random failure of part of the front of its frame led to a full vehicle recall. Not an easy decision, but one that ensured that the company took a responsible attitude. Sometimes the public see these well-publicised recalls as a sign that the manufacturer is inadequate. I believe just the reverse, and

The Lotus Esprit S4.

The Esprit X180R SCCA race car replica.

that it shows total commitment to quality, safety and the public.

The Excel was ageing and I tried to get a face-lifted car adopted with a turbocharged Lotus 2.2-litre engine. I felt that, with 220 horsepower, the car could have continued a bit longer. The Excel ceased production in 1992 with a total of 1327 units built, with the previous Elite and Eclat totalling 4886. The design we began in 1971 had served well. The Elite held the position of highest total production volume, with 2535 produced.

As part of the drive to improve the Elan, a production engineer, Derek Beamish, and I were invited to visit Saab's plant in Finland, where its convertible was made. The factory claimed the car was free of water leaks, which the Elan was not, but the main reason for the Saab's warterproof performance was that the side windows were nearly vertical and the roof overhung like a Tudor cottage. Over the years, just about every contemporary soft top car was tested in the Lotus water spray test, and they all were similar to, and many worse, than the Lotus – with the one exception: Mercedes.

In early August 1990, while I was in Dayton, I had been introduced to Jurgen Klenk, an Opel safety engineer. In February 1991, I was asked to visit Opel in Russelsheim, Germany, and present my safety credentials to Karl Jullig, the Director of Body Engineering. I was warned that Jullig was an efficient time user, and that he would not be detained for long.

I checked in at Norwich airport just after 6am, to find that fog had cancelled the flight to Amsterdam. I would undoubtedly miss my connection to Frankfurt, and the day would be lost. When I made my delayed arrival in Holland, Air UK rose to the occasion, and got me a seat on the Cathay Pacific, Frankfurt-Hong Kong flight. I settled myself into the 747, and only just had time to get all the goodies, before disembarking in Germany. Grateful that the airline had got me there, I rushed to the Opel Technical Centre with no time to spare. Herr Jullig was very interested in my presentation and extended the half hour room booking to two hours.

Shortly after this trip, on 28 of March 1991, Tony Rudd retired from Lotus. Tony and my lives had intertwined since the Lotus job offers in late 1970. With a wealth of experience, and always a raconteur, he was undoubtedly one of the fairest men I had worked for. It was a measure of his value that he didn't retire until the age of 68, although the term 'retire' hardly covered his subsequent energetic activities.

Nothing more was heard from Opel until late July. I flew over to see Jurgen Klenk, who said it was looking at installing airbags in the complete range of its cars, and planning was starting for the programmes. I returned and started to build a team.

Immediately after the Frankfurt Motor Show, I got a call from Jurgen. "Get yourself and Mark Easton (Programme Manager) over here by Monday and be prepared to stay some days – as long as it takes." The Show had highlighted the readiness of most of the German manufacturers to put airbag-equipped cars on to the European market immediately. Unlike Opel-Vauxhall, they sold most of their models with airbags in the USA already. Their systems were developed and available, and GM Europe's senior management was concerned it would be left behind.

Mark and I decided to go to Germany by road, as that would give us maximum flexibility. We left, with the boot of my car stuffed with black marker pens and graph paper. We checked into an Inn at Ginsheim, on the Rhine on the Sunday night, unaware of what lay ahead.

First thing on the Monday morning, Jurgen briefed us. Opel had three vehicle platforms in urgent need of airbag systems. It was short of experienced resource. Mark and I were to prepare programme timing, all dovetailed together to simultaneously develop driver and passenger restraints, with a fourth platform running a few months behind.

By the Wednesday morning, we had it all roughed out, crash and sled tests, abuse tests, electromagnetic compatibility tests, durability and supplier tooling lead times. Opel had expected it to take three years; we said it would take fourteen months.

A Lotus Esprit set up for a sales literature photograph at the Millbrook Crash Test Laboratory.

I went to see Karl Jullig, who simply asked, "Can you do it in the time?" I affirmed that we could. Jullig just said that we would get his full support.

We tidied the detail up on the Thursday and Friday, and Klenk told us to proceed immediately. Millbrook agreed to the timing, and we left for an overnight stop in Calais. Looking for somewhere to eat, we found a small family run restaurant in a side street near our hotel, and quietly – well initially anyway – celebrated the arrival of this huge contract.

As soon as we reached Hethel, the Lotus support started. A large temporary building was made available behind engineering. All safety work is commercially sensitive, so it was securely locked at all times. Three programme managers were needed initially. Mark Easton took one, Chris Harris another, and Bruce Wellings the third. Hundreds of vehicles would be coming through for crash preparation, many needing modifications, so Peter Davis became the Vehicle and Workshop Controller. Samantha, my secretary, moved in to look after the team. Mike Hague led the design activity, and John Cooper led the computer simulation group. Frank Wright returned to the group to run the test engineers and test procedures. Many of these people went on to become significant in the safety business.

We all needed the relevant tools for the job. A problem arose with the ability to transfer design data. Wymondham telephone exchange had gone digital, but the cables had not been laid for the three miles (5km) to Hethel. A temporary tower was built to beam the data to a local village, while the telephone company worked all hours laying the vital cables. They were operational in half the time originally promised.

While Hethel got into gear, there were many visits to Germany to clarify the details of the programme and to organise information. The first batch of vehicles was made ready for test, and off we went to Millbrook. After 14 months of, often, day and night work, we completed the task. The team received many letters and messages of thanks from Germany when the first cars went down the Luton production line, one week ahead of the original plan.

Shortly after the first cars went into public hands, John Cooper saw a report of a serious crash, where the driver had a miraculous escape. The car, a Vauxhall Cavalier, brand new with airbags, collided with a truck, on the A1. It rolled a number of times and came to rest, severely damaged on the grass verge. When the emergency services arrived, they asked the chap standing by the car, smoking a cigarette, where the driver was. He admitted to being the survivor, and explained the airbag had fired and saved him from any injury. The emergency services opinion from their long experience of such incidents, suggested that the usual outcome would have been fatal. It made it all worthwhile.

One morning in June 1992, the project team were called to a mass meeting in the big Engineering Vehicle Workshop, at Hethel. It was announced that due to it being unprofitable, the Elan would cease production instantly. Large numbers of staff were to be made redundant, and General Motors would be looking for new owners of the company.

Although it did not directly affect the safety team, it was a severe shock, as the Elan production was actually rising to new daily rates. The car was selling quite well, although the United States market was not as good as had been hoped. Over there, the selling price was little less than a Chevrolet Corvette, with 'hot' Japanese coupés around $15,000 less. In the UK, the car was selling at a loss, so instead of paying off the tooling and development costs, the debt was actually rising.

Adrian Palmer became Chief Executive at Lotus, Mike Kimberley moved on, working for GM in the Far East. With the completion of the safety work for the Germans, Adrian offered me the position of Head of Lotus Product Engineering, and charged me to come up with a five- and ten-year product plan. The Esprit was ageing, and the Elan and Excel out of production.

There was a great desire to bring the M100 Elan back. All the tooling still existed, and there were still many parts in the stores. I was not particularly keen on this, as the car had almost caused our demise, but the attraction of the stores full of parts was very strong. The problem was that when they were finished, there weren't any more – the engine having already gone out of production – so it would only hold the fort for a short time. My misgivings were over-ruled and the cars were built and sold under Bugatti ownership. I did, however plan a long-term replacement.

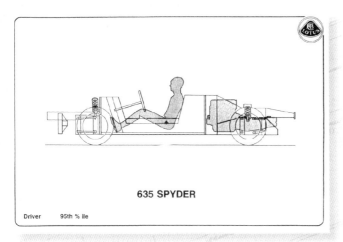

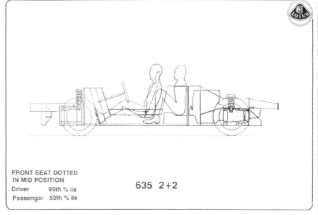

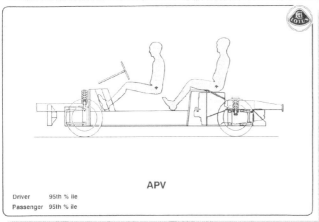

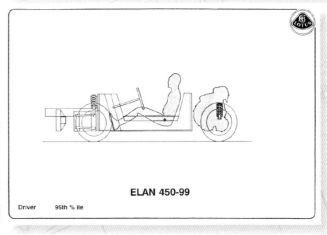

The proposed new Lotus model range in 1992.

My views on specialist product had not changed significantly over the years. Cars are very complex machines and, given limited funds, the specification should not be allowed to become so sophisticated that it is beyond the resource available to develop it. The second problem, again driven by cash constraint, is that small companies cannot afford to develop many different platforms. In fact, the larger ones hold the same view nowadays. With this in mind, I planned a range of vehicles around a modular platform. This used the same structure for the ends on all models, with variations in the simpler, middle section.

The modules were based around a new mid-engined package. Much time was spent deciding what the structure would be. Aluminium was a long-time favourite, as box sections could be extruded as a complete hollow section, removing the stiffness-sapping joints in a fabricated section. However, extruded aluminium sections had a

minimum thickness, required for manufacture, somewhat greater than the structure needed. We examined honeycomb aluminium sheet, but, besides material cost issues, there were others concerning water sealing of edges, and the availability of fittings, such as wiring grommets.

And then there was steel. It was cheap and very stiff. The box sections proposed were to be rolled profiles, seam welded to maintain structural stiffness. Corrosion proofing was a serious issue. The most effective steel treatment was zinc galvanising after the assembly was welded, but that could be prone to serious heat distortion. The resulting structure was known as a punt chassis. This was designed to have two different wheelbases, the longer to carry convertible and 2+2 variants.

There was also to be a version with a completely new centre section – a high-performance APV. The Elan S2

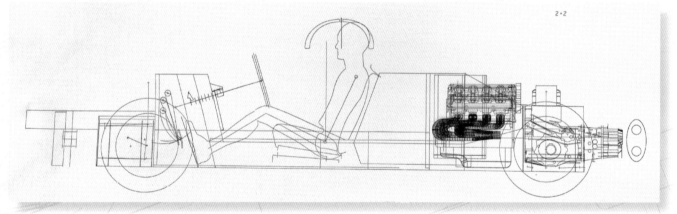

The 2+2 package computer-generated drawing. This type of presentation was much different to the traditional pencil on paper drawings I had been used to.

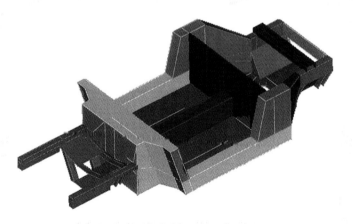

The structural model.

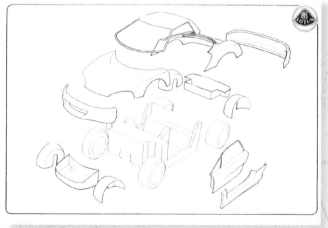

A drawing illustrating the body skins for Project 635.

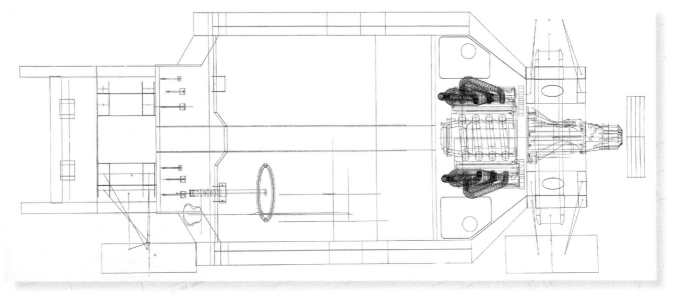

Computer drawings were unable to emphasise or delete levels of detail.

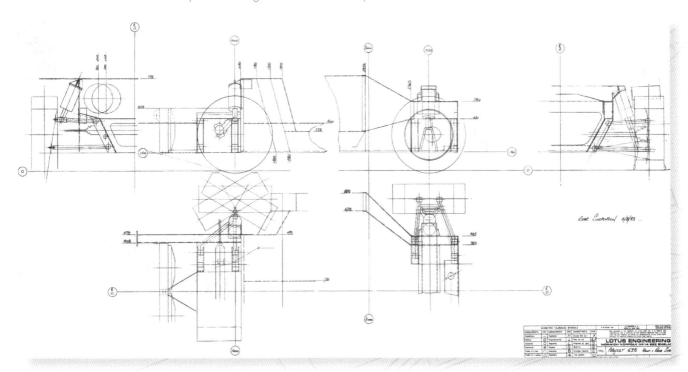

When drawing by hand only, details of interest are included. However, the accuracy of computer data cannot be doubted.

would be replaced by a car using the same punt, with a tubular frame carrying a 2-litre transverse mid-engine. The benefits of sharing nearly all components, to get a range of five products, was attractive.

The lion's share of the work, named Project 635, concentrated on the two-seat coupé. After the structure debate, the body material came under review. We felt that glass fibre didn't give the right tactile effects and visual finish for a mature car manufacturer. Aluminium was our preferred choice, but the cost was always an issue. Even the basic tooling for sheet metal was many times the cost of glass fibre moulds. We contacted various companies and examined a number of processes, and a wide variation of costs emerged.

John Miles, the ex-Team Lotus driver, advised on the suspension. He even had us study the current Lotus Formula One car, which featured very little track change between bump and rebound. Our design had long twin wishbones front and rear, with the coil spring damper units acting as closely to the hubs as possible, to improve road wheel movement/damper ratio, from 1.5:1 on the Esprit to 1.2:1. The front kingpin offset was reduced by 35mm from the Esprit, and featured a very low mass hub. Large Brembo brakes, with anti-lock, provided stopping power, and the car sat on 225 45 17 front tyres and 255 40 17 rears. The car was steered with the Esprit power rack, and a tilt and telescope steering column was incorporated.

The engine was the source of much research. We agreed that a V8 was a necessity. The United States had always been reluctant to accept the Lotus four-cylinder unit as appropriate for an expensive car, despite its horsepower and relative economy. Andrew Walmsley, as Lotus Cars Engineering Director, was my 'customer' and he agreed that a proprietary unit was the most sensible choice.

Which unit to chose was a more difficult decision, but we felt it needed a quality name. For the production numbers that we envisaged, it just did not make sense, to us, for Lotus to manufacture and maintain development of an engine on its own. After some discussion, BMW agreed to supply its 4-litre V8, and to accept Lotus durability data as proof of adequate installation development.

We visited BMW and had a price quotation which, to say the least, was very competitive. We then called on Audi's transmission supplier, which agreed to modify its unit to become a two-wheel drive transaxle capable of handling the expected torque.

However, when we got back to Hethel, we faced much resistance to the purchase of an engine from an outside source, as Lotus Engineering wanted the product to reflect its capabilities. First, there was a plan to build a unique engine using proprietary GM components, and then we had discussions for a new V8 with Rover. Eventually Lotus did design and build its own V8.

The most radical vehicle in the plan was the APV, All Purpose Vehicle. Studies were made of luxury saloon and coupé rivals. The luxury opposition would be hard to beat in the saloon and coupé market. The resources of companies such as BMW, Jaguar, etc, were far beyond us, but a full four-seater vehicle would extend the Lotus range.

To package four seats in the project 635 module, the rear passengers sat on top of the V8 engine, with the front ones similarly raised, with the floor at the height of the centre tunnel. The centre section of the punt was new, connecting to the ends of the Esprit modules.

The double-skinned floor would house 130 litres (28 gallons) of fuel, and a supplementary air conditioner for the rear compartment. With most vehicle systems mounted as low or lower than in the Esprit, it would have had a centre of gravity only a little higher.

As a much more sporting vehicle than its rivals, such as the Renault Espace, it had a lower roof 200mm (8in) less than the Renault. With an estimated 241 horsepower per ton, the maximum speed would be limited to 155mph (250kph) and the acceleration was calculated to see 60mph (100kph) in 5.5 seconds, just 0.1 longer than a BMW M5.

Our projections did not anticipate the Lotus APV being huge seller, with the market estimated at 800 per year for the UK, Europe and the USA. This was in a total world market for MPV's of one and half million vehicles.

My proposed plan in 1993 was published as follows:

Model	Available	Markets	UK price
Esprit 635	Autumn 1996	World	£45,000
Esprit 635 2+2	Autumn 1997	World	£48,000
635 APV	Autumn 1997	World	£60,000
Esprit 635 Spyder	Spring 1998	World	£50,000
Esprit 635 Turbo	Mid 1998	World	£55,000
635 Elan	Mid 1999	European	£28,000

In March 1993, I took a sabbatical from Product Engineering work, and went with Chris Harris to Italy, to present Lotus safety capabilities to potential Italian clients. We visited a number of companies in Turin, and the new Bugatti Company at Campogalliano.

A month later, Bugatti's Mario Barbieri paid us a visit at Hethel. He was shown into the directors' dining room (used for VIP meetings), and started a noncommittal conversation about vehicle safety. Adrian Palmer, Andrew Walmsley and I realised he was not really there for that. He then asked to speak to Adrian Palmer privately, so disappeared into his office. Andrew looked at me, and we both guessed the reason for his visit. Palmer and Barbieri returned after about 20 minutes, and Mario made his excuses and left.

Adrian came back into the room, rejoicing that Romano Artioli, the Bugatti saviour, wanted to buy Lotus. As the Opel importer for Italy, Romano was known to General Motors. We were both sworn to total secrecy, of course.

Chapter 12
The Italian job

I had to contain my excitement at work, but, at home, doodled emblems joining the two names. I saw Bugatti as a company with a history similar to Lotus, and thought heaven was round the corner. The new Bugatti company was apparently committed to engineering excellence, and had unlimited finance.

Romano Artioli had negotiated the rights to the Bugatti name, and created a new business to produce the finest exotic cars, and a range of expensive 'designer' personal accessories. Having already visited the lavish, purpose-built headquarters outside Modena, I had high hopes that Lotus would be carefully nurtured, and receive modernisation and investment.

On 28 August 1993, the deal was officially announced, and General Motors sold Lotus to Bugatti. Shortly after this milestone in Lotus history, Artioli announced that there would be a huge party to celebrate the new union. The Hethel site was scrubbed and polished for the event, and the production plant made ready to receive visitors.

Artioli certainly made it a weekend to remember. A Bugatti EB110 was brought over, attended by his brother-in-law, Arquitecto Benedini. Benedini had been responsible for the imposing buildings at Campogalliano, and had also taken on the job of re-styling the original Marcello Gandini Bugatti. Later, he became involved in detail changes to the Esprit, with much pain and anguish on Lotus' part, as we failed to 'sell' the need for fiscal, or engineering, practicality.

All the catering was to the highest standard, and dignitaries from the County of Norfolk, motorsport and the supplier industry were invited. The Bugatti Owners' Club and Lotus brought significant and historic cars to the test track, and Colin Chapman's son, Clive, displayed much of his collection of historic Lotus racing cars.

The highlight of the weekend was a banquet at the local Dunston Hall Hotel. Huge marquees housed well over 300 invited guests, with Lotus senior management and their wives as hosts. Waiters hovered at the four bars, supplying only the finest beverages, while the food was exceptional. We certainly thought that Bugatti and Lotus were going places.

Each department in Engineering put on a display of its activities; I put together one that included the sled buck for the Esprit passenger airbag development. The company had been reluctant to spend money on this project, but I knew passenger airbags had to be in the USA market by September 1993 to meet legislation. A semi-mid-mounted airbag and a passenger knee bolster had done little to change the appearance of the interior, but there were structural reinforcements behind the façade, to take the increased loads from occupant impacts. What was significant about the display was that none of the senior management staff had seen it before, due to their indifference to it. However, it was on the production line and in American showrooms on time.

Three weeks early, in August 1993, while behind-the-scenes discussions dragged on, Adrian Palmer had asked me to go and see Romano Artioli in Campogalliano, and present the Lotus new model strategy. The factory was on its summer holiday and all the air-conditioning was switched off, so I was uncomfortably hot by the time Romano joined the meeting.

He immediately threw out any suggestion of mid-engined cars, and said Lotus would be doing a front-engined 2+2 estate car. Despite Romano not being the type with whom one argues, I fought my case for nearly two hours, but he was adamant. He said mid-engined sports cars were passé; what people needed was a sporting estate. Indeed, that market was strong in Italy, but I was not so sure how well it would be accepted elsewhere. I certainly felt concerned that he did not want to support a replacement Esprit, which had been the Lotus flagship for so long.

Come September, with my product plan in the dustbin, my team got down to work on the 2+2 front-engined estate car mooted to replace it. Work began on the official project, Lotus M220, but it was a coupé not an estate car! The mid-engined 635 structure was modified to suit the new package, while Artioli supported the design of a unique new Lotus V8 engine. The American-built Warner six-speed transmission was drawn in, and Lotus Styling designers got to work.

Work progressed on the drawing board quickly; Artioli asked us to examine a version with a front-mounted Bugatti V12 engine and four-wheel drive transmission. Whether this was to replace his planned EB112, or to be a Lotus, we never found out, but it would certainly have set new heights on Lotus prices. It altered the front suspension and the structure significantly, while increasing the bulk and weight of the front of the package.

Two problems arose in the 2+2 design. Firstly, with the package as low as possible and the propeller shaft enclosed in a flat-bottomed centre tunnel, there was nowhere to run the exhaust system. The flat floor was for both structural and aerodynamic purposes. The best we could think of was to run it down the outer sills, but there were a number of compromises with that. Interestingly, Chrysler appeared to have the same problem with its Viper.

The second packaging issue was the location of a direct-acting brake servo. This drum-shaped device

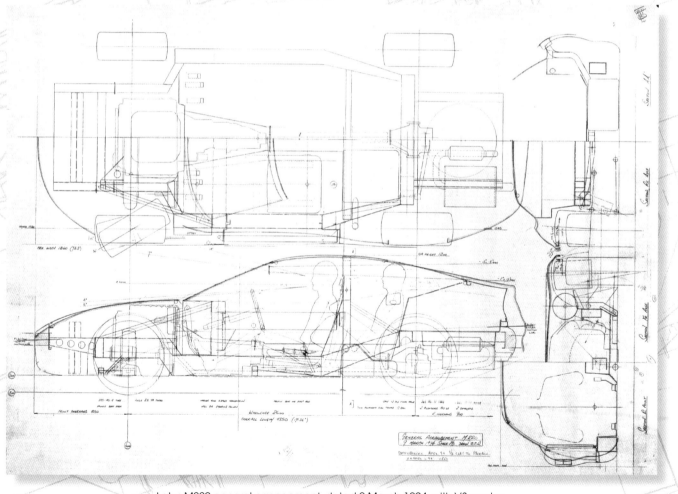

Lotus M220 general arrangement, dated 9 March 1994, with V8 engine.

needed to be aligned to the brake pedal, and, while it could just about be squeezed in alongside the cylinder head for right-hand drive, it had no home in the left-hand drive version. Some designs run a cross link to one side for all models, but the air conditioner blocked that route.

Adrian Palmer was keen to raise internal and external morale, after the disaster of the Elan close down, and sale from GM. Julian Thompson's styling designers put a major presentation together, to show the employees that there really was a future being planned. There was nowhere large enough to accommodate the whole workforce at Hethel, so St Andrews Hall, in Norwich, was hired for the event. The factory was closed for half a day, and the staff briefed on the 'brave new world.' I found it unusual for all future plans and scale models to be shown to the whole company, before the designs were even solidified. It was also strange to view them in a medieval hall remote from the business. The event did, however, begin to revive morale.

The first tangible evidence that things were improving was the return of the Elan to production. Tony Shute led the engineering team, which incorporated many improvements to produce the S2 model. By using as many of the remaining parts left after the sudden demise of the original, some 800 cars were built, filling the period to the announcement of the Elise. The run was limited to match the number of Isuzu engines sitting in the stores.

Once the S2 Elan was running, the company took further advantage from it, by arranging to sell the design and tooling to the Korean manufacturer, Kia. Although the Kia version was changed in many detail areas, and was powered by its own, less powerful engine, it could have damaged Lotus's reputation. I was among those that felt that, if the car were brought to Europe, it would debase the real Lotus version. Fortunately (for those of us with these views), Kia had enormous difficulty building them, and those it did were restricted to its home market. Shortly afterwards, it got into financial difficulties, and the sports car was axed – yet again.

By the beginning of 1994, work was proceeding on project Clubsport. It started as a very simple vehicle, with no doors. Doors had been regarded as 'difficult' for years, and I remember Martin Lilley being concerned about them, when I was drawing up the TVR Tasmin. In this case, they were seen as excessive weight and complication. Originally called 'Step In,' I did some very basic layout work for it, with the assumption of a tubular steel chassis.

However, through client work, Lotus Engineering was introduced to the possibility of an extruded aluminium

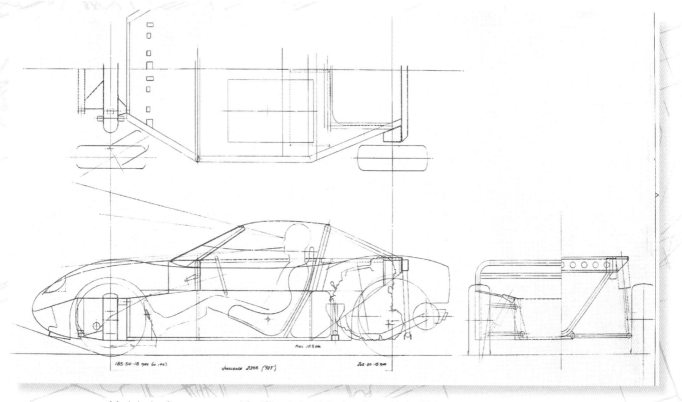

My tubular frame concept for 'Step In,' which developed into Clubsport and then the Elise.

frame, which was being researched for its weight-saving potential. (At one stage, Lotus was to build a series of these for the client, but that came to nothing.) Hydro Aluminium became involved in Clubsport, and the Elise project took off.

Julian Thompson had a clay model built very quickly and the engineering team started to refine the design. 13 senior management staff gathered in the Studio and the clay model put to the vote. One was against, and that was me. I felt that while the car had superb basic lines and proportion, the detailing was too exaggerated. It was a small car, which, I felt, didn't need over-embellishing. The design was released to proceed to prototypes on the nearly unanimous vote. Subsequent popularity suggests I was wrong!

With Lotus product work gaining pace, the engineering teams moved out into Portacabins (temporary portable buildings), with the M111 Elise upstairs under Tony Shute's leadership, and the M220 (2+2 Estate) downstairs under Malcolm Powell, and alongside the Lotus V8 engine team, working under John Owen. John had a hard time with the V8 project, because, although it had been approved, there was few suitable staff available. It was required in a very short time, to meet the introduction of new American exhaust emission legislation, so any shortage of manpower threatened to be serious. Somehow, John got it done on time, with significant help from co-operative suppliers. These were integrated into his team, and a celebration was shared with them, when the first engine ran, at the beginning of November 1994 – exactly 12 months after the project started.

The frame material for the M220 was still undecided: steel construction had support from Thompson Chassis, in Wolverhampton. Body panel studies led by Chris Dunster were supported by various suppliers, but the costs were still too high. I tended to be more involved with this project, possibly because it had grown from my original Esprit replacement work.

In the spring of 1994, Lotus carried out a survey to try to determine what its target customers expected from a Lotus Product. A market research company organised a series of fact-finding sessions at various venues. Two were held at Millbrook, with an audience consisting of people who had recently bought new cars similar to a Lotus. They were subjected to questions and discussion on their views on specialist cars, while Lotus remained anonymous. The answers were often very interesting, and, after lunch, Lotus was introduced as the host. This again brought further interesting comment, before they were given the chance to drive the current models. Virtually unanimous in their praise, they said they had no idea the Lotus cars were so good.

I also supported a market research event in Hamburg, taking an Esprit to Germany, unaccompanied. All went well, until I tried to get the right-hand drive car into the Hamburg hotel car park. The barrier control was naturally positioned on the left, but I was sitting on the right. There was no space to open my door and I was too big to climb across the tunnel. After much horn sounding, a passer-by rescued me. The market research message from the Germans was: no one will buy a car which costs a lot in depreciation. It was not the initial purchase price that affected them, but the cost of ownership.

As well as having responsibility for Lotus Product, I also took on the Legislation group. Lotus had dispensed with its Canadian importer, believing that Lotus USA in Atlanta could serve that market as well. For whatever reason, shortly after parting with the importer, the Canadian government authorities put a spotlight on the Esprit, and wanted full evidence of legal compliance to its regulations. The car was fully approved for America, but Canada had some exceptional requirements. Mountains of documents were sent to Transport Canada in Ottawa, but a couple of issues remained. We spent many hours on the telephone, until I felt that these would only be resolved with a personal visit.

Through Bugatti, Lotus had been introduced to an American vehicle regulation expert, Lance Tunick. The Canadian visit would be a good test for him, so he joined Arnie Johnson of Lotus USA and me for the fun. We had a deep and meaningful discussion with Transport Canada officials, after which the only issue outstanding concerned certain aspects of some testing that had been conducted years before. I agreed to write a report presenting our reasons for why the vehicles complied, and we got up to leave their office. The parting shot from the Canadian official was that, of course, he "would be talking to the Americans in Washington on the issues." We returned to our hotel, and immediately booked tickets for Washington.

Once there, officials from the National Highways and Transport Safety Authority (NHTSA) were very supportive and said they had no problems as I said that we would be retesting for the new V8 Esprit within a year, they suggested they would be keeping an eye on that! I was not too concerned, as I knew the car had wide margins for all aspects of its legal and safety compliance.

Back in England, Lotus Esprit Sport 300s were doing well on the race circuits. A headline, from 2 October 1994, underscored the success had by the Esprit, in both American and Europe: "Torkild Thyrring wins British GT

Challenge series at Silverstone in Lotus Esprit Sport 300 at the end of 1st full year."

The Lotus Esprit Sport 300s were prepared and entered by Chamberlain Racing, with covert support by Lotus Engineering. Despite their success, the factory relationship was not as wholehearted as one would have expected. The main problem was a lack of Lotus finance. I went up to Silverstone in anticipation of the victory, as did Patrick Peal, the Lotus PR manager. We appeared

to be the only factory interest, and, when Patrick had to leave immediately after the race, I felt obliged to stand the Chamberlain Racing mechanics a beer.

Later, Artioli set up a racing effort using a GT1 car based on the Elise. The team was located at Ketteringham Hall, under the patronage of Dutchman Toine Hezemans. Lotus was desperately short of money, and members of staff were warned to keep clear. The lack of cash and commitment meant the cars only showed the occasional flash of promise and generally did nothing to credit the company's reputation.

Lotus was struggling to keep adequate cash flow despite the commitment of all the staff, so the Elise was rushed to the Frankfurt Motor Show, in September 1995. The car wasn't ready for production – it didn't start coming off the line until the following June. The Elise was the second vehicle ever to get the new full European Type Approval, with a certificate supplied with every car produced. An enormous amount of work had to be done by Ken Evans to get the approvals, and a similar amount done by production staff at Hethel to satisfy the conformity of production rules. They got ISO 9000 recognition, without which, it was doubtful the legal certification would have been granted.

It meant that the Elise could be sold throughout Europe, and transferred between member states without difficulties in registration. Specialist vehicle manufacturers usually opted for National Type Approval in each country, which sets limits on sales volumes, and paperwork specific to each car.

The Elise was a showstopper. Besides its beguiling looks, the aluminium frame and light overall weight captured the imagination of the press. The light weight was aided by a minimal specification and, had I not insisted, it would not have had either an interior light (to find the dropped keys at night), or a

Brochure picture of the original Lotus Elise.

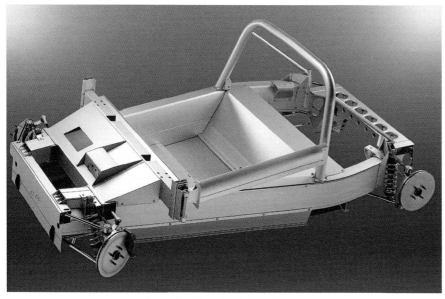

The Lotus Elise aluminium chassis.

cigar lighter (for phones, radar detectors, or even cigars). It didn't even run to an ashtray.

The aluminium frame had strengths and weaknesses. It was undoubtedly expensive – aluminium was an expensive raw material, and the metal finishing process that allowed the bonding to work was unique and very precise; the extrusion process had thickness limitations, which made many sections thicker than structurally necessary. There was much precision machining of these sections to ensure that the frames met the high build tolerances specified. Initially, the frames were built in Denmark, which increased labour and transport costs, but when the car became a runaway success, Hydro built a factory in Worcester, England, to overcome some of the cost concerns. I had looked at market potential, and found no evidence the car could sell in high numbers. In fact, Lotus did not expect to sell more than 750 units per year, and we even wondered if we could manage that many – the Elise broke the mould, and opened up a new market.

The day after the Frankfurt Motor Show press day, I was on my way to the USA as guest speaker at the Lotus Owners' Gathering, at Pocono, Pennsylvania, an annual event which spanned a weekend. The Elise news was red hot, so a motorcycle courier met me, on route to Heathrow, to deliver the Reuters News picture coverage of the launch.

I was not the original choice for the privileged position of guest speaker, but the very high-profile American originally booked had to withdraw at the last moment! Arnie Johnson drove me to the Mountain Laurel Resort, where I was introduced to Lotus Ltd which organised the event. Lotus USA sponsored the reception on the first evening; I put the Elise pictures on display, and gave a short presentation of the Frankfurt launch. Everyone wanted to know when it would arrive in the States, and I had the difficult task of explaining that its design had not been compromised to include American requirements, such as airbags and low damage bumpers. The Saturday evening was the Grand Banquet. I delivered tales of my early life at Lotus, and my times with Colin Chapman until late into the evening. I then repaired to the bar, with an audience who kept me up until the early hours. I was struck by the enthusiasm of the Americans.

Bugatti Automobili had asked Lotus to develop a Federal version of the EB 110 for North America. Due to other commitments, the small safety group had made no progress with airbag installation, so Adrian Palmer asked me to sort it out.

I contacted a number of test houses and asked if they could give immediate support. Most were too busy with scheduled work, so it was that TNO in Holland got the job. It provided the computer modelling and did the barrier crash testing, but did not have a Hy Ge sled. This was subcontracted to Keiper Reccaro, which had the latest hydraulically controlled accelerator.

The sled testing at Reccaro was difficult. The hydraulic sled was installed to support the design and development of its well-known vehicle seating. Its test team were not used to complete vehicle hulls as a buck – the Bugatti carbon fibre structure was too expensive – it cost more than a showroom-complete Esprit – to scrap by cutting the ends off. It took a long time to fit to the sled and the rebuild time of each hand-built interior took many hours compared with the minutes usual for a mass-produced design.

Worse, the safety component suppliers were not interested. Morton, a supplier in the USA hoped it could use airbags from an existing customer. We offered to pay significantly above the usual price to cover all the 'low volume' extra handling costs. That issue resolved, we then needed permission from the original user to use its airbag module, suitably badged.

Despite involvement by Lotus' Chief Executive, we never resolved the issue. I was most concerned that we had to meet a piece of American legislation, but could not get anyone to supply the components. One car was built and shipped to the States for EPA exhaust emissions approval, before Bugatti Automobili ceased production.

All through 1996, rumour was rife that Artioli was in financial difficulties. Bugatti had finally succumbed to its financial woes, in 1995 (eventually, its factory gates were locked – with some of the employee's personal goods, including their cars, inside). Simon Wood, who, as an ex-Lotus man, had always been a strong point of contact, returned to Hethel, and became a key member of senior management. With my move to run vehicle safety again, in the autumn of 1995, he took over the product group.

Artioli appointed ex-Ford Specialist Vehicle guru, Rod Mansfield, as Lotus Managing Director. Romano had removed Adrian Palmer, and Mansfield looked like the perfect person to keep the business happy. He was an advocate of personal empowerment. You knew your job, and you should therefore be allowed to do it with the minimum of interference.

Mansfield arrived in time for the launch of the Elise, but, despite being a boost to the company, failed to see it into full production. He was 'posted missing' on 21 February 1996, much to the dismay of the staff. On 27 February, the company had to issue an official statement that Lotus had not been sold.

The staff's constant uncertainty over the future dated back to Adrian Palmer's attempts to arrange a management buyout, before General Motors sold to Bugatti. The optimism of the new order had not lasted very long; and plans for product and factory improvements kept coming to nothing, due to lack of funds.

The Lotus V8 engine and the Elise were fortunately funded from engineering research budgets, but the 2+2 M220 never got one penny of the millions promised, so gradually died. This meant there was no successor to the Esprit in the pipeline, which, as the only product eligible for America, was serious.

My return to safety engineering was marked by a visit to the USA for the Stapp Safety Conference, five weeks after the Elise launch, in September 1995. Lotus Engineering had been contracted to assist a major American company with the installation of occupant protection for one of its customers. Initially the project had gone well. However, an oversight regarding the basic cockpit layout meant that a plateau had been reached, where performance could not be improved. The situation emphasised the 'whole vehicle approach,' as no amount of tuning to the available components would provide any progress. I was asked to return to the Vehicle Safety Group, and try and move the projects forward.

Our American partner had appointed a project manager, who used verbal aggression with the Lotus team to try and solve the problems. This did little to solve anything, and had lowered the morale of the team to one of despair. I had to try and get the team to understand that the customer was always right, despite his sometimes 'difficult' demeanour. The content behind the aggression was usually flawless, but its delivery was unpleasant.

The vehicle producer had a programme manager for each platform. One of these was a Solomon-like character, who listened to all the evidence regarding the need for a change, weighed up the pros and cons, and made a timely judgement. The offending area was redesigned, and the development of a robust safety system was completed.

The other chain of command was, perhaps, even more aggressive than our Colonial friend, and refused to contemplate any changes that would have helped

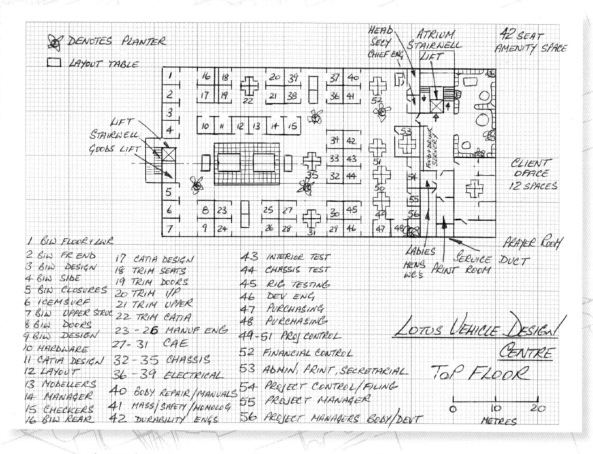

A page from my notebook: the design room in the never-finished project centre.

the technical performance. In due course, a system was released, but it had been a painful process. My job was not helped by the general condition of Lotus as a company, which meant I had to give morale-raising presentations to all parties on a far-too-regular basis.

The safety group was working on a number of projects, including an airbag for motorcycles. This joint project was inspired by the Road Research Laboratory, and involved engineering an airbag housed at the front of the machine's fuel tank. Geoff Grose led the work for Lotus, and the project was completed with extremely good results. Later, we tried to get motorcycle manufacturers interested, but even BMW turned it down.

Events took a dramatic turn in summer 1996: Mark Easton and I were just descending the entry ramp to the M4 motorway, returning from a motorcycle test at Crowthorne when my mobile phone rang. It was Tuesday 23 July, and Mark took the call. He relayed the content to me; the news was serious. Five directors had been asked to resign, their actions to try to avert the deepening financial plight at odds with Artioli. Mark related the basic news to me, as thunder, lightning and torrential rain raged around us, making navigation difficult, so we waited until we were clear of London, and then called Lotus security staff. They had no comment, but it was true.

Ownership and solvency issues were a tedious part of our life, but they also became a concern to our engineering clients. We were kept briefed on the official line, and had to pass this on to our clients. That we were successful at this, said much about Lotus' reputation, as consultants, but the prevailing atmosphere did not help with recruitment of new business. Eventually, after far too long, the waiting and the rumours and were over. My diary for the 30 October 1996 bluntly states "Yes, its Proton." Romano Artioli had sold most of his Lotus holding to the Malaysian carmaker, Proton, and the next era was dawning.

The arrival of Proton brought more work to Lotus Engineering, and, by the New Year of 1997, its PVR Project was under way. With the arrival of this major project for a conventional sheet metal car, I was invited to create a Body Engineering Division.

Lotus Engineering had already got defined departments for styling, powertrain and chassis development with smaller groups covering NVH, electrical, safety and legislation. Although some sheet metal project work had been successfully carried out, most of the body activity had been in the glass fibre-based Lotus Product group. Now that Lotus was owned by a company committed to sheet metal bodywork, there was an urgent need to strengthen its capabilities in that field.

I celebrated leaving the safety group by attending a business breakfast, hosted by my American client – I had to leave home at five o'clock in the morning to attend it. The meal was notable for some vocal critical observations from my host, which the hotel proprietor recalled very clearly, when I revisited the venue three years later! It marked a suitably embarrassing end to that project for me.

As Head of Body Engineering I was working under Simon Wood, Engineering Director, while the Senior Executive was a Malaysian, Mohammed Zainal. They gave me their full support. Initially, we were housed in a range of Portacabin temporary buildings. These tended to be warm in summer, and the reverse in the winter. They were, however, intended as a short-term home, while the new Vehicle Project Centre was built and equipped.

In early February 1997, I became involved in the detailed planning and specification of this new building. Its temporary foundation stone (but little else) had been laid alongside the test track. The chosen site was not ideal, with the proposed location for car parking situated beyond the dangerous stretch of tarmac, and office windows that would overlook this high security facility. I set out to try and get it relocated, and to come up with detailed plans for what it would contain. The first objective had plenty of support, and the building was re-sited on Potash Farm, at the front of the Hethel complex.

The long-term plan for the Vehicle Engineering Project Centre involved huge growth. The heart of it on the first floor was to be the central design area. This was to be the nerve centre of the project, where all parties could gather and debate, with an overall view of the design. Two complete cars could be housed on a reinforced section of the floor, alongside semi-vertical layout boards long enough for two whole vehicles. We envisaged that the building would be occupied by April 1998, when the Proton PVR Project would emerge from its concept phase.

The staff planning estimated that the project room would contain 210 souls. The client offices were laid out for ten visiting staff, and the ground floor workshops would need up to 50 staff; facilities were planned accordingly.

The creation of a vehicle engineering team, fully capable of developing modern metal-bodied cars, brought with it, for me, the introduction to CAD – Computer Aided Design. Although the Lotus V8 engine had been designed on computer, virtually all its other products had continued to use hand-drawing processes. These older processes had become unacceptable, and indeed, were totally unusable, for our high-volume vehicle clients.

A major aspect, which became serious, was the

cost of these CAD systems. The computer hardware, with its associated licensed programs, came to tens of thousands of pounds each per year. Staff training to use them generated further costs. Then we had to decide which design programs, from among the various ones throughout the industry, we would invest in.

IBM invited three of us to its seminar in Paris. After a highly impressive journey on the TGV, we were deposited at Disney World. IBM featured its Catia system and demonstrated its virtues, and detailed its long and distinguished client list. It was the system we adopted, although the excitement of having Mickey Mouse leap out at you on the way to breakfast nearly changed our minds.

As well as the staff and the buildings to house them, investment was needed in the computer equipment needed to allow them to operate. This list was long and very expensive, and the first cracks in the plan appeared shortly after the recruitment drive started to succeed. New staff appeared, but, despite every effort, there was no furniture or computer equipment upon which they could work. It became a regular, tedious battle and the managers became adept at stretching resources. Proton also wanted Lotus staff to work out in Malaysia, which called for yet more personnel.

Meanwhile, in the latter part of April 1997, problems emerged in Canada, again, with the improper import of Lotus Esprits. Despite the lessons of our previous experience, cars to American and not Canadian specification had, again, been imported from the USA. Transport Canada had found out, and wanted to exclude all of them immediately. Trucks with cars for delivery were held at the Canadian border or turned back. Mohammed Zainal was very concerned, and asked me to become involved.

I managed to get the authorities to agree that, if the cars were updated correctly with metric speedometers and the relevant French/English dual language labels, they could stay in Canada. They would only accept this, if I would personally inspect and sign for each vehicle already there. I left hurriedly, to inspect the first cars in Vancouver. I then flew to Toronto, and from there Montreal. All the cars affected had been inspected and rectified, so on to Ottawa, and the ministry. The signed papers were handed in, and I was told the cars could stay. A severe warning was issued regarding the company's attitude to the Canadian legislative requirements, which we dutifully accepted. Canadian Customs could then open the borders to Lotus again.

Lotus had been running without a Chief Executive since the Proton acquisition. On 13 August 1987, senior management was invited to meet the prospective incumbent, Chris Knight, who was not due to take up

residence until September. We all thought he was just what Lotus needed. He brought years of experience as a trained business manager, and promised that the company would be changing: plans were to be thoroughly researched, and business cases proven, before proceeding. Things were looking up.

Chris Knight brought Price Waterhouse into Lotus to accelerate the fresh approach to running the business. Over the winter of 1997, it oversaw a major planning exercise on the future of the business. All aspects were analysed, and plans discussed and reconfigured. Every senior manager's objectives and proposals were scrutinised. From it, the company put together an imposing presentation handbook of its future strategy. I was trying to build up the Body Engineering sector, but was still having to fight for every computer, table and chair. The new Project Centre construction was progressing with speed, and selection of the interior furniture was under way. We expected to take up residence by September 1998.

In early 1998, I also visited Proton's factory and engineering centre outside Kuala Lumpur, with Kevin Elgood, the Body Engineering Manager. Our trip gave us the opportunity to meet many of its departmental heads, all of whom were charming. Some aspects of the business, however, were less than perfect. It had a large factory building under conversion, for the Malaysian build of the Lotus Elise, which was nearly ready to start production. Proton made a few Elises for its home market, but they were expensive. At the time, they had no air-conditioning, and I couldn't imagine touching the raw aluminium in the cockpit, after a day in the sun, would have been soothing to the skin. The project ground to a halt soon afterwards.

Just before Kevin and I left for Kuala Lumpur, Chris Knight called a senior staff meeting, where we were told that projected company income did not balance expected capital expenditure. The new Finance Director showed a chart with massive expenditure looming in the approaching spring; it appeared to be most of the following year's commitment, rolled into one month. A number of us were sceptical at this apparently sudden disclosure, so my fellow departmental heads and I asked to be kept in the picture of how the revenue and expenditure was being maintained. Despite repeated attempts to get it, we were never given any more information.

At the meeting, we were told it would be touch-and-go for survival, so belt tightening was, again, the order of the day. The new Vehicle Project Centre was to be made weatherproof and put in 'mothballs.' Portacabin life was obviously set to remain for some time.

In February 1998, the Proton PVR project had reached the conclusion of its concept phase. The car was styled inside and out, and technical and manufacturing feasibility completed. All body surfaces were refined, and the body engineering schemes complete. Unfortunately, Proton decided not to proceed with the project, and the team, which was still expanding, was left with little to look forward to.

Instead, the company instituted a redundancy programme. I had a miserable time trying to satisfy corporate targets for headcount reductions. It was, to say the least, embarrassing to be selecting victims, who had, in one case, only been at Hethel for one week. Roger Becker's chassis group headcount was hit even harder, and resulted in a vastly reduced vehicle safety group. Just as the future had looked brighter, run as a better business, and totally planned, it went into reverse. However, a new vehicle engineering client project was on the horizon, and it was secured a month later. Some of the departed skilled expertise returned, but many ex-staff declined to go through it all again.

As part of a cost-saving initiative, Knight announced that the small collection of historic vehicles, which Lotus had gathered over the years, was to be sold. I believed, adamantly, that these could never be replaced, and were part of the Lotus heritage. Some were ordinary road cars: Colin Chapman's personal Elan +2, and the last Europa produced. Some were styling models, including the Italdesign Etna; and the collection included the M90 prototype.

Potash Farm, Hethel, prior to demolition, to make way for the new Engineering Project Centre.

The Engineering Project Centre ready to be 'mothballed.'

It was argued, by people who had never known him, that Colin Chapman and Lotus did not look to the past. Unfortunately, they neglected to remember (or never knew) that it was he who had preserved his own Elan +2, ordered the retention of the last Europa and founded the collection in the first place.

I talked to Clive Chapman, Colin's son, to see if there was a chance of launching a Lotus Museum at Ketteringham Hall. This could have amalgamated his racing collection with the company's vehicles. We put a comprehensive study together, but the indications suggested there was not a business case to support it.

In June 1998, I discussed the future with my director, Simon Wood. I didn't feel very comfortable with the new atmosphere at Hethel, and I was tired of the boom and bust, new ownership, and crisis round every corner, that had characterised the company's recent history. I saw little that was going to change for the better, so I decided to resign.

Some of the Lotus historic collection, at the Coys Silverstone auction, August 1998.

The Lotus M90 prototype, at the Coys auction at Silverstone, August 1998.

I left Lotus at the beginning of August 1998, and, shortly afterwards, went to the Coys auction at Silverstone, where the Lotus Collection was up for sale. I had mixed feelings, when the M90 prototype was sold to a good home in Texas, well above its expected price.

Looking back at my latter period at Lotus, I felt there were a number of factors that led to my gradual lessening of enthusiasm. There were a growing number of people, who were very ambitious, in positions where they had little hands-on experience, but a lot of personal confidence. They began to exert great power, and played internal politics as a profession.

I always believed in my staff and I cared for their well-being. Supporting my staff was sometimes seen as a weakness; if that was what it was, I was happy to suffer from it. Probably the biggest wrench was that management activities were taking me away from the technical aspects of work. Hours were spent discussing where employees could park their cars, and how to stagger canteen lunch times.

Chapter 13

Consultant

I was facing life post-Lotus, and needed to find a new occupation. I had completely fallen out of love with the motor business. I missed being at the sharp end of the creative process, and I had tired of the endless management meetings. It had stopped being fun.

My first idea was a pub, but my wife felt it was not a good plan. We considered a proposed luxury specialist travel company, but our research suggested that it would struggle. I even considered property development in France, but, after a visit, that idea also went into the waste-bin.

Millbrook Proving Ground had telephoned me in the autumn of 1998 and suggested a meeting, but I was keen to avoid the motor industry at the time, and declined the meeting, though left open the option of calling for a 'cup of tea.' Some months later, in April 1999, I phoned and asked to take up that offer of a warm beverage. We discussed the possibility of me assisting its Crashworthiness Department, and I left to mull it over.

It didn't take long for my enthusiasm to be rekindled, and I agreed to help. I had come to the conclusion that I should do what friends and family had been saying all along: "Go back to the motor industry as a consultant." So, on 5 July 1999, Norfolk Automotive Limited was born, and my keenness had returned.

At the same time, I talked to Lance Tunick, who had helped us so much at Lotus. He had founded COSVAM, an association to voice the interests of the specialist car industry in the USA. The major manufacturers had extensive means for lobbying the American government, but the small firms could not afford to do so. As more high technology-based legislation was introduced, their ability to develop compliant systems was constantly reducing. The difficulties we had getting airbags for the Bugatti EB110 had shown that, in some cases, the means to comply had become virtually impossible. Various initiatives were adopted with success – with both the clean air authorities and the NHTSA regulators. Lance offered me the position of COSVAM Membership Director, and I gladly accepted. It was another move back to the world of the automobile.

Now my task was to find clients. I created a brochure, outlining my experience, and began to contact potential customers. The responses were varied, and many led to dead ends. I was also elected as a member of the SMMT (Society of Motor Manufacturers and Traders) Engineering Consultants Group, maintaining a vigilant eye on the industry's movements.

In the ten years that Norfolk Automotive Limited operated, it brought me many interesting clients. In most cases, the work was confidential, so I can't expand on it here. Among other things, I spent a year with Gibbs Technologies, of amphibious car fame, in Nuneaton.

Automotive safety brought work as diverse as an appraisal of the crash test facilities at Autovaz, in Russia; project strategies for heavy trucks, and a Korean SUV in the USA; to consultancy with such companies as McLaren Cars and Prodrive. However, my work could be as varied as examining site redevelopment at Group Lotus, and brochure copywriting for the engineering company.

Work with the Tommy Kiara brought me back into contact with Mike Rawlings, with whom I had built the first TVR Tasmin. He and a long standing ex-Lotus colleague, Mark Easton, were building these lightweight

A concept proposal sketch for the Phipps sports car project.

The last Esprit ceremonial photograph at Hethel 20 February 2004.

sports cars for Japan, in a factory in East Dereham, Norfolk. The facility was busy developing other products, and eventually built a number of Moslers. I brought in Paul Mickleborough, and we started building developed Kiaras, as The Leading Edge Sports Car Company. Despite exhibiting, advertising and press coverage, the sales weren't there. We looked at developing the Kiara, but, alas, after months of negotiation, the cash was not forthcoming.

Another stillborn project was for a sports car with David Phipps, a delightful gentleman, with Lotus connections going back to its earliest days. Sadly, he passed away shortly after the proposal was submitted.

In the summer of 2003, I met up with Clive Roberts, who, following the Lotus Elan project, was working for General Motors at its China Engineering operation, in Shanghai. We discussed an opportunity for me to visit the Pan Asia Technical Centre (PATAC) to work on concept design. At the beginning of October, I stepped from the Shanghai flight out into the exciting 'new China.' As well as the excitement of working in a new culture, Shanghai was a connection to my family's past – my grandfather living there from 1912-1920, and my father attending school there.

20 February 2004 saw me back at Hethel for the ceremony marking the last production Esprit. Hazel Chapman was guest of honour for what I found a sad occasion. In the 32 years since the first concept discussions in Turin, the Esprit served Lotus well. It became a real supercar, and was a delight to drive. However, apart from Peter Stevens' restyle and the later V8 engine, nothing had come along to replace it, despite numerous attempts.

The spring of 2004 took me to Holland. TNO, in Delft, had given Lotus good service with its crash testing, and I was invited to report on future expansion. Taking a flat in the centre of Delft, it became my home for the rest of the year. Perhaps not surprisingly, I recommended expansion into China. After a number of lengthy research visits, I accepted the position of General Manager TNO China, with an office in Pudong, Shanghai.

XJ Liu was the able manager, and we set about building contacts and confidence throughout the year. Living in a pleasant apartment overlooking Century Park, I thoroughly enjoyed the people, food, architecture and history of this massive nation. To create the contacts required, we visited companies throughout the country, from the freezing north to the boiling south. I think we ranged from minus 20°C to plus over 40° in our travels. With TNO China set up and operating, I moved on to Wanxiang Electric Vehicles.

This move took me to the delightful city of Hangzhou, where the Wanxiang Group occupied premises in the suburb of Xiaoshan. This group manufactured all things chassis, from bearings to brakes, and had created the EV Division to develop electric vehicles. It's General Manager, Chen Jun, and his staff went out of their way to welcome me. Wanxiang wished to start a customer design and development facility, for complete vehicle underpinnings, and that was my first assignment. Its customer wanted to build a MPV/SUV, based on a common structure with a proprietary powertrain.

Back in Xiaoshan, my small team worked to design and verify a robust platform frame. Part of my assignment was to give these young engineers the benefit of my experience, so I made a number of presentations on the design and development process. Although China is turning out large numbers of graduates, there is no structure for exposing them to the 'real job.'

By July, we had a completed design and awaited further instructions. It was well received by the client, but his plans were cooling. By September, they froze and the project stopped, but Wanxiang wanted to build a 'demonstrator' platform, so that kept us busy.

In Xiaoshan, I lived 'native' – there were no Westerners in the industrial part of the city. I was apprehensive at first, but soon came to enjoy the enthusiasm and politeness of the locals. With my Chinese limited to essentials such as "beer," "please" and "thank you," it was surprising how much can be communicated by theatricals and pencil sketches.

An interesting effect of the Chinese habit of copying showed itself with a distinct lack of co-operation with potential suppliers. Most would not provide any drawings, and even other Wanxiang Group divisions would 'cut off' most of the information on the ones supplied to us.

Following the successful completion of the demonstrator chassis, I set to work on an electric vehicle. Wanxiang EV already had a fleet of buses running in Hangzhou, using its own lithium ion batteries. A number of Mazda Premacy vehicles had been converted as electric vehicles, and were in daily use. The loan of a hybrid Toyota Prius had not impressed me – even the three miles to work seemed mainly petrol-powered.

I had a strong belief that an electric car needed to be designed specifically round its strengths and weaknesses. Modern fossil-fuelled vehicle systems have all been developed round the available self-generated power sources – hot water, vacuum, and copious amounts of electricity. The electric car has none of these. In exchange for virtually no cooling or exhaust systems, it has to house batteries. These are large and heavy. Trying to specify and package these different requirements demanded, I believed, a new approach.

My EV proposal put the batteries under the floor. I suggested non servo drum brakes, heat pump climate control, LED lighting and above all, a low mass basic vehicle. It used a simple steel platform, with twin wishbone suspension all round. The motor was at the rear, as that simplified the driveshaft design. I also thought that it needed to be a full four-seater – anything less would compromise sales. In view of the need to access the underfloor batteries and to be city practical, I specified a large single sliding door.

This was to be another 'car that never was.' Its selling price was competitive, with China-produced batteries and an assembly cost of 12 yuan per hour – about £1. However, it was seen as a step too far for a company with no whole-vehicle experience. So, with useful work coming to an end, I regretfully left Wanxiang. Instead, I immediately took up a position halfway back to Shanghai, with London Taxi (LTI)'s Shanghai operation, working with the Geely Group at Fengjing.

This joint venture to build London taxis in China was not successful in my case. After a month at the LTI factory in Coventry, I was back in China representing LTI's interests. After some months of difficult relationships, I left – although, happily, the taxi was launched successfully in early 2009.

One more Chinese occupation came with SAIC, the owner of various Rover designs (badged as Roewe), which was designing a luxury car at its technical centre, in Anting.

As it was situated well out of Shanghai, a bus was provided as transport. This required one's presence at the bus stop at 6:30am, which was a challenge. Five months after my arrival, the project was abandoned.

Shortly before this sad end, I celebrated my 65th birthday, with a cake from SAIC, a cake from good friends, and a cake from Greame Allen, the proprietor of the Flying Fox Irish bar, in Shanghai. A small gathering there, with friends including Clive Roberts, assisted me with both cake and lubricants, until I assume I was

65 years and at least part of one day older! Three weeks later, I flew home, to retirement, my family, and the design and build of a house in my garden. In China, it is nearly impossible to work beyond that age.

Working as a consultant had brought plenty of variation in work content, location and quantity. My career has seen tremendous changes in the way things are done, and I count myself lucky to have been part of these changes. Over the years, I visited many foreign countries, and lived in some of them. From time to time, I see my old designs 'on the road' and talk with their (usually) happy owners. That made it all worth while.

As a postscript, my Lotus X100 resides in Texas with an enthusiastic owner. He and his predecessor have expertly restored and maintained it. One's creations are like one's children (although they take a bit longer to create). They become part of one's life, so it is heartwarming to see one's work appreciated.

The Lotus X100 prototype survives in Houston, Texas, September 2016.

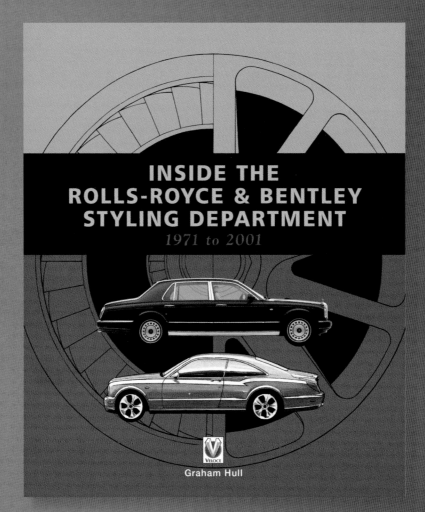

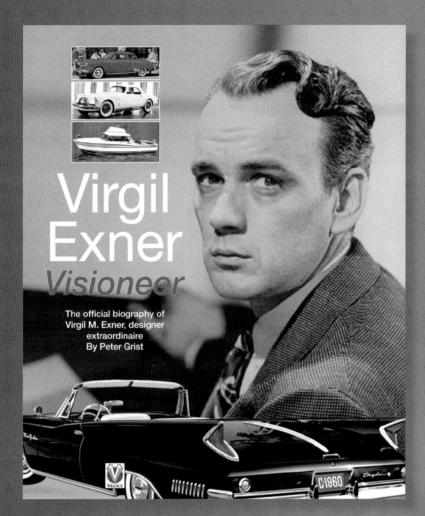

Virgil
Exner
Visioneer

The official biography of Virgil M. Exner, designer extraordinaire By Peter Grist

An in-depth look at the last of the great auto designers of the 20th Century, his glorious achievements and personal tragedies. With many previously unseen works of art and family photos among the 150 colour images throughout, this is a unique and fascinating insight into a pivotal player in the development of the modern automobile.

ISBN: 978-1-845848-63-7
Paperback • 25x20.7cm • £25* UK/$40* USA • 176 pages • 336 colour and b&w pictures

For more info on Veloce titles, visit our website at www.veloce.co.uk • email: info@veloce.co.uk • Tel: +44(0)1305 260068
* prices subject to change, p&p extra

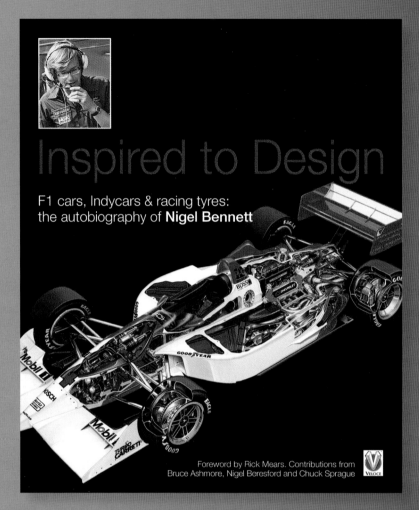

Inspired to Design

F1 cars, Indycars & racing tyres:
the autobiography of **Nigel Bennett**

Foreword by Rick Mears. Contributions from
Bruce Ashmore, Nigel Beresford and Chuck Sprague

Nigel Bennett's unique autobiography describes his life and career, from growing-up influenced by car design, to his education and the building of his 750 specials. He describes his work as Firestone Development Manager, recounting many tales of the outstanding designers and drivers of the period. Detailing his work in Formula 1, as a Team Lotus engineer, and then as Team Ensign designer, he also covers his Indycar designs at Theodore, Lola Cars and Penske Cars. Life after his retirement, his involvement in boat design and with modern F1 teams, are also recounted.

ISBN: 978-1-845845-36-0
Hardback • 25x20.7cm • £35* UK/$54.95* USA • 176 pages • 194 colour and b&w pictures

For more info on Veloce titles, visit our website at www.veloce.co.uk • email: info@veloce.co.uk • Tel: +44(0)1305 260068
* prices subject to change, p&p extra

Index